Brief Group Psychotherapy for Eating Disorders

In the treatment of Anorexia Nervosa, delivering psychological interventions in a group format can bring unique benefits in addition to those associated with working with patients individually. These include: sharing experiences and learning from others in a safe and therapeutic environment, becoming accustomed to being with other people and practising interpersonal skills. However, these aspects of group treatment also represent a challenge for group facilitators as it is exactly these interpersonal and relational demands that patients find difficult to tolerate. Facilitators are likely to be confronted with low motivation, or complete disengagement, as a result of the discomfort evoked by spending time in psychological groups. Nonetheless, once these difficulties are successfully overcome, the group setting can be effectively utilised to address the specific aims of a given psychological intervention, as well as tapping into these wider benefits.

Drawing upon research carried out by the Maudsley national inpatient eating disorders programme, *Brief Group Psychotherapy for Eating Disorders* brings together expert contributions in order to review the evidence base, as well as discussing how the challenges of the group setting can be overcome. This book outlines newly developed protocols for group interventions aimed at providing brief but effective treatment for an increased number of patients, and addresses the need to develop and evaluate cost-effective psychological interventions for patients with Anorexia Nervosa.

Brief Group Psychotherapy for Eating Disorders is designed to offer therapists, clinicians and researchers in the field a synopsis of the available evidence along with guidance on how to put theory into practice effectively. It will also be an invaluable resource for students, trainees and teachers in the clinical, counselling, psychology, psychiatry, nursing, occupational therapy and other allied professions.

Dr Kate Tchanturia, Fellow of the Academy of Eating Disorders and Fellow of the British Psychological Society, is Lead Clinical Psychologist in the South London and Maudsley NHS Foundation Trust Eating Disorders National Service and Reader in the Psychology of Eating Disorders at King's College London. She is actively involved in several postgraduate programmes within King's College London (PhD, Clinical Psychology doctoral training programmes and lead of the Women's Mental Health module for the Mental Health Studies MSc programme). Kate's research centres around translation, applying research findings in cognitive and emotional processing in eating disorders in order to develop novel treatment interventions, such as cognitive remediation and emotion skills training modules in individual and group formats. For further details please see: http://www.katetchanturia.com.

Brief Group Psychotherapy for Eating Disorders

Inpatient protocols

Edited by Kate Tchanturia

Routledge
Taylor & Francis Group

LONDON AND NEW YORK

KH

First published 2015
by Routledge
27 Church Road, Hove, East Sussex, BN3 2FA

and by Routledge
711 Third Avenue, New York, NY 10017

Routledge is an imprint of the Taylor & Francis Group, an informa business

British Library Cataloguing in Publication Data
A catalogue record for this book is available from the British Library

Library of Congress Cataloguing in Publication data
   Brief group psychotherapy for eating disorders : inpatient protocols / edited by
   Kate Tchanturia.
     p. ; cm.
   Includes bibliographical references.
   I. Tchanturia, Kate, editor.
   [DNLM: 1. Eating Disorders–psychology. 2. Eating Disorders–therapy.
   3. Psychotherapy, Brief–methods. 4. Psychotherapy, Group–methods. WM 175]
   RC552.E18
   616.85'260651–dc23
   2014047231

ISBN: 978-1-138-84888-7 (hbk)
ISBN: 978-1-138-84891-7 (pbk)
ISBN: 978-1-315-72036-4 (ebk)

Typeset in Times
by Out of House Publishing

Printed and bound in the United States of America by Publishers Graphics,
LLC on sustainably sourced paper.

11/17/16

Contents

List of figures   vii

List of tables   ix

Notes on contributors   x

Acknowledgements   xiv

1 An introduction to brief group psychotherapy in
   intensive care programmes for eating disorders:
   gathering research evidence   1
   KATE TCHANTURIA AND KATHERINE SPARROW

2 A short description of the adult clinical treatment service
   at the Maudsley   24
   KATE TCHANTURIA

3 Flexibility workshops – cognitive remediation therapy (CRT)
   in group format: adults   26
   KATE TCHANTURIA AND ELI DORIS

4 Group cognitive remediation therapy format for adolescents   51
   ZOE MAIDEN, LAURA BAKER, JONATHAN ESPIE, MIMA SIMIC
   AND KATE TCHANTURIA

5 Thinking about emotions: CREST group   74
   KATE TCHANTURIA, AMY BROWN AND CAROLINE FLEMING

6 Perfectionism short format group for inpatients   107
   SAMANTHA LLOYD, CAROLINE FLEMING
   AND KATE TCHANTURIA

7 Single session groups   121
   SUZI DOYLE

8 An introduction to compassion group for eating disorders   133
   JANE EVANS

9 BodyWise: a low intensity group to address body
   image disturbance   162
   VICTORIA MOUNTFORD AND AMY BROWN

10 Recovery/discovery oriented group   184
   KATE TCHANTURIA AND CLAIRE BAILLIE

   Final thoughts   218

   Index   222

Figures

1.1	Snapshot of the individual and group attendance	3
1.2	Flow diagram in line with PRISMA	17
1.3	The number and type of groups reported before 2000	18
1.4	The number and type of groups reported after 2000	18
2.1	The individual and group programmes in the ward	25
3.1	The average length of admission has not only decreased in our service, this is a general trend across the UK	27
3.2	Describing task figure	32
3.3	Describing task figure	32
3.4	Occupations task example diagram	37
3.5	Group 'mind map' example	39
4.1	How many squares task	59
5.1	Think, be, do positive things	92
5.2	Positive emotions	95
6.1	Model of perfectionism	112
6.2	Changes in FMPS score following the 'Living with Perfectionism' group (N = 28)	116
6.3	Changes in CPQ score following the 'Living with Perfectionism' group (N = 16)	117
6.4	Responses to the question 'What did you learn from attending the group?'	117
6.5	Responses to the question 'What would you change about the group?'	118
8.1	Comparison of compassion to selves and others scale	137
8.2	Three types of affect regulation system	138
8.3	Interactions between our thoughts, images and our emotions	148
9.1	Bell curve to demonstrate normal distribution within a population	170
10.1	The ten point ladder of change	198
10.2	Work and Social Adjustment Scale results before recovery group and after the group	205

10.3   How to meet new people   205
FT.1   The most common theme in each of the four groups and
        overlapping themes which were common across all these groups   219
FT.2   Magnitude of change between time 1 (pre-group) and time 2
        (post-group) assessments   220

Tables

1.1 Systematic review of the published work in group format
in eating disorders   5
3.1 The average length of stay in the inpatient programme has
decreased over time   27
3.2 Outcome data from the 'Flexibility group' pilot work   40
3.3 CRT group therapy qualitative feedback from the patients attending
this group from the different runs   41
3.4 Themes emerging from patient feedback   45
3.5 Summary of the results from a qualitative study conducted by Lounes
(2014), assessing feedback from 11 therapists who had been trained to
deliver both individual and group CRT   47
4.1 Session content   53
5.1 CREST – Thinking about Emotions Group Therapy, some qualitative
feedback from the participants in the inpatient ward   76
8.1 The pros and cons of self-criticism and self-compassion   141
10.1 WSAS between-groups comparisons   204

Contributors

Claire Baillie (PsychD, CPsychol) is a chartered counselling psychologist who has worked in the eating disorders field for 15 years. Most recently she worked for 2 years in the National Inpatient Eating Disorders Service at the Bethlem Royal Hospital. Before qualifying as a psychologist she spent 12 years working in the South London and Maudsley NHS Foundation Trust Eating Disorders National Service's intensive residential rehabilitation service based in the community. During this time she also undertook secondments in day care and outpatients settings for the same service.

Laura Baker (BNurs) is a clinical nurse specialist working in the Child and Adolescent Eating Disorders Team at the Maudsley Hospital where she facilitates the Flexible Thinking (CRT) group as part of the Intensive Treatment Programme. Prior to this she worked at Snowsfields Adolescent Unit at the Maudsley and was the eating disorders team leader. She completed her Bachelor of Paediatric Nursing degree (Hons) at the University of Manchester.

Amy Brown (BSc, MSc, DClinPsy) is a clinical psychologist at the South London and Maudsley NHS Foundation Trust Eating Disorders National Service. After completing her doctorate at Royal Holloway University of London, she obtained a postgraduate diploma in cognitive behavioural therapy from the Institute of Psychiatry, King's College London. She has published in peer reviewed journals and presented at conferences on research that she has conducted in the field of eating disorders. Her current interests include cognitive behavioural therapy, the therapeutic alliance and body image.

Eli Doris (BA) is currently working as a care quality coordinator for the National Inpatient Eating Disorders Service at the Bethlem Royal Hospital, under the supervision of Dr Kate Tchanturia and is doing an MSc in the Mental Health Studies programme at King's College London. She has been contributing to new and ongoing research projects in the field of eating disorders. Prior to this she completed her BA in Experimental Psychology at the University of Oxford.

Suzi Doyle (DCPsych, CPsychol) is a chartered counselling psychologist who works for the National Inpatient Eating Disorders Service at the Bethlem Royal Hospital. Prior to this position, she worked as a registered integrative psychotherapist in the field of general psychological therapy, including the treatment of eating disorders. As a member of Professor Janet Treasure's team of volunteer coaches, she has offered coaching for carers of people with eating disorders within a number of research projects. Alongside her position within the National Health Service, Suzi Doyle works in private practice in central London.

Jonathan Espie (DClin) is a clinical psychologist and part of the senior management team in the Child and Adolescent Eating Disorder Service at the Maudsley Hospital. Jonathan is experienced in working with children and families across a broad range of behavioural, developmental and mental health difficulties. His publications include papers on cognitive biases in adolescents, parenting, and psycho-education for parents of children with autism spectrum conditions. Alongside his systemic approach to eating disorders, Jonathan offers specialist input as a CBT therapist.

Jane Evans (BSc, DClinPsy) is a senior clinical psychologist and is based at the Adult Outpatient Eating Disorder Service at the Maudsley Hospital. Jane has worked in the field of eating disorders for over ten years, having worked in a number of specialist services in London, across in, day and outpatient settings and conducting both individual and group therapy. She completed her doctorate in Clinical Psychology at University College London in 2007 and since then has completed her diploma in Cognitive Behavioural Therapy at Royal Holloway University of London. Her publications include book chapters and papers in the area of CBT for eating disorders.

Caroline Fleming (PsychD, CPsychol) is a chartered counselling psychologist who has worked in the field of eating disorders for eight years. For the past five years she has worked for the National Inpatient Eating Disorder Service at the Bethlem Royal Hospital with Dr Kate Tchanturia in the translation of research into clinical practice, and is working to develop novel individual and group therapies within the inpatient setting. Prior to this she worked within the day and outpatient services for adults with eating disorders for Surrey and Borders NHS Foundation Trust. Caroline is Associate Fellow of the British Psychological Society.

Samantha Lloyd (BA, MSc) is a current PhD student investigating perfectionism in adolescents and adults with Anorexia Nervosa, including potential associations between perfectionism and neurocognition. In the process of her PhD she conducted a systematic review of the literature and experimental studies on the topic. Before joining Dr Tchanturia's team she completed an MSc in Mental Health Service and Population Research at the Institute of Psychiatry and has worked as a research assistant in both chronic fatigue and eating disorders services.

Zoe Maiden (BSc) is currently working as an assistant psychologist in the Child and Adolescent Eating Disorder Service at the Maudsley Hospital. She has been a member of the Intensive Treatment Programme for a year, contributing to ongoing research and audit projects. Prior to this, she worked as a research and clinical coordinator at the Centre for Anxiety Disorders and Trauma in Maudsley Hospital. She completed her BSc in Psychology at the University of Surrey and is starting clinical psychology training at Royal Holloway University of London.

Victoria Mountford (BA, DClinPsy) is Principal Clinical Psychologist at the South London and Maudsley NHS Foundation Trust Eating Disorders National Service. She has co-authored two books including a leading guide to cognitive behavioural therapy for adults with eating disorders and authored a number of book chapters. Her research interests include cognitive behaviour therapy, treatment outcomes and body image. She has published on these topics in peer reviewed journals and presented at international conferences.

Mima Simic (MD, MRCPsych) is Head of the CAMHS National and Specialist Child and Adolescent Eating Disorder Service (CAEDS) and Consultant Child and Adolescent Psychiatrist for the adolescent DBT service at the Maudsley Hospital. For more than 25 years, her clinical work has been focused on the treatment and development of new treatments for disorders in adolescence with the specialist interest on eating disorders and self-harm. Her main research interest has focused on testing the efficacy of the newly developed treatment modalities for eating disorders and self-harm, and results of the treatment trials she participated in continue to be published in the peer reviewed journals.

Katherine Sparrow (BSc) is currently undertaking the Mental Health Studies MSc at Kings College London. She is working on a research project on the group therapy offered at Bethlem Royal Hospital's Eating Disorders Unit under the supervision of Dr Kate Tchanturia. Prior to this she completed her BSc in Psychology at the University of Nottingham.

Kate Tchanturia (PhD, DClin) is a chartered clinical psychologist who has worked in the field of clinical and experimental psychology for 30 years. Over the last two decades, her clinical and academic work in the King's College London Department of Psychological Medicine and the South London and Maudsley NHS Foundation Trust Eating Disorders National Service has focused on translational research to promote excellence in clinical practice. Dr Tchanturia has published over 120 peer reviewed papers reporting experimental studies of cognitive processing and emotion in eating disorders, as well as their cultural presentations. In this book, she reviews the emerging evidence of brief group interventions for eating disorders with her collaborators and colleagues from the South London and Maudsley NHS Foundation Trust Eating Disorders National Service. Dr Tchanturia is the lead clinical psychologist for the Eating Disorders National Service at the Maudsley Hospital and a Reader in the psychology of eating disorders at King's College London. She is a Fellow of the Academy of Eating

Disorders, a Fellow of the British Psychological Society and a visiting professor of Clinical Psychology in Tbilisi Illia University, Georgia. She is a recipient of Royal Society, Wellcome Trust, NHS Innovation, Maudsley Charity, Psychiatry Research Trust, BRC and Swiss Anorexia Foundation awards. She has lectured internationally and trained clinicians and researchers in the UK, USA, Europe, South America, New Zealand, Australia and in her country of origin, Georgia, in the neuropsychology of eating disorders and how to translate it into remedial approaches.

She has contributed seven chapters in various manuals on eating disorders and edited the book *Cognitive Remediation Therapy (CRT) for Eating and Weight Disorders* (Routledge: http://www.routledge.com/books/details/9781138794030/).

For more details visit: http://www.katetchanturia.com.

Acknowledgements

I have many people to thank for their general support and help with this book. Books such as this one reflect the hard work of a team and I was very lucky to have many talented, compassionate people around me to complete this exciting project.

First of all, many thanks to my lovely family: Simon, Alex and Sophie, for putting up with me finishing book chapters and edits during our wonderful holiday in Tuscany. Many thanks to my son Alex Surguladze who designed the book cover. We are now making a habit of working as a team and using his skills wherever possible in my work. Sophie also worked on some images, graphs and editing in the book.

This book was inspired and strongly supported by my wonderful colleagues and great friends, Professors Janet Treasure, Ulrike Schmidt and Iain Campbell, Dr Niki Kern, Dannie Glennon, Lynn StLouis, Caroline Norton and many wonderful clinicians from our great multidisciplinary team.

Almost all psychologists from my clinical and research teams worked hard and contributed chapters, and coped with my clumsy grammar (in my third language). It is a great privilege and honour to work with you, many thanks for your great team work. A big thanks to my fantastic postgraduate students. I hope they will forgive me not to list them all here. Your names and hard work appear on different pages of this book.

I would like to thank all of our patients for taking part in the studies and for their helpful comments, feedback, participating in the focus groups, permission to use anonymous cases, stories and examples.

I have been supported financially by different funding resources throughout the research: Swiss Anorexia Foundation, BIAL, the Psychiatry Research Trust, the NIHR Biomedical Research Centre for Mental Health at South London and Maudsley NHS Foundation Trust and the Institute of Psychiatry, King's College London, NHS Innovations, Maudsley Charity Health in Mind.

This is a great opportunity to express my gratitude to all of them.

An introduction to brief group psychotherapy in intensive care programmes for eating disorders: gathering research evidence

Kate Tchanturia and Katherine Sparrow

Eating disorders are severe mental health problems with devastating consequences. The high mortality rates associated with these disorders emphasise the relevance of developing successful treatment interventions. The existing literature regarding psychological treatment programmes for eating disorders is still limited, and this is particularly true for group interventions.

Delivering psychological interventions in a group format can bring unique benefits that are not achievable when working with patients individually. These benefits include: sharing experiences and learning from others in a safe and therapeutic environment, being with other people and practising interpersonal skills. In the treatment of anorexia nervosa (AN), these therapeutic benefits also represent a challenge for group facilitators as it is exactly these interpersonal and relational demands that patients find difficult to tolerate (Tchanturia *et al.*, 2012, 2013a; Fleming *et al.*, 2014). Facilitators are likely to be confronted with low motivation and a reluctance to engage, which are not only characteristic of the illness itself, but are also a result of the discomfort evoked by spending time with others in a group setting (Genders and Tchanturia, 2010). It has been observed that patients with AN often remain isolated and avoid communicating with other patients in inpatient settings. Our recent research also shows that people with anorexia have difficulties making social contacts and forming friendships well before the onset of the illness (Doris *et al.*, 2014). We also know that people with eating disorders report high levels of social anhedonia – an absence of pleasure derived from being with people (Tchanturia *et al.*, 2012; Harrison *et al.*, 2014). In our recent study when we compared IQ matched controls and patients with anorexia, we found that patients with a higher than normal IQ scored lower on emotional intelligence tasks (Hambrook *et al.*, 2012). This task called MSCIT is widely used in human resources and by organisational psychologists. A combination of many factors such as being shy, socially anxious and having a long-term eating disorder creates social difficulties. The majority of patients in our inpatient programme tell us about their discomfort when engaging in group discussions, whether inside or outside of the hospital environment. In one of our recent studies exploring how eating disorders affect work and social adjustment we found that most people experienced the largest detriment to their social relationships and social leisure, whereas the work domain was less affected by their eating disorder (Tchanturia et al., 2013a; Harrison et al., 2014). One interesting piece of research conducted by our group suggests that patients with anorexia have very low facial expressivity in the acute stage of the illness. While watching an amusing film clip, patients with anorexia did not express smiles compared to non-eating-disordered controls (Davies et al., 2010). Interestingly, the results of this original study conducted with adults were replicated in an adolescent patient group (Rhind et al., 2014). The absence of facial emotional expression hugely affects the quality of patients' relationships. We have therefore used these research findings to inform our group interventions and tailor group treatment in the best possible way for our patients. For example, we developed psycho-education materials and specific exercises informed by research findings to help patients address their social difficulties.

Group therapy is unique in providing a safe opportunity to address social problems, which is important for improving patients' quality of life and relapse prevention. For this reason we have summarised the relevant literature in this book to enable us to reflect on our own practice and develop a stronger, more robust group treatment programme.

We utilise a stringent clinical audit system in our treatment programme in order to evaluate the efficacy of both individual and group interventions. Over the years we have been considering how to improve the group programme and tailor it to our patients' needs. This is an ongoing process and we have shared our insights in this book with the aim to help both ourselves and our colleagues working in the field of eating disorders to learn from this research and develop group treatment programmes further.

In Figure 1.1 we have presented a brief snapshot of the number of individual vs group therapy sessions attended by inpatients on our ward in 2013. This provides a visual demonstration of the challenges faced by clinicians regarding patients' willingness to engage with group treatment. On examination of the individual cases presented in Figure 1.1, it appears that patients who attended a relatively greater number of individual therapy sessions are those who failed to gain significant weight during their inpatient admission and remained on the ward for a long time. It is notable that the number of group therapy sessions attended by these patients is very low.

In contrast, patients who attended relatively fewer individual therapy sessions and a relatively greater number of group therapy sessions were more likely to gain weight and have a shorter admission period. These observations are very preliminary and complex, but nevertheless emphasise the importance of encouraging patients to attend group therapy. This approach holds great therapeutic value for patients. The group format encourages them to be with others and to develop the skills to eat in a social environment. Patients also have the opportunity to discuss topics directly related to the disorder or to broader aspects of recovery. In addition, given the busy ward environment, a meaningful and evidence-based group

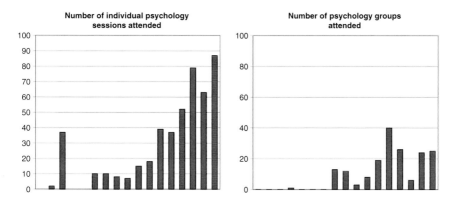

Figure 1.1 Snapshot of the individual and group attendance

programme is a more efficient use of the therapist's time; a necessary consideration which will be further explained later.

Having highlighted these difficulties, we believe it would be therapeutically beneficial to use the time during an inpatient's admission to address not only the core symptoms of the illness, but also the broader issues which often act as maintaining factors. Therapeutic interventions which improve interpersonal skills and confidence in being with others, and create a more cohesive sense of identity and reduce feelings of isolation, are likely to facilitate the complex process of functional reintegration into the community. Some authors believe that interventions which encourage the direct expression of feelings are clearly warranted in this patient group, as they are inclined to express feelings through indirect or somatic channels (Lieb and Thompson, 1984). Therapeutic groups are the ideal place to practise and implement social and communication skills, and to receive social feedback (both verbal and non-verbal). In the context of inpatient adult services, the majority of patients have a chronic eating disorder and have been unwell for many years (Chapter 3 has more specific information about our national clinic demographics), therefore their social network is limited and their social confidence is low. To add to these difficulties, the prevalence of autistic traits is high among eating disordered inpatients (e.g. Huke *et al.*, 2013; Tchanturia *et al.*, 2013c).

There has been a great deal of research and clinical debate regarding what works best in terms of treatment for eating disorders in adults. This is particularly true for patients with a diagnosis of anorexia due to the lack of a strong first choice treatment (NICE, 2004). Another problematic issue related to this is that it tends to be the more severely unwell patients who disengage from treatment. Given that AN has a high mortality rate and is a huge burden for patients, their families and society, further research and new recommendations are needed.

With regard to the existing literature for group interventions, the majority of recently published studies focus only on individual forms of treatment. Indeed, our systematic appraisal of the literature showed that only 38 studies have reported group therapy treatments in eating disorders. Moreover it is difficult to form any conclusions from the available studies for the following reasons: they report on different patient groups (anorexia, bulimia, binge eating disorders), the content and therapeutic model varies hugely, sample sizes are small, and outcome measures are very different (Genders and Tchanturia, 2010; Pretorius *et al.*, 2012; Fleming *et al.*, 2014).

We decided to appraise the available literature and present the studies we were able to find systematically before publishing this book. Table 1.1 summarises the studies we were able to find up to and including 2014 (May).

Systematic literature review of the group treatment of EDs: method

Two systematic literature reviews were conducted according to the 'PRISMA statement' (Moher *et al.*, 2009) for this study. The first was a review of studies on group therapy for eating disorders. Figure 1.2 (on page 17) shows the consort diagram for the study selection.

Eligibility criteria

Studies of group therapy for eating disorders published in peer reviewed journals in English were included. Studies were included if they examined the outcome or efficacy of a group therapy or examined the feedback of patients regarding group therapy. Studies were excluded if they:

- examined the dynamics of the group in group therapy (e.g. group cohesion);
- examined multifamily group therapy;
- focused on binge eating disorder and obesity;
- examined the feedback of the therapist or parents regarding the group therapy;
- explored challenges in implementing group therapy generally.

Information sources and search strategy

Electronic databases of PsycINFO, Medline, Embase and SCOPUS were searched up to July 2014 using the following keywords: ('group therapy' or 'group treatment') and ('eating disorders' or 'anorexia').

Selection

Studies identified in the search were then screened by the content of their abstracts and potentially relevant articles were selected. Duplicates were excluded at this stage and full text articles were then assessed for suitability. Studies were excluded

Table 1.1 Systematic review of the published work in group format in eating disorders. We used a broad strategy because of the limited amount of research on this topic

Authors	Year and journal	Group intervention/aims	Outcome
Brennan et al.	2014 Counselling and Psychotherapy Research	Emotion-focused therapy group. The purpose of this qualitative study was to explore the perspectives of six women with eating disorders regarding their experiences of participating in a 12-week emotion-focused therapy group. The purpose of the group was to help participants find the connections between their eating disorder symptoms and feelings, facilitate the development of increased self-awareness, and teach the participants to relate to themselves and their emotions in accepting, healthy ways. The main focus of the group work was on helping the women change their vast self-criticism.	A qualitative analysis of the patients' letters to their inner self-critics illustrates their growth and development in the ability to foster a sense of self apart from the critic, separate from and confront the criticism, listen to their feelings and act on their needs. This group was well received by participants.
Fleming et al.	2014 Advances in Eating Disorders: Theory, Research and Practice	Cognitive behavioural therapy-based self-esteem group. The group was designed to address low confidence, low self-worth and low assertiveness in inpatients with AN. Six group sessions were designed and piloted within an inpatient eating disorders ward. Sixty-three inpatients participated.	Qualitative feedback demonstrated that both patients and group facilitators found the group to be acceptable, useful and an overall positive experience. The clinical outcome measures showed no statistically significant improvements in patients' self-reported self-esteem or motivation to change; though with regard to self-esteem, a change in the positive direction was observed.

Table 1.1 (cont.)

Authors	Year and journal	Group intervention/aims	Outcome
Goss and Allan	2014 *British Journal of Clinical Psychology*	*Compassion-focused therapy for eating disorders (CFT-E).* The article describes how CFT-E uniquely addresses the issues of shame, self-criticism, self-directed hostility, and difficulties in generating and experiencing emotion in patients with an eating disorder. The article also discusses the current evidence base for CFT-E and provides an outline of recent and potential future developments in CFT-E.	Conclusions: CFT-E offers a promising group treatment for adult patients who present to specialist eating disorder services with restricting and binge/purging eating disorders. CFT-E has a specific protocol and interventions to address the biological, psychological and social challenges of recovery from an eating disorder.
Tchanturia et al.	2014 *European Eating Disorders Review*	*Cognitive Remediation and Emotions Skills Training (CREST) group therapy for AN.* Seventy-one adult inpatients suffering from AN took part in the five-session group (36 patients provided pre- and post-intervention outcome measures). Sessions were one hour long and took place once a week.	Results showed that social anhedonia decreased significantly between pre- and post-intervention, with effect size (d = 0.39). Motivation (perceived 'importance to change' and 'ability to change') was found to have increased with small effect sizes (d = 0.23 and d = 0.16), but these changes did not reach statistical significance. The CREST group had positive feedback from both the patients and the therapist delivering this structured intervention.
Morgan et al.	2014 *European Eating Disorders Review*	*Ten-session manualised body image therapy.* Fifty-five adult inpatients at two national centres received the group-based manualised body image therapy.	The group achieved statistically significant changes in body checking, body avoidance and anxiety, and shape- and weight-concern. The examples of body checking include frequent self-weighing, self-examination of specific body parts, using clothes that fit to judge the shape and the pinching flesh. Examples of body avoidance include concealing mirrors and averting eyes from reflective surfaces such as shop windows. Conclusion by authors: this is a feasible, effective and acceptable manual-based therapy.

| Bhatnagar et al. | 2013 Journal of Clinical Psychology | A cognitive-behavioural group intervention for the treatment of body image disturbance in women with eating disorders. The intervention was an eight-session CBT group called for Body Image Disturbance (CBT for BID). The treatment was designed for use in an outpatient clinic with an adult eating disorder population. The intervention targeted attitudinal and behavioural components of body image disturbance using psychoeducation, self-monitoring, systematic desensitisation and cognitive restructuring. Primary outcomes included multidimensional body image assessment (effectiveness) and treatment adherence and satisfaction (feasibility). | Participants undergoing manualised group treatment reported significantly less body image disturbance than participants randomised to a waitlist control condition. An inspection of mean scores indicated that those in the immediate intervention group (in comparison to those in the delayed intervention group) reported more satisfaction in overall appearance, greater satisfaction with individual body parts, less of a discrepancy between perceptions of their current body and their ideal body, and fewer maladaptive body image avoidance behaviours. However, differences disappeared after both groups had been through intervention. Participants also reported less depression and eating disorder pathology from baseline to post-treatment; however, this difference was not considered statistically significant. Feasibility outcomes suggest the intervention was well received and highly acceptable to participants. |
| Juarascio et al. | 2013 Behavior Modification | Acceptance and commitment therapy (ACT) – group-based. 140 patients with AN and bulimia (BN) either received treatment as usual (TAU) or TAU plus ACT. | Individuals in the ACT condition trended toward lower global eating pathology, shape concerns and weight concerns by post-treatment, as well as greater willingness to consume a distressing food. Patients in this condition also trended toward greater increases in psychological flexibility as measured by the AAQ-II. Although relatively small effects, it is notable that the addition of a small number of ACT group sessions showed a consistent pattern of reduced eating pathology by post-treatment over and above the effect of a much broader and more comprehensive treatment programme (i.e. TAU). ACT patients also showed lower rates of rehospitalisation during the six months after discharge. |

Table 1.1 (cont.)

Authors	Year and journal	Group intervention/aims	Outcome
Ohmann et al.	2013 Neuropsychiatrie	A cognitive behavioural therapy (CBT) group for AN. The authors examined the emotional problems of patients with AN during the course of a CBT group therapy programme. Twenty-nine outpatient females with AN participated in four groups of manual-based CBT group therapy. The multimodal group–CBT programme included nine modules: therapeutic motivation, psycho-education, individual problem analysis, teaching of problem-solving strategies, communication skills, hedonistic training, elements of awareness, body and schema psychotherapy.	Sixteen patients were successfully treated, five had a poor outcome, eight dropped out. Emotional deficits were resistant to change. Comorbid disorders and parental psychopathology were negative prognostic factors.
Zuchova et al.	2013 Eating and Weight Disorders	Explored the feasibility and acceptability of group cognitive remediation therapy (CRT) for AN inpatients. Ten 45-minute CRT sessions took place once a week, in two consecutive groups of adult inpatients. Groups consisted of 14 and 20 patients respectively.	Found that: 1) group CRT could be well incorporated into the therapeutic programme of the Eating Disorders Unit; 2) CRT group was well received by the patients.
Juarascio et al.	2013 Journal of Contextual Behavioural Science	Investigated whether more severe baseline eating pathology moderated the effect of an acceptance and commitment group-based therapy in 140 women with AN/BN.	Those with more severe symptoms at baseline showed greater improvements in eating disorder symptomatology in the ACT condition than in the TAU condition; however, the effect size was relatively small. This was also the case for patients with more previous hospitalisations and those with AN with lower body weights. Therefore ACT may be beneficial for patients with more severe eating disorder pathology.

Pretorius et al.	2012 *European Eating Disorders Review*	Seven *CRT groups* for 30 adolescents with AN were carried out.	Cognitive flexibility and motivation were assessed before and after each group. There were changes with small effect sizes in self-reported cognitive flexibility post group ($t(18) = -1.8$; $p < 0.09$). Adolescents found the group interesting and useful; however, some wanted more support with application to real life.
Lavender et al.	2012 *PLoS ONE*	*Emotional and Social Mind Training for BN.* Seventy-four participants were randomised to either Emotional and Social Mind Training (ESM) or CBT group programmes.	The primary outcome measure was the Eating Disorder Examination (EDE) global score. Assessments were carried out at baseline, end of treatment (four months) and follow-up (six months). Found no differences in outcome between the two treatments. Adherence rates were higher for participants in the ESM group. ESM might be a viable alternative to CBT for some individuals.
Wood et al.	2011 *Clinical Child Psychology and Psychiatry*	*One-off CRT group* for nine adolescent inpatients with AN.	Ten-session course of group-based CRT was well received by the participants, who reported it to be useful. They engaged well with the therapy and felt empowered by achieving tasks better than the facilitating therapists. This helped to develop a positive therapeutic relationship and allowed patients to see facilitators/fellow participants as being imperfect and supported the fact that this is normal, human and acceptable. The participants appeared to be more aware of individual cognitive deficits and open to discussion about thinking styles. There were definite improvements in performance on some of the CRT tasks.
Lázaro et al.	2011 *European Eating Disorders Review*	*Self-esteem and social skills group therapy* in 160 adolescent eating disorder patients attending a day hospital treatment programme.	After the group therapy both groups presented significant improvements in their perceptions of physical appearance, their self-concepts related to shape and weight and to others, happiness and satisfaction, social withdrawal and leadership. BN and BN related patients presented more changes on many of the variables.

Table 1.1 (cont.)

Authors	Year and journal	Group intervention/aims	Outcome
Legenbauer et al.	2011 European Eating Disorders Review	Examined the impact and change of dysfunctional cognitions during a *body image group therapy*, which included 41 patients with an eating disorder. The treatment programme included 10 group sessions which took place once a week in an outpatient setting. There were 4–8 participants in each of the 10 treatment groups.	Results indicate a significant reduction of dysfunctional cognitions relating to 'body and self-esteem', 'dietary restraint', 'eating and loss of control', as well as 'internalisation and social comparison'. Furthermore, the changes in dysfunctional cognitions were associated with a reduction in eating disorder psychopathology.
Nowoweiski et al.	2011 Behaviour Change	Evaluated the efficacy of a day treatment programme for eating disorders which consisted of *group-based dialectical-behavioural therapy and short-term dynamic psychotherapy*.	Compared pre- and post-treatment data outcome measures for eating disorder pathology and patient satisfaction was also evaluated using qualitative methods. Results indicated a significant reduction in depressive symptoms post-treatment using a Wilcoxon Sign Test ($W = -2.032, p < 0.05$), along with a high degree of satisfaction with the treatment.
Katzman et al.	2010 Psychosomatic Medicine	Compared *CBT versus MET* (Motivational Enhancement Therapy) in phase 1 followed by group versus individual CBT in phase 2 in 75 patients with BN.	Patients improved significantly across all of the interventions. However, no statistical differences in either outcome measure or treatment compliance were found across the treatment conditions. Dropout rate tended to be lower for those in group treatment; however, it was not statistically different from those in individual treatment.
Genders and Tchanturia	2010 Eating and Weight Disorders	Report the development and acceptability of a pilot of *CRT for AN in a group format*. Four group sessions were designed and piloted with 30 patients in an eating disorder service.	Statistically significant improvements were found in self-reported ability to change (p = 0.03). Both patients and group facilitators found the group acceptable, useful and a positive experience.
Proulx	2008 Eating Disorders	The experiences of six women with BN were examined after they participated in an *eight-week mindfulness-based eating disorder treatment group*.	The women reported less emotional distress and improved abilities to manage stress. This treatment may help the 40% of women who do not improve with current therapies and might be useful to prevent symptoms in younger women.

Author	Year / Journal	Aims and methods	Results
Prestano et al.	2008 European Eating Disorders Review	Aimed to examine the effectiveness of group analytic therapy for patients with AN and BN. Eight patients (three AN and five BN) entered group-analytic treatment, meeting weekly for two years. Eating behaviours, overall psychological distress and group process variables were regularly assessed using quantitative and qualitative measures, with comparisons made at the beginning and end of the therapy.	Results: treatment was discontinued in two cases. In terms of eating disorder symptoms, three patients were recovered, two were unchanged and one had deteriorated. Patients experienced an overall positive group climate and a positive group alliance. Perception of being understood by the therapist appeared to play an important role in the therapeutic process. These preliminary results suggest that group analytic therapy may be effective in helping patients with eating disorders.
Dean et al.	2008 European Eating Disorders Review	Examined group MET as an adjunct to inpatient treatment for eating disorders. Twenty-three inpatients completed a four-session MET group programme in addition to routine hospital care. A control group of 19 participants completed TAU.	Despite an absence of significant differences between the MET and the TAU groups on the overall formal outcome measures, there were nevertheless differences between the groups. Specifically, the MET groups appeared to foster longer-term motivation and engagement, and to promote treatment continuation. The results tentatively suggest that MET could be valuable for the treatment of inpatient eating disorder patients and further research is warranted.
Richards et al.	2006 Eating Disorders	Compared the efficacy of spirituality, cognitive and emotional support groups for treating eating disorder inpatients. Participants = 122 women receiving eating disorder inpatient treatment. Several outcome measures were administered at admission and discharge (post-treatment), including the Eating Attitudes Test (EAT; Garner and Garfinkel, 1979), Body Shape Questionnaire (BSQ: Cooper et al., 1987), Outcome Questionnaire (OQ-45; Lambert and Burlingame, 1996), Multidimensional Self-Esteem Inventory (MSEI; Epstein and O'Brien, 1983), and Spiritual Well-Being Scale (SWBS; Ellison and Smith, 1991).	Paired t-tests on the mean scores of pre- to post-treatment outcome measures for all three treatment groups combined revealed that the patients reported statistically significant improvements on all of the outcome measures – most with large effect sizes. Patients in the Spirituality group tended to score significantly lower on psychological disturbance and eating disorder symptoms at the conclusion of treatment compared to patients in the other groups, and higher on spiritual well-being. On weekly outcome measures, patients in the Spirituality group improved significantly faster during the first four weeks of treatment. The findings indicate that the Spirituality group did enhance the overall effectiveness of the eating disorder inpatient programme – somewhat more so than did the Cognitive and Emotional Support

Table 1.1 (cont.)

Authors	Year and journal	Group intervention/aims	Outcome
			groups. There was a consistent pattern of findings, many of them statistically significant, which favoured the Spirituality group. Attending to eating disorder patients' spirituality growth and well-being during inpatient treatment may help reduce depression and anxiety, relationship distress, social role conflict and eating disorder symptoms.
Nevonen and Broberg	2005 European Eating Disorders Review	*Compared individual and group psychotherapy for EDNOS.* Thirty-five female patients were matched according to eating disorder severity and then randomly assigned to either group or individual therapy. Each condition consisted of 10 CBT sessions (providing psycho-education and dietary regulation) followed by 13 IPT sessions (targeting interpersonal problems).	Participants were assessed at pre- and post-treatment and at 1- and 2.5-year follow-up. Found no significant differences between the two treatment approaches. Therefore the group approach is more cost-effective.
Clark et al.	2003 Nursing Times	*Evaluation of the Priory EDU which runs an extensive group therapy programme involving cognitive groups, small psychodynamic groups, assertiveness groups, body image groups and psycho-educational groups.* The audit was completed at the end of 2001 and looked into the outcomes of treatment for all patients with AN who were admitted to the unit in 1997.	Patients found the intensive group programme helpful as they could receive support from others. It increased their confidence and improved their social interaction. The follow-up study showed that 85% of patients were successfully helped to return to their normal weight. Four-fifths of the patients who were followed up were doing reasonably well four years later.

Author	Year / Journal	Description	Outcome
Chen et al. Reviewed by Tasca and Bone (2007) – please see reference list	2003 *International Journal of Eating Disorders*	*Compared group and individual CBT for 60 patients with BN. Participants were randomly assigned to: (1) group therapy that was manualised, conducted in 90-minute sessions, and delivered in a closed format; or (2) individual therapy that consisted of 19 semi-structured 50-minute sessions during a 4.5-month period.*	Measures of eating disorder psychopathology, general psychiatric symptoms, self-esteem and social adjustment were administered to assess changes in functioning at post-treatment and at three- and six-month follow-up sessions. Although individual therapy produced significantly greater reductions in binging and purging behaviours post-treatment, no significant differences remained at three- or six-month follow-up. The group condition produced greater improvement for social adjustment and anxiety at the follow-up assessments among treatment completers.
Wiseman et al.	2002 *Eating Disorders*	*Compared a short-term CBT group with a psycho-education group in an inpatient eating disorder unit. Forty patients were assessed at hospital admission and after two weeks of group participation.*	Both groups showed improvement over the two weeks; however, no significant differences were found. Both staff and patients preferred the CBT treatment.
Crafti	2002 *Behaviour Change*	*Evaluated a group treatment programme incorporating both cognitive behavioural and interpersonal components for post-adolescent women.*	Outcome was determined by measures of behaviour change, changes in eating psychopathology and measures of general psychopathology. Group data indicated improvement on most outcome measures at both post-treatment and follow-up for treated clients (in both settings) compared to a waiting-list control group.
Waisberg and Woods	2002 *Canadian Journal of Dietetic Practice and Research*	*Examined the effectiveness of a short-term nutrition and behaviour change outpatient group for patients with AN. The group was developed and co-led by a dietician and a psychologist on a general hospital eating disorders team. The main goal of the short-term nutrition and*	The group was evaluated by monitoring group members' weights, collecting pre-treatment and post-treatment scores on the Eating Attitudes Test-26, and comparing earlier and later food records. Statistically significant changes were found in the consumption of calories ($p < 0.01$), fat ($p < 0.005$) and protein ($p < 0.02$). The group was designed to provide

Table 1.1 (cont.)

Authors	Year and journal	Group intervention/aims	Outcome
		behaviour change group was weight gain through normalisation of eating. Interventions included didactic teaching, cognitive-behavioural approaches, emotionally focused comments and facilitation of group discussion. The aim was to improve dietary knowledge and skills while addressing cognitive and emotional barriers to change.	treatment that was adjunctive to psychotherapy. Patients were taught practical skills they could use to monitor their own future behaviour. The group was successful and warrants further refinement and investigation.
Laberg et al.	2001 Scandinavian Journal of Behavioural Therapy	Qualitative study on patients' experiences of group therapy. The group therapy was CBT-focused with interpersonal themes for BN.	Patients found being treated in a group as opposed to individual sessions very helpful as they felt supported by other group members. Patients found the psychoeducation aspect of the treatment very helpful. The negative criticism that patients reported about the treatment was that they wanted to be treated for longer in order to make more progress.
Mussell et al.	2000 Journal of Consulting and Clinical Psychology	The aim was to investigate potential patient variables that predict favourable response to group CBT in a sample of 143 women seeking treatment for BN.	Pre-treatment desire to discontinue bulimic behaviours and expected success were associated with good treatment outcome. The primary variable found to predict longer-term outcome was symptom remission at the end of treatment and at the one-month follow-up.
Fernandez-Aranda et al.	1998 Eating and Weight Disorders	Examined the effectiveness of CBT group therapy for outpatients. Twenty-six outpatients were assessed at the beginning and end of treatment, and at one year follow-up.	Good EAT scores were observed in 70% of patients after the treatment and in 60% at follow-up. The results substantiate the effectiveness of the CBT approach.

Study	Year / Journal	Method	Findings
Vanderlinden and Vandereycken	1988 *Psychotherapy and Psychosomatics*	Compared the perception of changes by the patients themselves, the group members, and the therapeutic team in 53 eating disorder patients during an inpatient group treatment programme.	Patients tend to deny problems or to evaluate their progress optimistically, whereas fellow patients and staff members are much alike in their sceptical evaluations.
Marner and Westerberg	1987 *Journal of Family Therapy*	Eight families referred to a child psychiatric outpatient ward were offered *group therapy and family therapy simultaneously*, one group for patients with AN and one for their parents.	The participants from both groups reported that they had learned a lot from the experience but felt that group therapy could not replace family therapy. The girls with AN were interested in meeting other girls with the same problem. As the girls in the group were at different stages of their illness they could support each other, but at the same time some girls felt threatened when patients joined the group who were thinner than they were.
Kirkley et al.	1985 *Journal of Consulting and Clinical Psychology*	Compared the efficacy of two group treatments *(CBT and non-directive)* for BN. The CBT group was instructed to make specific changes in their eating and vomiting behaviour, whereas the non-directive group was given no such instructions. Both treatment groups met weekly for 16 weeks.	The CBT group tended to have fewer dropouts and yielded significantly greater decreases in binging and vomiting than the nondirective treatment. At three-month follow-up, 38% of the CBT and 1% of the non-directive group participants continued to abstain from bingeing and vomiting, but these differences were not statistically significant.
Roy-Byrne et al.	1984 *International Journal of Eating Disorders*	Nine patients with BN participated in a year-long group therapy which combined *behavioural and psychodynamic approaches*.	By the end of the year, six had complete cessation or considerable improvement of their bulimic symptoms.
Connors et al.	1984 *The American Journal of Psychiatry*	Treatment of BN with a brief *psycho-educational group therapy*. Two groups of ten normal-weight bulimic women received short-term, structured group treatment. Treatment incorporated education, self-monitoring, goal setting, assertion training, relaxation and cognitive restructuring.	Results showed an overall reduction of 70% in binge-purge episodes. There were significant improvements in psychological functioning, including self-esteem, depression, assertiveness and pathological attitudes about eating.

Table 1.1 (cont.)

Authors	Year and journal	Group intervention/aims	Outcome
Lieb and Thompson	1984 *International Journal of Group Psychotherapy*	*Group therapy of four adolescent anorexia nervosa inpatients. The group met twice weekly for one hour per session.*	Patients were resistant to the idea of group therapy at first. They were reserved during the initial group sessions but their resistance and isolation dramatically decreased as the sessions progressed. At first they discussed their strategies for dieting and exercising, but then the focus shifted to common emotional difficulties and conflicts their families shared. They realised they all felt a high pressure from their families to achieve and used dieting to cope with this. Outside the group, they also began to interact in a less hostile way with staff and other patients. They began to eat meals together and to steadily gain weight. All four patients maintained their weight at discharge or had a slight gain in weight at follow-up. All four patients felt that the group was very helpful.
Stevens and Salisbury	1984 *American Journal of Orthopsychiatry*	Describes the structure, process and outcome of a group therapy project involving eight bulimic women. A closed group which met weekly for 90-minute sessions. The group focused on eating behaviour during the early sessions and then moved on to gaining awareness of connections between feelings and eating behaviour.	Five of the six members of the group who continued beyond the 16th session reported symptom control.

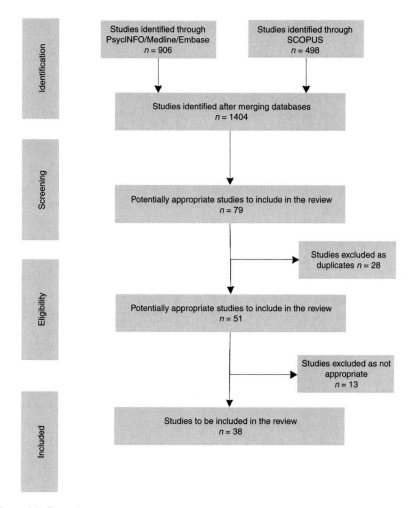

Figure 1.2 Flow diagram in line with PRISMA

as being inappropriate for the review if they did not meet the eligibility criteria at this stage.

As depicted by the table, it is very hard to synthesise the findings from the literature. It is also clear that pre 2000 there were only nine studies examining group therapy and after 2000 this figure tripled.

However, the evidence is still very limited. The modest number of publications since 2000 is highlighted by the table.

Figures 1.3 and 1.4 visually present the state of the literature on group interventions for eating disorders, emphasising the gaps in our knowledge.

To summarise, the evidence base for treatments of AN remains limited (e.g. Berg and Wonderlich, 2013; Kass *et al.*, 2013). Therefore, there is a need to

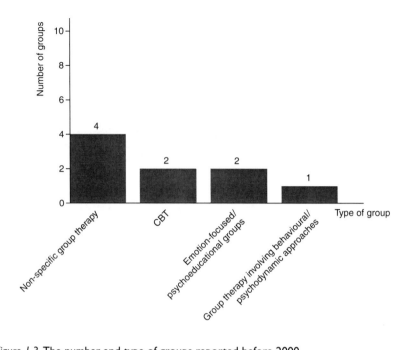

Figure 1.3 The number and type of groups reported before 2000

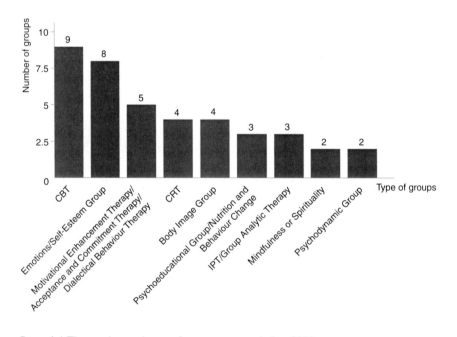

Figure 1.4 The number and type of groups reported after 2000

develop and clinically evaluate cost-effective psychological interventions for patients with AN (NICE, 2004). As a starting point, research investigating the cognitive, socio-emotional profile of individuals with eating disorders has yielded promising results and identified key areas for therapies to target (Davies *et al.*, 2010, 2012; Money *et al.*, 2011; Tchanturia *et al.*, 2013b; Fleming *et al.*, 2014; Lloyd *et al.*, 2014).

In this overview we reflected on the need to conduct more systematic research, evaluate groups and generate further evidence regarding group interventions that are beneficial for eating disorders. In the following chapters of the book we will:

1. provide group intervention protocols;
2. evaluate existing audit data on the therapeutic groups we run in the inpatient ward;
3. analyse quantitative and qualitative data;
4. plan future studies to inform our clinical practice.

In our opinion, the importance of this evaluation and of sharing short group treatment protocols is timely. First, it will contribute to the limited existing literature on group interventions designed specifically for eating disorders. Furthermore, in the current economic climate, mental health services in the UK and other countries are under pressure to provide brief but effective treatment packages for an ever increasing number of patients. Mental health services differ between countries, but the time pressure and demand for better tailored treatments are nevertheless similar regardless of geography.

We will discuss group protocols and available evidence in the following chapters and summarise where possible what we have learned.

Acknowledgement

Kate Tchanturia would like to thank the Swiss Anorexia Foundation for their help in this study.

References

Berg, K. C. and Wonderlich, S. A. (2013). Emerging psychological treatments in the field of eating disorders. *Current Psychiatry Reports*, 15(11), 1–9.

Bhatnagar, K. A. C., Wisniewski, L., Solomon, M. and Heinberg, L. (2013). Effectiveness and feasibility of a cognitive-behavioral group intervention for body image disturbance in women with eating disorders. *Journal of Clinical Psychology*, 69(1), 1–13.

Brennan, M. A., Emmerling, M. E. and Whelton, W. J. (2014). Emotion-focused group therapy: Addressing self-criticism in the treatment of eating disorders. *Counselling and Psychotherapy Research*, 1–9.

Chen, E., Touyz, S. W., Beumont, P. J., Fairburn, C. G., Griffiths, R., Butow, P., … Basten, C. (2003). Comparison of group and individual cognitive-behavioral therapy for patients with bulimia nervosa. *International Journal of Eating Disorders*, 33(3), 241–254.

Clark, S., Oxbrough, J., Smith, P. and Rowan, P. (2003). Anorexia nervosa and the efficacy of an eating disorder service. *Nursing Times*, 99, 34–36.

Conners, M. E., Johnson, C. L. and Stuckey, M. K. (1984). Treatment of bulimia with brief psychoeducational group therapy. *The American Journal of Psychiatry*, 141(12), 1512–1516.

Crafti, N. A. (2002). Integrating cognitive-behavioural and interpersonal approaches in a group program for the eating disorders: Measuring effectiveness in a naturalistic setting. *Behaviour Change*, 19(1), 22–38.

Davies, H., Schmidt, U., Stahl, D. and Tchanturia, K. (2010). Evoked facial emotional expression and emotional experience in people with anorexia nervosa. *International Journal of Eating Disorders*, 44(6), 531–539.

Davies, H., Fox, J., Naumann, U., Treasure, J., Schmidt, U. and Tchanturia, K. (2012). Cognitive remediation and emotion skills training for anorexia nervosa: An observational study using neuropsychological outcomes. *European Eating Disorders Review*, 20(3), 211–217.

Dean, H. Y., Touyz, S. W., Rieger, E. and Thornton, C. E. (2008). Group Motivational Enhancement Therapy as an adjunct to inpatient treatment for eating disorders: A preliminary study. *European Eating Disorders Review*, 16(4), 256–267.

Doris, E., Westwood, H., Mandy, W. and Tchanturia, K. (2014). Patients with anorexia nervosa show similar friendships difficulties to people with autism spectrum disorders: A qualitative study. *Psychology, Special issue: Autism*, 5, 1338–1349.

Fernandez-Aranda, F., Bel, M., Jimenez, S., Vinuales, M., Turon, J. and Vallejo, J. (1998). Outpatient group therapy for anorexia nervosa: A preliminary study. *Eating and Weight Disorders*, 3(1), 1–6.

Fleming, C., Doris, E. and Tchanturia, K. (2014). Self-esteem group work for inpatients with anorexia nervosa. *Advances in Eating Disorders: Theory, Research and Practice*, 2(3), 1–8.

Genders, R. and Tchanturia, K. (2010). Cognitive Remediation Therapy (CRT) for anorexia in group format: A pilot study. *Eating and Weight Disorders*, 15(4), 234–239.

Goss, K. and Allan, S. (2014). The development and application of compassion-focused therapy for eating disorders (CFT-E). *British Journal of Clinical Psychology*, 53(1), 62–77.

Hambrook, D., Brown, G. and Tchanturia, K. (2012). Emotional intelligence in anorexia nervosa: Is anxiety a missing piece of the puzzle? *Psychiatry Research*, 200(1), 12–19.

Harrison, A., Mountford, V. and Tchanturia, K. (2014). Social anhedonia and work and social functioning in the acute and recovered phases of eating disorders. *Psychiatry Research*, 218, 187–194.

Huke, V., Turk, J., Saeidi, S., Kent, A. and Morgan, J. F. (2014). The clinical implications of high levels of autism spectrum disorder features in anorexia nervosa: A pilot study. *European Eating Disorders Review*, 22(2), 116–121.

Juarascio, A., Kerrigan, S., Goldstein, S. P., Shaw, J., Forman, E. M., Butryn, M. and Herbert, J. D. (2013). Baseline eating disorder severity predicts response to an acceptance and commitment therapy-based group treatment. *Journal of Contextual Behavioral Science*, 2(3), 74–78.

Juarascio, A., Shaw, J., Forman, E., Timko, C. A., Herbert, J., Butryn, M., … Lowe, M. (2013). Acceptance and commitment therapy as a novel treatment for eating disorders: An initial test of efficacy and mediation. *Behavior Modification*, 37(4), 459–489.

Kass, A. E., Kolko, R. P. and Wilfley, D. E. (2013). Psychological treatments for eating disorders. *Current Opinion in Psychiatry*, 26(6), 549–555.

Katzman, M. A., Bara-Carril, N., Rabe-Hesketh, S., Schmidt, U., Troop, N. and Treasure, J. (2010). A randomized controlled two-stage trial in the treatment of bulimia nervosa, comparing CBT versus motivational enhancement in Phase 1 followed by group versus individual CBT in Phase 2. *Psychosomatic Medicine*, 72(7), 656–663.

Kirkley, B. G., Schneider, J. A., Agras, W. S. and Bachman, J. A. (1985). Comparison of two group treatments for bulimia. *Journal of Consulting and Clinical Psychology*, 53(1), 43–48.

Klump, K. L., Bulik, C. M., Kaye, W. H., Treasure, J. and Tyson, E. (2009). Academy for Eating Disorders position paper: Eating disorders are serious mental illnesses. *International Journal of Eating Disorders*, 42(2), 97–103.

Laberg, S., Törnkvist, Å. and Andersson, G. (2001). Experiences of patients in cognitive behavioural group therapy: A qualitative study of eating disorders. *Scandinavian Journal of Behaviour Therapy*, 30(4), 161–178.

Lavender, A., Startup, H., Naumann, U., Samarawickrema, N., DeJong, H., Kenyon, M., … Schmidt, U. (2012). Emotional and social mind training: A randomised controlled trial of a new group-based treatment for bulimia nervosa. *PLoS ONE*, 7(10), e46047.

Lázaro, L., Font, E., Moreno, E., Calvo, R., Vila, M., Andrés-Perpiñá, S., … Castro-Fornieles, J. (2011). Effectiveness of self-esteem and social skills group therapy in adolescent eating disorder patients attending a day hospital treatment programme. *European Eating Disorders Review*, 19(5), 398–406.

Legenbauer, T., Schütt-Strömel, S., Hiller, W. and Vocks, S. (2011). Predictors of improved eating behaviour following body image therapy: A pilot study. *European Eating Disorders Review*, 19(2), 129–137.

Lieb, R. C. and Thompson, T. L. (1984). Group psychotherapy of four anorexia nervosa inpatients. *International Journal of Group Psychotherapy*, 34(4), 639–642.

Lloyd, S., Fleming, C., Schmidt, U. and Tchanturia, K. (2014). Targeting perfectionism in Anorexia Nervosa using a group based cognitive behavioural approach: A pilot study. *European Eating Disorder Review*, 22(5), 366–372.

Marner, T. and Westerberg, C. (1987). Concomitant group therapy with anorectics and their parents as a supplement to family therapy. *Journal of Family Therapy*, 9(3), 255–263.

Moher, D., Liberati, A., Tetzlaff, J. and Altman, D. G. (2009). Preferred reporting items for systematic reviews and meta-analyses: The PRISMA statement. *Annals of Internal Medicine*, 151(4), 264–269.

Money, C., Genders, B., Treasure, J., Schmidt, U. and Tchanturia, K. (2011). A brief emotion focused intervention for inpatients with anorexia nervosa: A qualitative study. *Journal of Health Psychology*, 16(6), 947–958.

Morgan, J. F., Lazarova, S., Schelhase, M. and Saeidi, S. (2014). Ten session body image therapy: Efficacy of a manualised body image therapy. *European Eating Disorders Review*, 22(1), 66–71.

Mussell, M. P., Mitchell, J. E., Crosby, R. D., Fulkerson, J. A., Hoberman, H. M. and Romano, J. L. (2000). Commitment to treatment goals in prediction of group cognitive-behavioral therapy treatment outcome for women with bulimia nervosa. *Journal of Consulting and Clinical Psychology*, 68(3), 432–437.

National Institute for Clinical Excellence (NICE). (2004). Eating disorders: Core interventions in the treatment and management of anorexia nervosa, bulimia nervosa, and related eating disorders. https://www.nice.org.uk/guidance/cg9.

Nevonen, L. and Broberg, A. G. (2005). A comparison of sequenced individual and group psychotherapy for eating disorder not otherwise specified. *European Eating Disorders Review*, 13(1), 29–37.

Nowoweiski, D., Arthey, S. and Bosanac, P. (2011). Evaluation of an Australian day treatment program for eating disorders. *Behaviour Change*, 28(4), 206–220.

Ohmann, S., Popow, C., Wurzer, M., Karwautz, A., Sackl-Pammer, P. and Schuch, B. (2013). Emotional aspects of anorexia nervosa: Results of prospective naturalistic cognitive behavioral group therapy. *Neuropsychiatrie*, 27(3), 119–128.

Prestano, C., Lo Coco, G., Gullo, S. and Lo Verso, G. (2008). Group analytic therapy for eating disorders: Preliminary results in a single-group study. *European Eating Disorders Review*, 16(4), 302–310.

Pretorius, N., Dimmer, M., Power, E., Eisler, I., Simic, M. and Tchanturia, K. (2012). Evaluation of a cognitive remediation therapy group for adolescents with anorexia nervosa: Pilot study. *European Eating Disorders Review*, 20(4), 321–325.

Proulx, K. (2008). Experiences of women with bulimia nervosa in a mindfulness-based eating disorder treatment group. *Eating Disorders*, 16(1), 52–72.

Rhind, C., Mandy, W., Treasure, J. and Tchanturia, K. (2014). An exploratory study of evoked facial affect in adolescents with anorexia nervosa. *Psychiatry Research*, 220(1–2), 711–715.

Richards, P. S., Berrett, M. E., Hardman, R. K. and Eggett, D. L. (2006). Comparative efficacy of spirituality, cognitive, and emotional support groups for treating eating disorder inpatients. *Eating Disorders*, 14(5), 401–415.

Roy-Byrne, P., Lee-Benner, K. and Yager, J. (1984). Group therapy for bulimia: A year's experience. *International Journal of Eating Disorders*, 3(2), 97–116.

Stevens, E. V. and Salisbury, J. D. (1984). Group therapy for bulimic adults. *American Journal of Orthopsychiatry*, 54(1), 156–161.

Tasca, G. A. and Bone, M. (2007). Individual versus group psychotherapy for eating disorders. *International Journal of Group Psychotherapy*, 57(3), 399–403.

Tchanturia, K., Davies, H., Harrison, A., Fox, J., Treasure, J. and Schmidt, U. (2012). Altered social hedonic processing in eating disorders. *International Journal of Eating Disorders*, 45(8), 962–969.

Tchanturia, K., Hambrook, D., Curtis, H., Jones, T., Lounes, N., Fenn, K., Keys, A., Stivenson, L., Davies, H. (2013a). Work and social adjustment in patients with anorexia nervosa. *Comprehensive Psychiatry*, 54(1), 41–45.

Tchanturia, K., Lloyd, S. and Lang, K. (2013b). Cognitive remediation therapy for anorexia nervosa: Current evidence and future research directions. *International Journal of Eating Disorders*, 46(5), 492–495.

Tchanturia, K., Smith, E., Weineck, F., Fidanboylu, E., Kern, N., Treasure, J. and Baron Cohen, S. (2013c). Exploring autistic traits in anorexia: A clinical study. *Molecular Autism*, 4, 44.

Tchanturia, K., Doris, E. and Fleming, C. (2014). Effectiveness of Cognitive Remediation and Emotion Skills Training (CREST) for anorexia nervosa in group format: A naturalistic pilot study. *European Eating Disorders Review*, 22(3), 200–205.

Vanderlinden, J. and Vandereycken, W. (1988). Perception of changes in eating disorder patients during group treatment. *Psychotherapy and Psychosomatics*, 49(3–4), 160–163.

Waisberg, J. L. and Woods, M. T. (2002). A nutrition and behaviour change group for patients with anorexia nervosa. *Canadian Journal of Dietetic Practice and Research: A publication of Dietitians of Canada = Revue canadienne de la pratique et de la recherche en dietetique: une publication des Dietetistes du Canada*, 63(4), 202–205.

Wiseman, C. V., Sunday, S. R., Klapper, F., Klein, M. and Halmi, K. A. (2002). Short-term group CBT versus psycho-education on an inpatient eating disorder unit. *Eating Disorders*, 10(4), 313–320.

Wood, L., Al-Khairulla, H. and Lask, B. (2011). Group cognitive remediation therapy for adolescents with anorexia nervosa. *Clinical Child Psychology and Psychiatry*, 16(2), 225–231.

Zuchova, S., Erler, T. and Papezova, H. (2013). Group cognitive remediation therapy for adult anorexia nervosa inpatients: First experiences. *Eating and Weight Disorders*, 18(3), 269–273.

Chapter 2

A short description of the adult clinical treatment service at the Maudsley

Kate Tchanturia

The eating disorders unit (EDU) adult service at the Maudsley has different departments: outpatient, day care step-up and inpatient treatment programmes. The inpatient ward has 18 beds and accepts patients from many parts of the UK and locally which means that it is a national service for eating disorders (ED).

The Psychology team is formed of a consultant (lead), clinical and counselling psychologists and a psychology assistant of different grades according to training and years of experience working in the field. They offer psychological treatment including Cognitive Remediation and Emotion Skills Training (CRT and CREST), Motivational Enhancement Therapy (MET) and Cognitive Behavioural Therapy (CBT). Some of the therapists in the department are trained in Cognitive Analytical Therapy (CAT), Schema Therapy, and some of them in Dialectical Behavioural Therapy (DBT). We have a large multidisciplinary team with many skills, offering occupational therapy based groups, and a family therapist jointly with a social worker delivers the carers workshops developed by Professor Janet Treasure, consultant psychiatrist and clinical director of the eating disorder service. We also have a very experienced team led by dietician Kate Williams delivering individual and group sessions. The Maudsley adult team is research active and has an evidence-generated approach. A good example of this is the outpatient manualised treatment intervention (MANTRA) developed by Professor Ulrike Schmidt. Professor Schmidt is head of the research unit and consultant psychiatrist in the outpatient department.

In this book we choose to focus on the group interventions that we deliver in our treatment programme in brief format. This book is mainly written by the psychology team and represents part of the work we do.

The multi-disciplinary team (MDT) includes: the Medical team (consultant psychiatrists and doctors); the Management team (specialist clinical lead and ward manager); the Nursing team; the Psychology team (that provides individual and group psychological work as well as assessments); the Occupational Therapy team (that provides individual sessions, reviews and group interventions); the Family Interventions team; and access to a dietician.

In the inpatient programme treatment as usual includes:

• Individual care plans, daily weigh-ins and dispensing on any medication by the Nursing team.

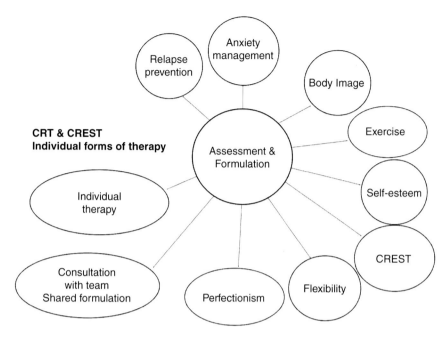

Figure 2.1 The individual and group programmes in the ward

- Communal meals (three main meals and three snacks) every day in the dining room. Patients must stay in the dining room for the duration of the meal and are supported by members of the MDT. Each meal is followed by a rest period which is for one hour after main meals and 20 minutes after snacks. During this time patients must remain in the communal areas of the unit.
- Aims of the eating programme: to make eating as manageable as possible, to restore nutritional health safely, to establish a regular eating pattern, with a normal variety of foods and to gradually give the responsibility back to patients for feeding themselves. The eating programme is divided into four main stages: 1) a gradual re-introduction to eating; 2) gradual increase of meals throughout the day; 3) more substantial meal plans; 4) participation in trips to the canteen, cooking groups in the unit and buying and preparing meals.

The Psychology groups programme includes the Flexibility group (CRT), the Emotions group (CREST), Coping with worry group, Self-esteem group, Living with Perfectionism, Body wise, Relapse prevention, Coping with excessive exercise group as well as one-off groups. In the step-up programme a recovery star based programme is running as well as day care specific groups.

We mainly will describe the group programme that the Psychology team offers. Most of it is designed based on the psychoeducational materials and tools that target the psychopathology, cognitive and personality styles commonly described in anorexia and that facilitate the recovery process.

Chapter 3

Flexibility workshops

Cognitive remediation therapy (CRT) in group format: adults

Kate Tchanturia and Eli Doris

After the successful development and implementation of the individual format of cognitive remediation therapy (CRT), we decided to develop a group format of CRT with several clinical benefits in mind. First of all, to maintain and consolidate the knowledge, reflection and skills obtained in the individual format of CRT; secondly, we hoped that the group format would allow patients to practise social skills as well as thinking about thinking styles in a socially safe environment. Those of us involved in the development (please see acknowledgements section), delivery and supervision of this group decided to call the intervention the 'Flexibility workshop', to make it more accessible to patients who were not familiar with the term CRT.

We were mindful that the patients who would be receiving the group intervention may have already had, or be due for, individual CRT sessions; therefore it was decided to try to include some novel exercises in the group sessions. These exercises were designed to tap into 'bigger picture' thinking and cognitive flexibility, as with the tasks administered in individual CRT sessions. There was also a need to make sure that the exercises were acceptable to patients in a group situation, as well as being interactive in nature, in order to make the most efficient use of the group format. As with individual CRT, the aim of the group sessions was to practise global and flexible thinking, but with the support of peer group members and group facilitators. All sessions were designed to include the following elements: psycho-education, practical exercises, reflection and discussion within the session, and the planning of homework tasks. Continual discussion relating the exercises and homework tasks to real life thoughts and behaviours also remained an essential part of the reflection process.

The aims of the pilot work (a short four-session intervention with 18 patients, which was reported in our first paper: Genders and Tchanturia, 2010) were not only to explore whether participation in the group would enhance cognitive skills, but also whether there were any secondary gains in improving motivation and self-confidence. Outcome measures were used to evaluate the group's effectiveness in improving these areas as well as its acceptability to the patient group. The outcome measures we used are outlined after the session plans on p. 29.

Table 3.1 The average length of stay in the inpatient programme has decreased over time; data sourced from the last nine years of our inpatient programme audit

	2005	2006	2007	2008	2009	2010	2011	2012	2013
Average length of admission (weeks)	21.7	25.1	23.0	17.3	19.7	17.2	20.4	16.3	16.9

Length of stay in the inpatient unit in weeks

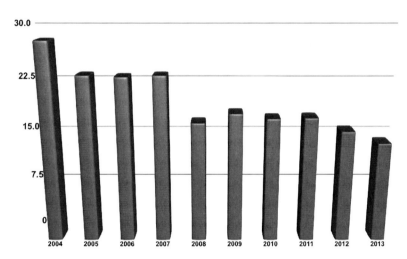

Figure 3.1 The average length of admission has not only decreased in our service, this is a general trend across the UK. We know from the literature that hospital stay has shortened even in the USA. In some European countries it is longer.

The length of the intervention was decided to be four weekly sessions, which was later extended to six weekly sessions (Tchanturia and Smith, 2015). This decision (for a short format) was influenced in part by the fact that the group was an unfunded pilot clinical project and also by the average length of inpatient admission at the time of the pilot (2009), which had been decreasing (please see Table 3.1 and Figure 3.1). Once we had piloted the four-session format, we collected qualitative evaluation from the patients in the inpatient clinical programme (Genders and Tchanturia, 2010; Tchanturia and Smith, 2015) as well as from the clinicians who had delivered the intervention (Lounes DClin Thesis, 2014; Lounes and Tchanturia, 2015). Both patients and clinicians highlighted the importance of extending the four-session format and at present we are evaluating the six-session format.

It might be helpful to outline the general context and patients' characteristics from the audit data over the past nine years (this is the 'bigger picture' which varies from year to year, but is a close approximation to our clinical reality based on the mean percentages calculated from the audit data). Of our patients, 95.5% have anorexia nervosa (AN), of which 61.1% are AN Restrictive, 23.4% are AN Binge-Purge and 11% are atypical AN; while 1.1% have Bulimia Nervosa and 3.4% have Eating Disorder Not Otherwise Specified (EDNOS). In terms of severity, 33–40% typically are national referrals (usually more severely unwell) and around 25% are treated under the Mental Health Act. Regarding admission by Body Mass Index (BMI, defined as weight/height^2) severity, 4.4% are in the underweight range (BMI 17.5–20), 17.4% are in the AN range (BMI 15–17.5), 37.4% are in the severe range (BMI 13.5–15), 30.1% are in the critical range (BMI 12–13.5), and 9.8% are in the life threatening range (BMI < 12).

The group was designed to be delivered by multi-disciplinary clinical team members with two facilitators per group (typically one with clinical/counselling psychology training). The facilitators' stance is aimed to be motivational, collaborative and interactive. The sessions are an *exploration* of the different thinking styles of the group members, and the facilitators should emphasise that there are no right or wrong ways of thinking but rather pros and cons of different thinking styles.

The main difference between the individual and group formats of CRT is that the group format is much shorter; therefore reflection and the relating of content to everyday life should be initiated much earlier. However, with several group members and two facilitators' contributions, these reflections tend to arise more easily in the early sessions.

Thus, six group sessions were planned and implemented; the outline of each is provided below. We do not have exclusion criteria for the Flexibility group, and regardless of the severity of the illness (as shown above) we include patients from the very early days of their admission, to ensure that psychological work starts immediately upon arrival to the inpatient programme alongside nutritional treatment. In traditional treatment approaches it is common to wait until nutritional status has improved, given that cognitive functioning is limited when patients are in the severe range of BMI 10.5–15.00. Thus most of the individual talking therapies are delivered when patients are in the weight-restored stage. However, given that anorexia is an ego syntonic disorder (patients often identify with the illness and feel a sense of achievement and control from it), by the time weight is restored, the chances of therapeutic engagement and motivation for psychological treatment are pretty low. It seems to us that cognitive remediation in both the individual and group formats bridges this gap and helps patients to start psychological work early on in the treatment programme. This is due to the nature of CRT; both patients and clinicians from our qualitative study mention that it is fun, easy to engage with, has a focus away from eating and disorder-related symptoms, and yet is still relevant for the recovery journey. With regard to content, the main focus of the group is targeting cognition; in particular, awareness of cognitive inflexibility and the absence of bigger picture thinking are the targets of this psychological treatment.

Content of the group sessions

Session 1 – the brain, thinking styles and what research tells us about cognitive styles in eating disorders

Materials: paper, pens, flipchart and flipchart pens, laptop or computer, data projector, hand-outs, homework sheets and self-report questionnaires (outlined in the 'outcome measures' section).

1. Welcome to the group and ground rules

Group members are welcomed and a few minutes are spent discussing general ground rules for group attendance such as respect, time keeping and confidentiality. The group members are asked if they would like to keep the six sessions open or closed to new members. In most cases group members request closed groups and as facilitators we have discovered that this does indeed allow for greater continuity between sessions. Outcome measures should also be administered at the start of the session, for auditing purposes and the detection of cognitive and psychological changes over time.

2. Introduction to CRT

Group facilitators normally give a brief explanation of the basis of the group in the same way as one would introduce individual CRT sessions to a patient. It should be emphasised that the sessions are designed to be interactive and not necessarily focused on eating, weight and shape; for example:

> The idea behind this group is to help people *think* about *thinking*. In everyday life we don't often stop and think about *how* we think – we tend to do the things the same way day in day out without really thinking about it – like we are on autopilot. Our brains get used to these ways of thinking and this means we often find it difficult to adapt when we need to.
>
> The idea of this group is for us to do some games and puzzles that will help us to identify our thinking strategies in everyday life and explore whether there might be alternative ways of doing things.

A short task at the beginning of the session can provide a simple demonstration of the ideas behind the group and act as an ice breaker.

3. Handwriting task

Group members are given a sheet of paper and a pen and asked to write their name with their dominant hand. They are then asked to do the same but with their non-dominant hand. Facilitators can join in so as to demonstrate the interactive nature of the group and to engage participants in the process. Group members are then asked if they would like to share their writing with the rest of the group and discuss how it felt to write with their non-dominant hand. Facilitators can share their experiences too.

The aim of the exercise is to demonstrate how we all have certain ways of doing things which feel comfortable and that most of our everyday habits are automatic. However, the exercise also shows us that although we all find it difficult to do things another way, our brains will allow us to do so and with practice it should become easier.

After this exercise it is easy to introduce the brain plasticity idea, i.e. how we can develop new pathways and areas of the brain through practice and being aware of our cognitive styles. We often use examples from the research literature, such as how the working memory of taxi drivers becomes very efficient and how well their hippocampus develops; we also talk about musicians developing different brain structures depending on what instrument they play.

4. Psycho-educational film clip

We found in the first session (depending on the motivation and severity of the group) that patients are interested in learning about what is known from the research evidence on how anorexia affects the brain. There is a piece of psycho-educational material which sheds light on this and can be shown when access to PowerPoint and the Internet is possible during the session:

http://bodybrain.com.au/info/sites/default/files/Brain%20for%20Kids_0.pdf

This short film serves as a basis for interesting discussions.

5. Brain atlas/hand-out

If the group takes place in a room where these facilities are not available then we use stories and interesting/engaging materials illustrating the brain plasticity idea and how different parts of the brain can be trained and developed through practising and exerting brain function. We often present a brain atlas or hand-out with some comments, for example:

> There are special parts of our brain that are responsible for what we call 'executive functioning' (like a big boss organising his workers!)
> This includes planning, organising, problem-solving and self-control (if you find these things difficult, you may find that you're late for sessions, often act before thinking, forget to do things …).
> We mainly use our frontal lobes (at the top/front of the brain) when we're doing these things.

The brain is the hungriest organ in the body and in order to function it needs between 500 and 800 kcal. Often we discuss the Minnesota starvation experiments and what we know about the consequences of chronic food deprivation.

6. Planning homework

For homework, participants can explore the benefits of cognitive exercises and learn how we can change/train our brains.

In the session we also mention the benefits of flexible thinking; even if some people think they are flexible they can still think about how useful this skill is in the general context.

Dr Spencer Johnson's book *Who Moved My Cheese* (1999) is a manageable sized book to read for homework and discuss in the next session.

Session 2 – bigger picture thinking

Materials: paper, pens, flipchart and flipchart pens, laptop or computer, data projector, hand-outs and homework sheets.

1. Summary of the previous session and reflection on homework

This session starts with a brief reminder from Session 1 and thinking about how people think when they are at the most severe stage of illness compared to when they are in a better nutritional state. Group members who have attempted a homework challenge are encouraged to share their experiences.

Almost all groups comment that attention is very much affected when in the starved state. As an ice breaker the group can be shown the following clip, which provides good material to start thinking and discussion about how awareness alters perception and attention:

http://www.youtube.com/watch?v=IGQmdoK_ZfY

We endeavour to keep CRT sessions balanced between specific and concrete materials, role plays and games, and reflection and discussion. In the group setting we encourage DOING, then REFLECTING and planning homework.

In the second session the theme is about trying to see the 'wood for trees', and after group members participate in an exercise which targets this, we move to the discussion and behavioural experiments.

2. Describing task in pairs

Group members are asked to get into pairs and each is given a hand-out containing a set of line drawings of simple and more complex shapes (see Figures 3.2 and 3.3 for examples), and some blank paper and pens. It should be ensured that each participant has a different hand-out from their partner.

They are then instructed to take it in turns to choose a figure from their hand-out, without showing it to their partner, and describe it to them so that they can draw it. A facilitator should pair up with a participant if there are odd numbers.

This task should take about ten minutes or long enough so that each member of a pair has described and drawn at least one of the shapes.

EXAMPLE FIGURES FOR THE DESCRIBING TASK

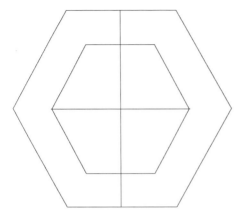

Figure 3.2 Describing task figure

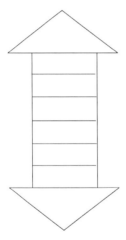

Figure 3.3 Describing task figure

REFLECTIONS

The facilitators can then ask the group for observations and reflections on the task to elicit discussion on detail-focused vs bigger picture thinking and the pros and cons of these, for example:

- How did people find it?
- Was it easy or difficult? Was it easier to draw or describe?
- What strategies seemed to help?
- How might you have done it differently?

- Which thinking styles were you using during this task?
- In which alternative ways could you approach this task?
- What are the advantages/disadvantages of these approaches?
- When do we need to use these thinking styles in everyday life?
- Can these thinking styles cause problems ever?

3. Planning homework

The session ends with some optional homework challenges. These should be introduced a few minutes before the end and a hand-out with suggested ideas can be provided (for a copy of the homework challenges see below). Participants are encouraged to try a *small* challenge for homework which should be treated as a personal experiment. The aim is not for participants to confront major difficulties associated with their eating disorder, but merely to practise simple tasks with the view of raising their awareness of their thinking styles and increasing their confidence in their own ability to change.

Flexibility group – homework challenges

Before the next group session, see if you can try one or two of these challenges.

Try to choose one that may be something you would not normally do, or that is different to how you would normally do it.

These challenges may help to break a rigid routine you have (e.g. tidying your room), or may help to break a rigid thinking pattern (e.g. worrying about the dining room).

- Get up or go to bed at a different time – maybe try not to set your alarm if there isn't something you need to get up for.
- Read a different magazine from usual.
- Watch a film or an episode of a TV show you haven't seen before.
- Use a different shampoo or shower gel.
- Style your hair in a different way.
- Listen to a different radio station.
- Try not to make your bed first thing in the morning – maybe try and leave it until later in the day or before you go to bed.
- Change where you sit in the lounge.
- Borrow a CD from someone else.
- Take a different route on a journey you are used to taking.
- Try a different colour eye shadow or lip gloss.
- Play a game of cards/board game.
- Change the time on your phone to 24hr or 12hr.
- Read a chapter in a book.
- Leave the house/room untidy when you go out and tidy up later.
- Choose a new ringtone on your phone.

Or choose your own *little* challenge that means something to you.

Let us know how it went.

Session 3 – switching

Materials: flipchart, flipchart pens, hand-outs and homework sheets.

1. Summary of the previous session and reflection on homework

Group members are asked if they can provide a summary of the previous session and what they learnt. Group members who have attempted a homework challenge are encouraged to share their experiences.

2. Illusions task

Visual illusions can be blown up and displayed on a flipchart, or they can be given as hand-outs if this is not possible. Around four or five illusions can be used in one session. The facilitators should encourage a discussion on each illusion, asking group members what they can see – this task is a good way to promote interaction between different group members coming to the board to point out different parts of the picture.

Following this, the group are then asked to reflect on what the task tells us about our ways of thinking, for example:

- What did people notice first? The bigger parts or the smaller parts?
- Could group members see the different perspectives?
- When do we need to be able to switch in everyday life?
- Is it hard sometimes to see things from another point of view?
- Do people find it hard to switch from their normal routines and habits? Any examples?

3. Planning homework

The session ends with the planning of homework. The list of homework challenges may be used again for those who have not tried one, but for others it may be appropriate to plan a more personal challenge within the session. The facilitators should try to discourage unrealistic goals to avoid the possibility of feelings of failure.

Session 4 – multi-tasking

Materials: flipchart, flipchart pens, packs of playing cards and homework sheets.

I. Summary of the previous session and reflection on homework

As with the previous sessions, begin with a reminder of the topics from the previous session and feedback from group members who attempted homework challenges.

2. Rub tummy/pat head

Ask group members to rub their tummy and pat their head at the same time (facilitators typically join in). Then ask group members to switch to rubbing their head and patting their tummy. Ask the group how easy or difficult they found the task.

Facilitators can then explain that this task is a short, easy way to demonstrate how our brains find it difficult to manage two things at once, especially when they are done in a way that we are not used to.

3. Card game task

The aim of this task is to practise multi-tasking further. Group members are asked to get into pairs; facilitators may pair up with participants if there is an odd number in the group. Each pair is given a pack of playing cards and asked to play snap with one another, awaiting further instructions. After group members have been playing for a few minutes, facilitators should then ask them to carry on playing snap but at the same time to take it in turns to describe their favourite film to each other. Allow group members to continue with this for a few minutes before commencing discussion about the task.

Reflections should elicit discussion on why the task was difficult, and how group members manage multi-tasking in everyday life, for example:

- How did everyone find the task?
- When did it become harder?
- Which skills do we need to be able to do both the card game and the discussion?
- When do we need to do this in everyday life? When is it difficult?

4. Planning homework

More personal challenges can be encouraged, this time they may focus on practising multi-tasking if this has been identified as a particular problem; otherwise the focus can remain on practising flexibility in everyday activities and routines.

Session 5 – summary and reflections

Materials: flipchart, flipchart pens, occupations written on postcards/post-it notes, hand-outs and homework sheets.

1. Summary of the previous session and reflection on homework

As before, the group begins with a summary of what was covered in the previous session and a discussion about the homework.

The aim of the session is to summarise and consolidate what has been covered in the previous sessions and to think about how group members can take what they have learnt forward. Facilitators can ask the group members if they remember the four different thinking styles that have been covered in the sessions: '*detail-focused thinking*', '*bigger picture thinking*', '*switching*' and '*multi-tasking*'.

The following task allows group members to reflect on some of those different strategies.

2. Occupations task

This task allows group members to explore four different thinking styles ('*flexible*', '*focused*', '*detailed*' and '*bigger picture*') and when they would be useful in everyday life. The overall aim is for patients to conclude that no particular thinking style is best; but it helps if we can have skills in all four thinking styles as they are all needed at different times in life.

Different occupations are written on postcards or post-it notes in preparation for the session, for example: brain surgeon, teacher, dinner lady, architect, student, editor, builder, chef.

To begin the task, four thinking styles are written in the four corners of a flip-chart sheet (Figure 3.4). The group members are then instructed to place the different occupations on the flipchart under the skill they would use most. Discussion over the occupational skills used by each one is encouraged until an agreement is reached over where each occupation should be placed. For example, an architect might need to take a bigger picture approach when looking at the building he is planning as a whole and how it will fit into its environment, but he also needs to take a detailed approach when drawing the very minute and complex parts of the plans. In this example, the architect may then be placed somewhere between the bigger picture and detailed points on the flipchart.

Discussions often conclude that several of the occupations use a variety of skills and can be placed in the middle of the flipchart or in between two of the skills. After all of the occupations are sorted on the flipchart, the facilitators should generate a discussion on what the group can conclude from this task about the thinking skills covered in these sessions. As mentioned previously, this allows group members to come to some useful conclusions about thinking skills, for example:

*   Everyone needs a combination of all the thinking skills.
*   Some people have strengths in some of the skills more than in others.
*   If we can practise having all of the skills in our thinking 'repertoire' then we are more likely to be able to handle different situations in life.

Occupations task – an example

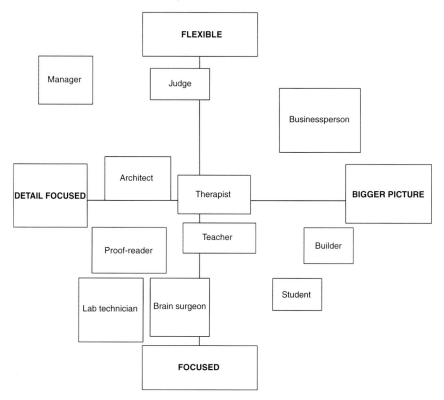

Figure 3.4 Occupations task example diagram

3. Proverbs and sayings

The aim of the final task is to provide some motivational messages for the group to discuss in the session. Proverbs and sayings that capture the aims and themes of the group sessions are presented to the group and provided on a hand-out (an example of the proverbs and sayings hand-out is provided on p. 38). Facilitators should encourage a discussion on these sayings and on how group members feel about the end of the group, for example:

- Do any of these sayings particularly stand out to anyone?
- Does anyone have a favourite?
- Does anyone have any other examples that are not on the list?
- Do any of them really summarise what this group has meant?
- Can everyone share the main message they will take from this group and how they will take it forward?

Proverbs and sayings – some examples

Nothing ventured, nothing gained.

Short words are best and the old words when short are best of all.

You will never get to the end of the journey if you stop to shy a stone at every dog that barks.

Never stand so high upon a principle that you cannot lower it to suit the circumstances.

Difficulties mastered are opportunities won.

Criticism is easy; achievement is difficult.

A picture is a worth a thousand words.

Actions speak louder than words.

All work and no play makes Jack a dull boy.

Habit is second nature.

Session 6 – mind maps, the meaning of life and the bigger picture of recovery

Materials: paper, pens, flipchart and flipchart pens, homework sheets, and self-report questionnaires.

The main objective of this final session is to bring together what was covered over the course of the previous group sessions. To help with this, the group members are introduced to three useful tools: mind maps, the recovery star and the professor's lesson.

Mind maps

Ask group members to think together and draw a mind map (see Figure 3.5 for an example) on the flipchart including ideas relating to the following questions: What was this group experience like? What was learnt and experienced and what are the take-home messages? How can this knowledge be consolidated in real life?

Outcome measures

Outcome measures should be administered at the end of the session, for auditing purposes and the detection of cognitive and psychological changes over time.

Outcome measures we use in the group format of CRT

We administer self-report outcome measures before the first and after the last session of this group. The measures for the final session include a feedback questionnaire. Verbal feedback can also be sought at the end of the group.

When deciding on appropriate outcome measures for evaluating this work, the team were mindful of choosing measures which would reflect change in the areas on which the group focused, while remaining practical to administer in the

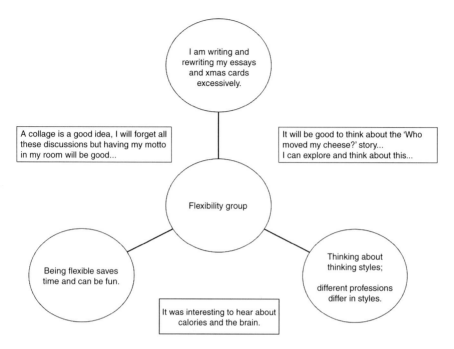

Figure 3.5 Group 'mind map' example

session. Neuropsychological assessment was not possible mainly due to the lack of resources.

To measure the development of cognitive skills, the Cognitive Flexibility Scale (CFS; Martin and Rubin, 1995) was the only brief measure we were able to find when we started to evaluate CRT groups. The CFS assesses participants' perceptions of the options and alternatives available to them in everyday situations. Higher scores represent greater cognitive flexibility. The authors found a mean score of 54.1 in a healthy population (Martin and Rubin, 1995). In our early work (e.g. Genders and Tchanturia, 2010; Lounes *et al.*, 2011) we reported results using this questionnaire, but we are increasingly using the DFlex questionnaire (Roberts *et al.*, 2011), because this measure captures both flexibility and 'bigger picture' thinking, and has now been validated.

We also use the motivational ruler (MR) which asks group members to rate on a scale of 0 to 10 how important it is to change and how confident they are in their ability to change. Please see Table 3.2 for outcome data from the Flexibility group pilot work.

In addition, we give participants a self-designed feedback form at the last session. This feedback form asks group members to rate on a Likert scale of 1 to 5 how much they enjoyed the sessions, how useful the sessions were and whether they felt they have learnt any new skills. There are also two open-ended questions

Table 3.2 Outcome data from the 'Flexibility group' pilot work

		N (% sample)	Pre-intervention	Post-intervention	p	Effect size
Flexibility	BMI	97 (100)	15.7 (2.06)	16.1 (1.91)	<0.001**	0.20
	CFS	69 (71)	44.3 (8.88)	46.0 (8.55)	0.09	0.20
	MR – I	73 (76)	7.85 (2.42)	8.03 (2.21)	0.45	0.08
	MR – A	73 (76)	4.86 (2.58)	5.58 (2.70)	0.02	0.27

that ask participants what they liked most about the sessions and what could be improved.

As can be seen in the other chapters, we try to use the motivational ruler and feedback questionnaire with most of the groups.

Group members' feedback from the pilot work

When asked what participants liked most about the sessions, 65 per cent mentioned that being able to talk and share experiences was helpful. They also mentioned liking the approach of using practical tasks to demonstrate thinking and behavioural styles. The educational aspects of the sessions, i.e. learning about thinking styles and the brain, were also cited as being useful. Four participants also mentioned finding the homework in between sessions helpful for practising new ways of approaching everyday activities.

Only some of the participants suggested something that could be improved. Half of them said that they would like more sessions and further practice at the skills covered in the sessions, while two participants mentioned the benefits of having individual CRT sessions in addition to the group, and the remaining participants said that nothing could be improved.

Some quotes from patients' feedback forms after the pilot CRT groups are presented in Table 3.3. The purpose of this snapshot illustration is to help clinicians who will be running the groups to plan and learn from earlier patient experiences.

Patient feedback following the CRT groups was organised into themes after qualitative analysis by one of KT's students (please see Table 3.4).

Feedback from patients and clinicians helps us to reflect on every group we have in the inpatient programme. We review groups once every year and try to synthesise outcomes and qualitative feedback from patients and the clinical team in order to make the appropriate changes. Here we have highlighted some recommendations which we either have already implemented or will be implementing in our future work.

Table 3.3 CRT group therapy qualitative feedback from the patients attending this group from the different runs (this audit has been firmed up over the years and is now conducted more systematically, with the same questionnaire administered after every type of group in the inpatient setting)

Date group commenced	What did you enjoy most about the sessions?	How can we improve sessions?
February 2009	• I liked the calm, relaxed atmosphere as it made it easier to talk about difficult issues. I liked the activities and games as it demonstrated the skills in everyday situations. • Helping to understand thinking styles and strategies and how to adopt new coping mechanisms.	• More sessions. Better attendance (as I think it would be useful for everyone to attend). • A balance between games and discussions. • Relaxed atmosphere, informal environment, colourful presentation, well-planned. • Nothing comes to mind.
May 2009	• The opportunity to share experiences. • Practical activities. Encouragement. • The chance to be able to speak out in a group. Also the challenges/tasks that we have been set. • I liked the size of the group. I thought it was a good open and sharing group and this was encouraged well. The tasks set and discussed were quite gentle but allowed for deeper reflection. I felt it wasn't too pressurised or formal but it was motivating.	• Both groups and individual workshops would be beneficial. • More sessions available and also more tasks, e.g. 'seeing two pictures in the one'. • More suggestions or ideas to try outside of group so that awareness can be raised about an individual's routines and flexibility.
September 2009	• The mixture of light-hearted exercises which could lead to some thought-provoking, deep discussions. Felt a 'safe' place to talk, non-judgemental. Open yet challenging fixed behaviour/thinking styles. • Group programme, share ideas. • Sharing ideas with peers. Provision of 'food for thought' and reflection. • It's nice to start and finish a whole group. • Seeing the bigger picture. • Group discussions. • During rest periods. • They were very open to changes. We were able to discuss things which people found helpful which were not in the session.	• For me, hearing about people's general experiences is helpful, not being stereotyped as having 'anorexic thinking'. • More homework, reminder of choice, include real-life situations. • No immediate ideas. • I don't know. • It should not be a closed group. • Do more practical tasks. Maybe bring in something from home life, college or work and try to solve the problem in the group using tasks discussed in sessions, i.e. multi-tasking making an important phone call. • More activities? • More solid ideas about flexibility and ways to be flexible.

Table 3.3 (cont.)

Date group commenced	What did you enjoy most about the sessions?	How can we improve sessions?
November 2009	• Focusing on the positive aspects of everyday experiences. Discussion about what I have changed. The group encouraged me to try to think more flexibly. • Talking about the practical implications of flexibility. • The focus on what we can change now. • Something different to groups I have attended before. Alternative ways of looking at things. • The talking and trying to look at things in a different way.	• More practical tasks in sessions. Goal setting in sessions. • Nothing. • The initial exercises, e.g. illusions and so on are quite basic when you already have done them or understand the principles so only doing this for new people. More in communication style and detail/getting to point.
January 2010	• Relaxed approach, combination of having plans but seeming open to discussion. • Relaxed and informative and helpful. • The practical element, e.g. games.	• More focus on difficult behaviour. • More sessions. • Extend length of programme, handbook of useful tips and practical tasks.
June 2010	• Sharing, fun, learning new skills. • The activity. • I learnt a lot about the things that I find difficult and brought them to light so I can use what I have learnt to be able to change in a way that will be easier to cope. • The activities especially the art and relating them to our behaviours. Being able to have a greater understanding of why I do certain things. The realisation that I do get caught up in detail and so do many people. Being able to make slight adjustments to routine – how this can be OK.	• More time – maybe five sessions rather than four. Thank you. • Different examples of applying new ideas and skills to real-life situations. • I think it should run for a longer period of time as it is a major issue for most of the people on this ward as well as give more practical solutions and tools. • Nothing, I thought it very well organised and found it easy to follow and understand. • More discussion over how we can relate the exercises to the illness, i.e. the multi-tasking – how can this be incorporated into treatments.
July 2010	• The 'safe space' given for people to talk about rules/routines. Also hearing advice from other people including Kate/Becca and Helen. • Exercise and games.	• It needs to be carried out on a more regular basis, e.g. eight-week cycles. Could also set people specific challenges each week. • Course could be longer.

	Feedback	Suggestions
September 2010	• The practical tasks: thinking about how one could use new techniques in everyday life. Thinking about little things you could change to start with. • They were interesting and also fun. I learnt things about myself. The staff were lovely. • Sorry, I cannot concentrate right now and cannot comment due to only attending one session. • The light-heartedness sometimes with exercises and games. • Sharing and hearing others' views, opinions and ideas. • Interacting and discussing instead of being talked at, because otherwise you lose your concentration. • The incorporation of tasks, it wasn't all passive. The group was small, therefore it was easy to talk and contribute.	• More sessions and a more regular rotation. • Run them more often and longer. • Set aims, goals, practical things. • Not assume everyone is really inflexible. • Encourage others to attend.
November 2010	• Practical skills, challenges and tools to practise being more flexible. Sharing and hearing others' experiences. • The approach to the group and the atmosphere it created. People felt comfortable to input their thoughts. • Session leaders were very knowledgeable and welcomed our thoughts and feelings. Were very understanding and sympathetic and gave us a very clear idea about what expectations we could reasonably have as a result of the workshop. • Thinking about introducing flexibility into my daily life. Kate's accent. Not forced to talk. Liked the 'quotes' hand-out, with positive affirmations on it. • Finding out about the different ways of seeing things and the ways of trying to change from one to another, i.e. detail and bigger picture and multi-tasking, etc.	• I strongly believe four sessions is not enough at all to cover such an important topic. I think group context should improve and develop after the end of each programme so those doing it more than once wouldn't find it boring. • A different variety of tasks if it is with the same people so it doesn't feel repetitive. • More sessions please – eight instead of four. • More hand-outs of flexibility. More tips and help on how one can include flexibility into our lives, and highlight the benefits of doing so. • More information such as hand-outs of each session so you can refer back to them again.
February 2011	• Interactive learning, sharing coping strategies and experiences. • Doing games and exercises. • Wasn't focused on food. Was enjoyable and didn't feel too invasive.	• Perhaps a couple of sessions longer and more work on putting skills into practice. • Longer group.

Table 3.3 (cont.)

Date group commenced	What did you enjoy most about the sessions?	How can we improve sessions?
May 2011	• Not too long and the challenge of thinking flexibly. • The ideas about trying new things each week.	• More discussion and tips on specific examples from patient experiences of when our thinking is stuck, e.g. too focused on detail and how we could have changed it in this situation.
September 2011	• Group communication and input. • Interactive, interesting exercises, relaxed, rewarding. • Group discussion.	• The ideas raised and work on them individually with key worker/therapist. • Did too few to comment. • Sharing more ideas.
January 2012	• The group used practical exercises. • Interactive games and visual images, well organised, fun, not too serious. • Tended to be repeated information and data from previous sessions attended. Personally I find a more practical group beneficial. • Thinking out of the box, bigger picture. • The sessions were very interactive. • Hearing other patients' points of views and their areas in which they struggle and sometimes being able to relate or realise my different ways of thinking to theirs. • I have done this group a number of times so I found it quite helpful but it helped me see what I still need to work on. • It was good to hear how other people perceived the same thing in different ways. • Physical activities, illusions, puzzles, mind games. • Interactive activities, discussing and describing, illusions, snap and multi-tasking. When the discussions were more animated and involved. • The different ways of looking at 'thinking' and the activities used to show that.	• More tasks and games, hand-outs. • Longer, more involvement from more people. • Do some different exercises so it is slightly different if you have already done the group. • I think it needs more sessions and more discussion about how inflexible/flexible thinking can impact on every aspect of your life. I felt a lot of the exercises were fun, but not really ones which made me think much about what/how I need to change. • Longer time frame to be able to put ideas into action and more work on individual issues, e.g. what people suffer and struggle with and more ideas on how to be flexible. • The two sessions I attended focused on a lot of things I had already covered in individual CRT. Perhaps an overall agenda for all the sessions discussed at the first group. • More activities. • More interactive activities, not just in a circle with a flipchart. More deep and interesting discussions to involve people. • Maybe discuss more about how flexible thinking comes up in our everyday lives and struggles and how we change them.
June 2012	• Interactive tasks. • Interactive tasks.	• To vary the content, as many people have attended the group previously.

Table 3.4 Themes emerging from patient feedback
Sparrow, 2014 MSc dissertation

What did you enjoy most about the sessions?

Themes within patients' qualitative responses	Frequency
Enjoyed the size and the relaxed atmosphere of the group as it made it easy to speak up and enjoyed sharing thoughts and feelings with others	22 (36%)
Enjoyed the light-hearted practical activities and games as they demonstrated how to use the skills in everyday situations and could lead to thought-provoking and deeper reflection and discussions	21 (34.4%)
Enjoyed learning to understand different thinking styles and strategies and gaining a greater understanding of why I do certain things in a certain way and why I find certain things difficult	7 (11.5%)
Felt it was not too pressurised/formal/invasive	7 (11.5%)
Enjoyed learning new skills and how to adopt new coping mechanisms and learning alternative ways of looking at situations	6 (9.8%)
Felt it was motivating/encouraging/rewarding as the focus was on what can be changed now	5 (8.2%)
Enjoyed animated and interactive group discussions rather than just listening to the group facilitator	5 (8.2%)
Enjoyed the challenge of thinking flexibly and thinking about the practicality of introducing more flexibility into my everyday life more and more	5 (8.2%)
Found the group fun and interesting, that it was different to other groups	4 (6.6%)
Enjoyed learning how to see the bigger picture	3 (4.9%)
Group facilitators were very knowledgeable and understanding.	3 (4.9%)
Liked the fact that the group was planned but the facilitators were also open to change – things which patients found helpful could be discussed which were not originally planned for the session	2 (3.3%)
Useful to identifying little things which you could change to begin with and learning how making slight adjustments to your routine can be OK	2 (3.3%)
Focusing on the positive aspects of everyday experiences and the positive affirmations hand-out	2 (3.3%)
Thought that it was helpful that the group was conducted or facilitated during rest period	1 (1.6%)
Enjoyed that the group was not focused around food	1 (1.6%)

How can we improve sessions?

Themes within patients' qualitative responses	Frequency
Would like more sessions/more frequent sessions/a more frequent rotation of the group	17 (32%)
Would like more tasks such as the 'seeing two pictures in one' task and more activities/games	7 (13.2%)
Would like more help with applying skills to real life and more practical solutions and tools	7 (13.2%)
Nothing comes to mind to improve	5 (9.4%)

Table 3.4 (cont.)

Would like a wider variety of tasks and more varied group content so that people repeating the group do not find it boring	5 (9.4%)
Would like a handbook or more resources/hand-outs to take away with useful tips and practical tasks	4 (7.5%)
Would like to work on the ideas raised in the group individually with a therapist/more work on specific individual issues	3 (5.6%)
Would like more discussion about how inflexible thinking can impact on your life and more discussion on why we need to change and how to change and be more flexible	3 (5.6%)
Feel that more patients should attend as they would benefit from it	3 (5.6%)
Would like to discuss patients' experiences more, e.g. when we are paying too much attention to detail and how we could have changed in that situation	3 (5.6%)
More suggestions to try outside of the group and more homework	3 (5.6%)
Would like more deep and interesting group discussions and would like more people to get involved	2 (3.8%)
Would like to be set goals each week	2 (3.8%)
Would like more of a balance between games and discussions	1 (1.9%)
More solid ideas about flexibility and ways to be flexible	1 (1.9%)

Summary of the individual vs group CRT differences

Individual and group formats follow CRT principles; for more details see Tchanturia *et al.* (2013, 2014) and: http://www.national.slam.nhs.uk/wp-content/uploads/2014/03/Cognitive-remediation-therapy-for-Anorexia-Nervosa-Kate-Tchantura.pdf.

Additionally, please see Table 3.5.

KT: I think that at least one group therapist needs to have solid clinical experience in order to be able to facilitate a group and contain the group processes in the best possible way. The main challenge with this group is to balance group member contribution, i.e. to make sure that the more talkative members do not take over the majority of the space in the group; to avoid competition and encourage collaboration and sharing; and to deal with criticism and turn it into curiosity. Group exercises are designed to help therapists go back to the specifics of the task/role play and bring the focus of the work onto cognitive styles.

Recommendations for improvement and suggestions on how to run this group

- Our clinical observation, which was supported by patients' feedback, told us that the original amount of four group sessions was a very small dose and that it would be more appropriate to run the group in a six-session format for adults (in the next chapter you will see that in the adolescent part of the clinic we are running eight sessions).
- In the context of our inpatient programme it is practical to run groups once per week (this frequency can be adapted depending on the clinical setting).

Table 3.5 Summary of the results from a qualitative study conducted by Lounes (2014), assessing feedback from 11 therapists who had been trained to deliver both individual and group CRT

Individual CRT	Group CRT
• tailoring the work to the individual • the benefit of creativity with the tasks to suit each individual patient • the therapist modelling flexibility in the sessions, for example with the use of the tasks • therapists recognising the variations in delivering CRT, mainly due to individualisation and therapist style • working from the manual is seen as both an advantage and as restrictive: it is a helpful tool however it can be restrictive, mainly in terms of what can be explored within the structure • therapists felt it may be safer for patients to open up in an individual setting	• patients can learn from others and share the work with others, thus also getting support with tasks in the session and with homework • the group can allow patients to discuss their thinking styles, thus normalising some of their experiences • the group can be an additional opportunity for patients to experience social activities and can boost self-esteem • therapists commented on the inevitable comparison to others in the group and the competitive aspects • therapists have to manage group dynamics and processes which can be difficult • less individual tailoring or focus is possible in the group

- The 45-minute session length is preferred in the ward setting (one of the reasons for this is that due to patients being very underweight it can be difficult for them to maintain concentration for longer than this). In the day care context one hour is suitable. We believe that small modifications are necessary depending on the context of the clinical setting.
- While it is important to connect sessions and recap on the previous session for the first few minutes, we endeavour to keep sessions as standalone and ensure that they each tap into flexibility and bigger picture thinking, as well as having relevance to functioning/recovery.
- It is important to have a balance between 'doing' and 'thinking' activities.
- Ten minutes for planning before group meetings and group debriefing are necessary.
- Weekly supervision for therapists running each group including CRT.
- When you add or create a new exercise it is important to ensure that it fits the purpose of tapping into thinking styles and the bigger picture of recovery. Supervision and reflective time after the groups help to keep 'innovations' on track and prevent deviation from the theoretical framework and the main aims of this work.
- Outcome measures: we have validated the Detail and Flexibility (DFlex; Roberts *et al.*, 2011) questionnaire and although it has not yet been formally used in the group evaluation, we would like to administer it at the beginning and end of the CRT group because it taps into both flexibility and bigger

picture thinking. This measure has been published and validated and will be easy to implement from now on.

- This is work in progress, but hopefully the self-report measures and qualitative evaluations will help to gather further evidence.

Additional materials and group exercises

1. Ice breaker: 'Brain clip' http://bodybrain.com.au/info/sites/default/files/ Brain%20for%20Kids_0.pdf

Discuss how the clip relates to the brain, what we know about the brain in terms of laying down new neural networks when we do new things, and how this helps us to think about things from different perspectives.

Initials............ Date........

Group Feedback Questionnaire

1. **Name of group**..
2. **How many sessions did you attend?** ....
3. **How much did you enjoy these sessions?**

Did not enjoy at all	Quite enjoyed		Really enjoyed	
1	2	3	4	5

4. **How useful were these sessions?**

Not useful at all	Quite useful		Really useful	
1	2	3	4	5

5. **Have you used any new thinking skills or strategies as a result of what you learnt in the group?**

No, none	Some		Yes, lots	
1	2	3	4	5

6. **What did you think about the length of the group (i.e. number of weeks)? Was this too long, too short or appropriate?**

Too short	Just right		Too long	
1	2	3	4	5

7. **What did you like the most about the sessions?**

....
....
....
....
....

8. **Please give your ideas about how we could improve the group in the future:**

....
....
....
....
....

9. **What other groups have you attended on the ward?**

....
....
....

10. **Are there any new groups you would like introduced into the programme?**

....
....
....

Acknowledgements

Kate would like to thank her students Naima Lounes, Katherine Sparrow and Rebecca Genders, as well as our colleagues from the South London and Maudsley NHS Foundation Trust Eating Disorders Adult National Service for their support, ideas and valuable input in the development of this group protocol as well as practical input in its implementation.

This work was supported by the NIHR Biomedical Research Centre for Mental Health, South London and Maudsley NHS Foundation Trust, the Institute of Psychiatry, King's College London, and by an NIHR Programme Grant for Applied Research (Reference number RP-PG-0606-1043). The views expressed herein are not necessarily those of the NHS, NIHR or the Department of Health. We are grateful to the Swiss Anorexia Foundation for funding awarded in 2015.

Bibliography

Bulik, C. (2014). The challenges of treating anorexia nervosa. *The Lancet*, 383(9912), 105–106.

Cognitive Remediation for Eating and Weight Disorders (2014) *Clinical Manual Cognitive Remediation for Anorexia Nervosa*, K. Tchanturia (ed.). London: Routledge.

Genders, R. and Tchanturia, K. (2010). Cognitive Remediation Therapy (CRT) for anorexia in group format: A pilot study. *Eating and Weight Disorders*, 15(4), 234–239.

Johnson, S. (1999). *Who Moved My Cheese?* London: Vermilion.

Lounes, N. (2014). Cognitive Remediation Therapy in anorexia nervosa: Patients' neuropsychological and self-report outcomes and therapist qualitative feedback. Clinical Doctoral Thesis.

Lounes, N. and Tchanturia, K. (2015). Clinicians' experience of cognitive remediation therapy: A qualitative study. In Tchanturia, K. (ed.), *Cognitive Remediation Therapy (CRT) for Eating and Weight Disorders* (pp. 62–79). East Sussex, UK: Routledge.

Lounes, N., Khan, G. and Tchanturia, K. (2011). Assessment of cognitive flexibility in anorexia nervosa: Self-report or experimental measure? A brief report. *Journal of the International Neuropsychological Society*, 17(5), 925–928.

Martin, M. M. and Rubin, R. B. (1995). A new measure of cognitive flexibility. *Psychological Reports*, 76(2), 623–626.

Miller, W. R. and Rollnick, S. (2002). *Motivational Interviewing: Preparing People for Change* (2nd edition). New York: Guilford Press. http://www.national.slam.nhs.uk/wp-content/uploads/2014/03/Cognitive-remediation-therapy-for-Anorexia-Nervosa-Kate-Tchantura.pdf.

Roberts, M., Barthel, S., Tchanturia, K., Lopez, C. and Treasure, J. (2011). Development and validation of the detail and flexibility questionnaire (DFlex) in eating disorders. *Eating Behaviours*, 12(3), 168–174.

Sparrow, K. (2014). Qualitative assessment of inpatient group programme. MSc dissertation.

Tchanturia, K. and Smith, E. (2015). Cognitive remediation therapy (CRT) for anorexia in group format: An evaluation from adult population. In Tchanturia, K. (ed.), *Cognitive Remediation Therapy (CRT) for Eating Disorders* (pp. 46–61). East Sussex, UK: Routledge.

Tchanturia, K., Lloyd, S. and Lang, K. (2013). Cognitive remediation in eating disorders. *International Journal of Eating Disorders, Special Issue*, 46(5), 492–496.

Tchanturia, K., Lounes, N. and Holttum, S. (2014). Cognitive remediation in anorexia nervosa and related conditions: A systematic review. *European Eating Disorders Review*, 22(6), 454–462.

Chapter 4

Group cognitive remediation therapy format for adolescents

Zoe Maiden, Laura Baker, Jonathan Espie, Mima Simic and Kate Tchanturia

Context and development

The following child and adolescent treatment programme was designed and developed within the South London and Maudsley (SLaM) Intensive Treatment Programme (ITP). This is part of the wider National and Specialist Child and Adolescent Eating Disorder Service (CAEDS). The ITP was set up in September 2010 for young people with anorexia nervosa (AN) or eating disorder not otherwise specified restrictive type (EDNOS-R), who require more intensive support than outpatient care and as an alternative to inpatient admission. The ITP aims to increase a young person's motivation for recovery, establish a regular and more flexible eating pattern, achieve consistent weight gain and/or maintenance, treat maintaining factors of the disorder and foster reintegration to school and with peer group. The programme also aims to disseminate skills to parents that can help them in meal supervision of the young person at home.

ITP is a day patient programme that runs from Monday to Friday, for up to eight young people each day. Young people usually attend the programme for five days initially and this is gradually reduced as they reintegrate back to school. If young people attend the programme for five days they receive ten hours of education per week. They are also given one individual therapy session per week for goal setting and motivational work, in addition to twice weekly family reviews with their parents and weekly parents' skills group. Work with families is based on the principles of Family Therapy for Anorexia Nervosa (FT-AN) that has been developed in our service. Regular physical monitoring, including weight and physical observations, is also provided.

Young people attend a variety of therapeutic groups based on cognitive behaviour therapy (CBT), dialectical behaviour therapy (DBT) including mindfulness, motivational interviewing (MI), mentalisation based art psychotherapy and cognitive remediation therapy (CRT) and yoga. The group programme aims to target maintaining factors of the illness. The CRT group was adapted from the adult group protocol and similarly was named the 'Flexible Thinking' group. For details see Chapter 3 on adult CRT groups, and our first publication (Genders and Tchanturia, 2010).

The adult group is based on neuropsychological data indicating that adults with AN have difficulties with flexibility of thinking and are overly concerned with finer details. It was introduced after encouraging results of the individual format of CRT (Tchanturia *et al.*, 2008, 2013 for more information). Research into the neurocognitive profiles of young people is still in its infancy and hence we are unsure if the same difficulties are present in young people with AN (for the systematic review of the literature see Lang and Tchanturia, 2014; Lang *et al.*, 2014). However, there is emerging evidence that at least some young people with AN share some premorbid temperament traits with adults with AN. These include increased inhibition, perfectionism and an inflexibility in thinking style. Also heightened attention to detail, and an exaggerated sensitivity to risk, mistakes and uncertainty were found. The CRT group described here aims to target these areas using various exercises which have been continuously developed to suit adolescent populations. Tasks are designed to promote interaction between group members and foster an active, fun-promoting, light-hearted atmosphere, which keeps young people engaged. At the same time care is taken in planning meetings and supervision to ensure that exercises tap into enhancing flexibility and 'bigger picture' thinking. Every exercise which was additional to those in the adult protocol (see Chapter 3 for more details) was planned and discussed amongst the authors of this chapter.

In 2010/11 for 12 months, CRT was delivered as a 'closed' group treatment, where young people all started the group at the same time and had only four weekly sessions. However, the group protocol has since been developed to adapt to the ITP becoming a rolling programme and young people attending the programme for two to three months. This has resulted in an 'open' group of eight sessions, where young people join and leave at different times. At present, the group is run by two facilitators from the multidisciplinary team (e.g. principal or senior clinical psychologist, an assistant psychologist and clinical nurse specialist (ZM, LB, JE)). They receive regular supervision from the last author (KT), who developed the adult one-to-one and group protocols. Sessions 1–3 and 5–7 each target a specific cognitive skill (bigger picture thinking, switching or multi-tasking) while Session 4 and Session 8 are 'summary' sessions. The sessions run for 45 minutes and include a combination of ice-breakers, psychoeducation, group exercises that practise the targeted skill, reflective discussions around the exercises, relating different thinking styles to real-life situations (including eating-related difficulties) and setting and reviewing of homework tasks. Session plans are followed, specifying what exercises are to be completed. However, we are also mindful of the combination of young people in the group each week and change the session plan if necessary (e.g. to accommodate those who have already completed several sessions as well as newcomers).

Each session follows a similar structure. For a full breakdown of each of our current sessions, please see Table 4.1.

- ice-breaker (five minutes)
- welcome new young people, explanation of why we do 'Flexible Thinking' (five minutes)

Table 4.1 Session content

Session	Content
1 – Bigger Picture	Bigger picture ice-breaker (message to the moon), introduction to CRT, bigger picture tasks (geometric figures, Qwirkle and/ or Blokus), reflections, homework (geometric figure)
2 – Switching	Switching ice-breaker (acting opposite), review of previous week's homework, switching tasks (Stroop task in pairs, illusions task), reflections, homework (one new behavioural task)
3 – Multi-tasking	Multi-tasking ice-breaker (multi-coloured ball game), review of previous week's homework, multi-tasking activities (drawing invisible circles, drawing real infinity signs, memory game), reflections, homework (practise a specific example of multi-tasking in everyday life)
4 – Summary	Ice-breaker (buzz), review of previous week's homework, summary of sessions so far, summarising task (adapted 'occupations' task), homework ('My Dream Job' worksheet)
5 – Bigger Picture	Ice-breaker (zip zap boing), review of previous week's homework, bigger picture tasks ('how to' text an alien, London landmarks), reflections, homework (difficult meal time worksheet)
6 – Switching	Switching ice-breaker (splat), review of previous week's homework, switching tasks (illusion cards, hand tapping game, switching in real life), homework (try as many behavioural tasks as you can)
7 – Multi-tasking	Multi-tasking ice-breaker (bip bap), review of previous week's homework, multi-tasking tasks (play-dough and directions, active listening game), reflections, homework ('pros and cons of flexible thinking' worksheet)
8 – Summary	Ice-breaker (slap clap click click), review of previous week's homework, summary of sessions so far, exercises for each targeted skill (bigger picture squares task, finer detail car task, twisted fairy-tale), team bigger picture vs team switch vs team multi-task, homework (flexible thinking motto)

*   review of homework (five minutes)
*   introduction to today's session (five minutes)
*   exercise 1 followed by reflective discussion/links with everyday life (ten minutes)
*   exercise 2 followed by reflective discussion/links with everyday life (ten minutes)
*   homework setting (five minutes)

Reflective discussions

Following each exercise, facilitators ask guiding questions to generate a discussion about what the young people just experienced, what they have learned from this and how they can use different skills to help them in different real-life situations. The choice and number of questions will depend on the exercise, the amount of prompting a group requires, and time restraints. A few examples of questions we might use are provided below:

1. What did you think of the task?
    *   Was it easy or hard?
    *   Which parts of it did you find particularly difficult?
    *   Why do you think we gave you this exercise?
2. Did you use or develop any strategies to help you complete the task?
    *   Could you have done anything different?
    *   If we did the same task again, would you go about it in the same way?
3. What does this task tell us about the way our/your brain works?
    *   Are you more likely to use one thinking style (e.g. finer detail) more than another (e.g. bigger picture)?
4. How can we apply these skills to everyday life?
    *   Is this type of skill always helpful? When is it/isn't this helpful?
    *   Do you think this skill is important to have in everyday life? If yes, why? If not, why do we think it's important?

Further questions are asked based on our knowledge of the young people in the group at the time. For example, if we know a young person in the group is struggling to think of the bigger picture in terms of her attendance at the ITP and what this means for her recovery, we may ask an open question about this to the group as a whole to generate discussion.

Ice-breakers

Ice-breakers were introduced to the group to set a light-hearted, interactive tone for the group. They also help to activate participants and get the group present-moment focussed. This can be particularly important after a difficult lunch time. The ice-breakers include one or more of the targeted thinking skills. Depending on the ice-breaker, one or both of the facilitators take part.

Body positioning game

Materials required: n/a

Young people are asked to spell out certain words, which could be seen from a birds-eye view, using only their bodies. This requires bigger picture thinking. All members of the group need to make up part or all of a letter and so effective communication and team work are also required. The group members are asked to spell out words including ITP (in both upper and lower case), brain and flexible.

Do the opposite

Materials required: n/a

This is a simple game whereby young people have to do the opposite of what we ask them to. Examples include:

- put left hand out
- stand on your right leg
- sit down
- jump in the air
- look up
- look down.

As the game progresses the facilitator picks up speed and tries to catch people out. If a player does the wrong action they are out; the game continues until one person is left. This ice-breaker requires switching and concentration.

Buzz

Materials required: n/a

We have adapted the classic game of 'Buzz' to allow the practice of switching. The aim is to count, as a group, from the number 1 to the number 30. Each attempt to count to 30 becomes more challenging as a new rule is introduced and participants have to switch from using one rule to another.

All group members stand in a circle and, going clockwise, take it in turn to say one number. For the first attempt, multiples of 3 (e.g. 3, 6, 9, etc.) are replaced by saying the word 'buzz' (they do not say the number). Once the team has successfully reached 30, a new rule is introduced; multiples of 5 (e.g. 5, 10, 15, etc.) are replaced with a clap. Again, once the team has successfully reached 30 using both rules, a third rule is introduced. Multiples of 4 (e.g. 4, 8, 12, etc.) are replaced with a stamp.

As it can be seen the game has switching and multi-tasking components and requires concentration.

Multi-coloured ball game

Materials required: three different coloured balls

The group is asked to stand in a circle and throw a pink ball between participants in a certain order, so that the group is always throwing the ball to and catching from the same person. Once a pattern is established, facilitators ask that when a group member makes eye contact with the person they are about to throw the ball to, they say the colour 'green'. Once the group is used to this, an additional ball is introduced, an orange one, which they must call 'pink' and continue to throw two balls around the group simultaneously. A final green ball is introduced which they must call 'orange', so all three balls are being thrown around the room with players saying colours which they are not. Generally only after many sessions of practice can the group manage to keep the balls in play and call them by their 'incorrect' colours. This ice-breaker requires concentration, switching and multi-tasking.

Slap clap click click

Materials required: n/a

This is a fast-paced word association game which asks players to think of a word associated with the prior word said. This is played sat down. Facilitators lead by starting the group off with a steady rhythm by slapping their hands on their knees, followed by a clap, then clicking their right hand and then clicking their left hand. On each click a word is said. The first click is the word that the previous person said. The second click is the 'new' word that is freely associated with it by that player. For example if the person starting the game says 'sea' the next person in the circle might say 'sea' on the first click and 'water' on the second click. The next player might say 'water, bottle' and so on. Multi-tasking is required to talk and continue the rhythm simultaneously and switching is required for the word association. Being flexible in general is also encouraged as young people have to find associated words.

Bigger picture thinking exercises

Qwirkle

Materials required: Qwirkle board game

Qwirkle is a board game that can be easily purchased online. It is often described as a pictoral version of Scrabble. Each participant takes it in turns to place tiles on the board, ensuring that these are either the same shape or colour as the row of tiles they are adding to. You get extra points for being able to fit tiles into more than one row, which is one way bigger picture thinking can be used in this game. The overall aim of the game is to create as many 'Qwirkles' as possible, for which the most points are awarded. This requires keeping the bigger picture in mind. For example, young people must decide if they want to risk putting tiles down, as their opponent may only need one tile to gain a 'Qwirkle'. Further instructions on scoring are provided with the game. If a group of young people are highly competitive, they are encouraged to work together rather than play against each other. Multi-tasking is also required in this game as players are required to hold many rules in mind at once. Young people are also required to be flexible and respond to the moves of the other players.

Blokus

Materials required: Blokus board game

Blokus is a board game that can be purchased online. It consists of a board with 400 squares on it. Each player is represented by a different colour and has 21 shapes varying in size. Each player has to fit as many of their pieces on the board as possible, each new piece must touch at least one other piece of the same colour. This game requires bigger picture thinking from the beginning. Young people are also required to be generally flexible and respond to the moves of the other players. The game ends when all players are blocked from laying down anymore of their pieces. Games typically last 20 minutes.

Geometric figures

Materials required: geometric figure packs

As described in the adult protocol (please see CRT adult manual from http://www.katetchanturia.com – publication section – http://media.wix.com/ugd/2e1018_f71866481f9f44e5a342fb068b891a8c.pdf).

'How to' text an alien

Materials required: 'how to' tasks written on pieces of paper

In this group exercise, the main aspects are to encourage good planning, prioritising, effective communication and team work. Split the group participants into pairs and give each pair a different 'task' to explain and ask them to keep it hidden from the rest of the group. Examples of tasks we have given out in the past are:

- how to make a cup of tea;
- how to create an event on Facebook;
- how to order a drink at Starbucks;
- how to plan an outfit for a party.

The tasks that we have used have depended on the ages and interests of the group. Any task that is relevant for adolescents would be suitable.

Instructions given: 'Imagine you are sending a text to an alien to explain the task that is written on your piece of paper. As it is a text, try to explain the task in as few words as possible.' Often, group participants initially write in a lot of detail. Once they have completed the write-up, they are instructed to now explain it in ten words. When this has been achieved, they are instructed to pick just three words for the text. Bigger picture thinking is increasingly required as the instructions progress to use fewer words to describe something that often requires a lot of detail.

Each pair then takes it in turn to read out their three words and the other young people try to guess what they are trying to explain. Here, the 'guessers' are required to use bigger picture thinking.

London landmarks (Taboo)

Materials required: London landmark sheets (x number of young people)

We have created our own, similar version of the well-known game Taboo. Each young person is given a sheet with a picture of a well-known London landmark. On that sheet is the name of the landmark and three words that are often used to describe it. The aim is for each young person to describe the London landmark, using only three words, but they are not allowed to use any of the words on the sheet. The rest of the group then has to guess what they are describing. Bigger picture thinking is needed by both the describer and the guessers. The London landmarks we currently use, with the three 'banned' words are:

- London Eye: big, Thames, wheel;
- the Gherkin: tall, shape, vegetable;
- London Zoo: animals, cage, walk;
- the o2: music, dome, gigs;
- St Paul's Cathedral: church, old, white;
- Tower Bridge: Thames, open, old;
- Big Ben: clock, tall, time;
- Harrods: shop, expensive, Knightsbridge.

We chose London landmarks as our service is based in London and all of the young people should therefore be able to participate. If you feel this would not be appropriate for your location, then we would encourage you to create your own version.

How many squares?

Materials required: squares picture for each young person

For this task, young people are each given Figure 4.1. They are then asked to work out individually the number of squares in the image. After a few minutes, young people are asked for their answers. This task requires bigger picture and finer detail thinking in order to get the right answer, which is 40.

Finer detail cars task

Materials required: car 'spot the difference' print-out for each young person

This is a difficult version of Spot the Difference. The material has been taken from the book *Left Brain/Right Brain: 50 Puzzles to Change the Way You Think* which is available to purchase from http://www.puzzlesociety.com. Young people are given a print-out of nine images of the same car, but only two are actually identical. Young people must use their attention to detail to notice which two are the same. Young people are often very good at this task, which generates an interesting debate about how their brains work and when their natural tendency for finer detail thinking can be helpful to them.

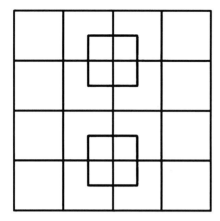

Figure 4.1 How many squares task

Switching exercises

Illusions

Materials required: illusions

Illusions are as in the adult group protocol in Chapter 3, p. 34. We have gathered a collection of illusions that we can use. Some of these are real-life examples, which particularly engage the young people. We have gained examples from various websites including brainden.com/optical-illusions.html, http://www.moillusions.com and http://www.eyetricks.com.

Our (and the young people's) favourite 'frog' illusion can be found at the following website: http://www.boredpanda.com/body-art-illusions-johannes-stoetter/.

The images are either presented to the group as a whole (as in the adult protocol) or each young person is given (face-down) the same image. They are then told to turn it over on the count of three and to shout out the first thing that they can see. We have found that this can be a more engaging way to generate discussion with quieter groups.

Illusion cards

Materials required: illusions

We own a selection of optical illusion cards called '50 Optical Illusions' by Usbourne Activities, which is available to purchase online. An optical illusion on each card is accompanied by text on the reverse explaining how the illusion works in tricking the eye. This title comes with a 'revealer' card, which can be used to measure and check the illustrations to increase understanding of how each illusion works. We ask the young people to get into pairs, and give them a few cards each to look at together. They are then asked to feed back to the rest of the group their favourite one and explain how it works. We try to stimulate discussions about which skills they need to use in order to see the illusion(s). This exercise can also lead to discussions about how what we see is not always 'true' and how this concept can relate to anorexia.

Stroop

Materials required: Stroop (please see CRT adult manual from http://www.katetchanturia.com – publication section – http://media.wix.com/ugd/2e1018_f71866481f9f44e5a342fb068b891a8c.pdf) http://en.wikipedia.org/wiki/Stroop_Effect http://faculty.washington.edu/chudler/words.html.

As in the adult group protocol, Stroop effect exercises help to practise switching, flexibility of thinking and provide specific materials for the reflection.

Twisted fairy-tale

Materials required: blank paper and pens

Young people are split into pairs and are asked to write down a summary of a fairy-tale of their choice. If they are struggling to think of a fairy-tale, an example may be provided by the facilitator (e.g. Cinderella, Red Riding Hood, Snow White, etc.). Although this exercise is used to practise 'switching', this initial instruction requires bigger picture thinking. Once the young people have completed this, they are instructed to now re-tell the fairy-tale from the viewpoint of the villain (e.g. the evil step-mum, the big bad wolf, etc.), with the intent to make the group feel very sympathetic towards that character. This exercise promotes flexible thinking and being able to 'switch' one's viewpoint from one extreme to the other. Using fairy-tales can be particularly powerful as they are often stories that people have known for their whole life. This can lead to useful conversations regarding 'switching' in everyday conversations or disagreements, particularly around the eating disorder. In terms of additional benefits of this exercise, it helps young people to develop theory of mind and shift perspective in the social domain, and develop mentalisation, which are critical and very useful skills in communication.

The hand tapping game

Materials needed: n/a

This game can be completed sat in a circle on the floor or sat around a large table. Young people and facilitators sit in a circle, with their hands placed out in front of them. Each person crosses hands with the person on either side of them, so that everyone has one hand from each neighbour between their own hands. A facilitator starts and chooses the direction (e.g. clockwise) for a single tap on the floor to be 'passed' around the circle. The tap travels in the order of the hands, not necessarily the order of the players. A single tap signals for play to continue to the next hand. Once the group has become accustomed to this and the tap is being passed with speed, a new rule may be introduced. Two taps of the same hand indicates a change in direction of play. Again, when this becomes familiar, a third rule is added. Three taps of the same hand would result in play 'skipping' a hand.

If the above explanation is not clear enough and you would like to see the game in action, please use the following link:

http://www.youtube.com/watch?v=DHMxfA2OivI

Switching in real life

Materials needed: list of predetermined real-life situations

Based on qualitative feedback that young people wanted the sessions to relate more to real life, a 'switching in real life' exercise was created. The facilitators brain-stormed to think of situations where being able to switch attention from one thing to another or switching your view of a situation may be helpful for group members. The following statements are read out and young people are asked tell us what an alternative behaviour/viewpoint could be.

1. My mum is trying to make me fat.
2. Looking in the mirror at the parts of me I dislike.
3. Everyone's looking at me.
4. No one likes me.
5. Focussing on the calories in the food I'm eating.
6. I am fat.
7. I'll never have a romantic relationship.
8. I'm going to fail all of my exams.

These statements can generate difficult conversations and it is recommended that this task is used when a good therapeutic relationship has been established and the group members know each other fairly well.

One, two, three

Materials required: n/a

Young people are asked to get into pairs and are given the following instructions:

In pairs, face each other. Start counting from one to three between yourselves, over and over. Once you get the hang of that part you are ready for the next stage. Instead of saying the number 'one', you should clap your hands – but you would still say 'two' and 'three' aloud.

Once this has been mastered, the next step is that instead of saying 'three', that person should bend their knees. You should still clap your hands for the number 'one'.

A: 'One' (claps hands)
B: 'Two'
A: 'Three' (bends knees)

B: 'One' (claps hands)
A: 'Two'
B: 'Three' (bends knees)

This task requires concentration and shifting.

Multi-tasking exercises

Memory game

Materials required: computerised portable tablet/alternative activity, list of 30 words, blank paper and pens

Recently, the ITP introduced computerised portable tablets for use in the therapeutic groups. For this task, young people are invited to start playing a simple game on the portable tablets. However, any non-computerised game or activity that is engaging would also be suitable. A facilitator gives instructions to the young people:

> I am going to read out a list of words. I want you to carry on playing the game and try to remember as many of the words as you can.

A list of 30 words is read out (e.g. bus, snowman, laptop, etc.). When the list has been read out, ask the young people to write down all of the words that they remember.

Active listening: Fruit-Ninja

Materials required: computerised portable tablet/alternative activity, song that has one word/phrase repeated a lot

The computerised portable tablets are also used in this task. Again, any non-computerised game or activity that is engaging would also be suitable. Young people are given a tablet each and instructed to start playing 'Fruit-Ninja', which is already downloaded and available. After a few minutes of playing, the following instructions are given:

> We are going to play a song. I want you to count the number of times the word 'X' is sung/spoken.

It is suggested that the song contains a large number of the word that is being counted. Previously, we have used the song 'Diamonds' by Rhianna, where the word counted is 'diamond'. We have also used the song 'I'm Blue' by Eifel 65, where the word to be counted is 'blue'.

Play-dough multi-task

Materials required: play-dough (enough for each young person)

Each young person is given a small ball of play-dough and is given the task of moulding it into a cat or dog and trying to make it as detail focussed as possible (fur, whiskers, features, etc.). At the same time, they have to follow the facilitator's instructions, for example: walk around in a circle, walk around the other way in a circle, stand in the corner, sit down, swap places with someone else, if your birthday is in the first half of the year, go to the window, if your birthday is in the second half of the year, go to the door, stand on your left leg, get into height order, get into birthday order, etc. The exercise ends with the young people comparing their models, discussing which part of the task they found easier and what this tells us about the way our brains work.

Snap

Materials required: packs of playing cards

As in adult CRT group, Chapter 3, p. 35.

Drawing opposite invisible circles (multi-tasking)

Materials required: n/a

Young people are asked to draw circles in the air, using their finger. The first set of circles are in a forward direction with their left hand. They are then asked to do the same with their right but in a backwards direction. They are then asked to do both at the same time. This task is trickier than it first appears.

Word search and colouring in

Materials required: n/a

Worksheets are prepared in advance with a small word search on one side of the page, and a small colouring-in image on the other. Young people are asked to do both at the same time (one with each hand) and notice which one they found easier and why. This can often generate interesting discussion about which task they thought more important to 'get right' which often correlates with different people's personality and thinking styles.

Summary sessions

Occupations task

Materials required: flip chart and pens/whiteboard

This is similar to the protocol in the adult group CRT, Chapter 3, p. 36. As well as giving the young people a 'random' job to plot on the axis, we ask each person to plot their own dream job. This helps to make the task more relevant to each individual and to begin thinking about what thinking skills they may need to work on in order to reach their goal. It also has a motivational element. We might also use jobs featured in popular culture to generate interest (e.g. *The Apprentice* or an *X Factor* judge).

Homework tasks

Bigger picture: geometric figure

Materials required: geometric figure

Young people are each given a different geometric figure to try at home with someone. This encourages them to share the 'bigger picture thinking' concept with their family so that they can support them in implementing it.

Switching: new pastime

Materials required: flip chart and pens/whiteboard

Ask each group member what they like to do in their spare time and write it on the flip chart. Each young person is then instructed to pick a pastime from the list that they do not usually do.

Multi-tasking: practise a specific multi-task at home

Materials required: flip chart and pens/whiteboard

Ask each group member for an example of when it is helpful for us to be able to multi-task in everyday life. Write the examples on the flip chart and then ask each young person to commit to practising one of them for homework (they do not have to be different from each other).

Summary session: 'My Dream Job' worksheet

Materials required: 'My Dream Job' worksheet (see Appendix A)

This is in order to consolidate what has already been talked up in the session and for the young people to further explore what thinking styles they will need to practise to match those needed in their dream job.

Bigger picture: 'A Difficult Meal Time' worksheet

Materials required: 'A Difficult Meal Time' worksheet (see Appendix B)

To help young people think about the thinking styles they usually employ during meal times and if they are helpful. It also challenges the group members to experiment and try something different during a difficult meal time.

Switching: 'Things I Can Try to Do Differently' challenge

Materials required: 'Things I Can Try to Do Differently' worksheet (see Appendix C)

The aim of this task is to encourage the young people to be generally more flexible in everyday life. The group often responds well if the homework is set with a small competitive element. The worksheet is split into three sections of 'difficult', 'medium' and 'easy' behavioural challenges for the young people to try. A tick box is next to each challenge so that they can keep track of how many they have tried. There is also space for the young people to fill in with any other challenges they can think of. They are given the instructions to try as many new things as possible before the next session.

Summarising: 'Pros and Cons of Flexible Thinking' worksheet

Materials required: 'Pros and Cons of Flexible Thinking' worksheet (see Appendix D)

This task aims to encourage young people to start thinking about what they have learned about flexible thinking. Specifically, they are asked to write the 'pros' and 'cons' of some of the skills we have targeted.

Summarising: flexible thinking motto

Young people are given a hand-out with quotes that relate to flexible thinking (see Appendix E). They are then asked, for homework, to think of their own 'motto' to summarise what they will take away from the flexible thinking groups.

Qualitative feedback

The eight-session protocol was developed based on qualitative feedback from young people. This was obtained from feedback sheets and focus groups. Suggestions for improvements were a larger variety of tasks in the sessions and relating the in-session tasks and discussions to more real-life examples. It was also clear from the facilitators' and supervisors' point of view that we needed to work on engaging the young people more in the material and help them to apply the skills outside of the group. Hence, this was the focus of the protocol's development.

We are keen to continue collecting specific qualitative feedback about the new protocol and are currently considering the most useful and efficient way to do this.

Recently we have begun to complete 'exit interviews' with young people who were discharged from ITP about their experience with treatment in ITP. One of the question that they are asked is 'Which groups did you find most helpful?'. Out of the nine interviews conducted so far, two of the young people have said that Flexible Thinking has been one of the most helpful groups. Young people were also asked 'Which group skills/ideas are you using in everyday life?' and two of them said being more flexible in their thinking and behaviour. As young people can attend up to 11 therapeutic groups during their time at ITP, this is very positive feedback.

Reflections from facilitators

While we feel it is important to have established eight clear session plans, it is also essential to be adaptive to the group of young people that we work with. For example, we have gathered a large collection of illusions so that if a young person has been in Session 2 before, we can use illusions that they have not seen. This allows the same concepts to be discussed with different examples. Additionally, we vary the level of competition to suit the needs of the group. If the group is well established and the young people have developed positive relationships with each other, an element of competition can help to engage them in the group content. However, if the group is less established and they are competing with each other in terms of eating disordered behaviours, we remove the element of competition in Flexible Thinking as much as possible.

Young people can sometimes be unclear about the purpose of the group and so we think it is essential to always ask them why they think we have made them do each task. Similarly, conversations about using the skills in everyday life, particularly in relation to their eating difficulties, are key.

Observations from the supervision

The Flexible Thinking group developed considerably from the adult to young people's version. It is clear that many tasks and exercises were developed to keep young people motivated and curious, while targeting critical thinking skills: flexibility, abstract, global thinking, being less perfectionistic, being and participating in the group discussion. Additional benefits of the group were to provide opportunities for young people to exercise theory of mind skills, reflect on their own journey to recovery and linking specific tasks to real life.

Through observation, the supervisors' main task was to ensure that the group was following CRT structure and principles and was not deviating to play (for the sake of play). The fun side and playful nature is an important component of CRT, but one needs to be very mindful that the main principles are still followed.

This specific group took place in an observation room, which allows supervisors to watch directly what is happening in the group. This was a great strength of the whole process; it made it easier to evaluate the fidelity of the group, provide direct feedback and develop the group further.

The additional exercises are an important strength and great development of this group but it is also important to note that the skills learned in the group are applied to the domain of eating and that the group helps the young people to implement these skills at the dining table.

Future work will be needed to calibrate outcome measures suitable for this age group that measure the concepts targeted.

APPENDICES: HOMEWORK WORKSHEETS

Appendix A

My dream job is: _____

The thinking styles needed for this job are:

(flexible/rigid, bigger picture/detail focussed, switching between rules?
Multi-tasking?)

_____

_____
_____
_____
_____

My current thinking styles are:

(flexible/rigid, bigger picture/detail focussed, switching between rules?
Multi-tasking?)

_____
_____
_____
_____
_____

How I can practise the thinking styles I need for my dream job:

_____
_____
_____
_____
_____

Appendix B

Think about a difficult meal time…

What thinking style/s do you notice that you use during difficult meal times? (e.g. focussed or stuck on details? Rigid thinking? Other thinking styles?)

What thinking styles might be more helpful to use at these times?

(e.g. standing back and looking at the bigger picture? Flexible thinking? Other thinking styles?)

What could I do to help me use these helpful thinking styles during difficult meal times?

What might be difficult when trying to use these helpful thinking styles during difficult meal times?

What can I do if this happens?

Now let's give it a go…

<u>Reflections</u>

How was the experiment?

Were you able to notice what thinking style you were using?

Was it a helpful thinking style for this situation? If not, were you able to choose a more helpful thinking style?

What have I learned from this experiment?

Appendix C

Things I can try to do differently

Look at the list below of ideas of things you can do differently. They are listed by difficulty level. Try to keep challenging yourself! Put a tick in the box of any that you try. There are some spaces for you to fill in any ideas you have too.

Difficult

☐ Choose a snack I have not tried before
☐ Eat my snack in a different order
☐ Choose to behave differently in a difficult situation and see if the response I get changes
☐ Use my compassionate voice instead of my critical voice
☐ Rearrange my whole bedroom

_____
_____

Medium

☐ Put on my clothes in a different order in the morning
☐ Do things in a different order in the morning (e.g. breakfast, then get dressed)
☐ Put my make-up on in a different order
☐ Read a newspaper/magazine from the back to the front
☐ Sit in a different seat (e.g. on the bus, in the living room)
☐ Go to bed at a different time
☐ Start and persevere with a new hobby

_____
_____
_____

Easy

☐ Change my profile picture on Facebook
☐ Change the background of my phone
☐ Change my ringtone
☐ Brush my teeth with my non-dominant hand
☐ Paint my nails a different colour
☐ Wear my hair differently
☐ Wear non-matching socks
☐ Use the TV remote with a different hand
☐ Watch a new TV programme
☐ Wear my watch/jewellery on the other wrist
☐ Take a different route to ITP
☐ Create a new playlist on my iPod/iPhone and listen to it
☐ Use a different shower gel/shampoo
☐ Only moisturise one half of my body

☐   Download and use a new app
☐   Wear new make-up/wear my make-up differently
☐   Move a small piece of furniture in my room

_____

_____

_____

_____

Appendix D

Pros and cons of flexible thinking
Bigger picture thinking

Pros	Cons

Finer detail thinking

Pros	Cons

Flexible thinking

Pros	Cons

Rigid thinking

Pros	Cons

Appendix E

Proverbs and sayings

- Challenges can be stepping stones or stumbling blocks… it's just a matter of how you view them.
- Don't limit your challenges… challenge your limits!
- Every truth has two sides; it is well to look at both, before we commit ourselves to either (Aesop).
- Without risk there is no opportunity for gain.
- Your current safe boundaries were once unknown frontiers.
- 'Tomorrow is another day.'
- Variety is the spice of life.
- 'Rules are made to be broken.'
- 'Nothing ventured, nothing gained.'
- 'Where one door shuts, another opens.'
- Attitude might not help you catch a fish… but it helps when you don't.
- Be not afraid of growing slowly, be afraid only of standing still (Chinese proverb).
- Better to bend than to break (Indian proverb).
- Chains of habit are too light to be felt until they are too heavy to be broken.

References

Genders, R. and Tchanturia, K. (2010) Cognitive remediation therapy (CRT) for anorexia in group format: A pilot study. *Eating Weight Disorders*, 15(4): 234–239.

Lang, K. and Tchanturia, K. (2014) A systematic review of central coherence in children and adolescents with anorexia nervosa. *Journal of Child and Adolescent Behavior*, 2: 140.

Lang, K., Stahl, D., Treasure, J. and Tchanturia, K. (2014) Set shifting abilities in children and adolescents with anorexia nervosa: An exploratory systematic review and meta-analysis. *International Journal of Eating Disorders*, 47(4): 394–399.

Tchanturia, K. and Lock, J. (2011) Cognitive remediation therapy (CRT) for eating disorders: Development, refinement and future directions. *Current Topics in Behavioural Neuroscience*, 6: 269–287.

Tchanturia, K., Davies, H., Lopez, C., Schmidt, U., Treasure, J. and Wykes, T. (2008) Neuropsychological task performance before and after cognitive remediation in anorexia nervosa: A pilot case series. *Psychological Medicine*, 38(9): 1371–1373.

Tchanturia K., Lloyd S. and Lang K. (2013). Cognitive remediation in eating disorders. *International Journal of Eating Disorders* Special Issue, 46(5): 492–496.

Chapter 5

Thinking about emotions: CREST group

Kate Tchanturia, Amy Brown and Caroline Fleming

Cognitive Remediation and Emotion Skills Training (CREST) takes an interactive approach to helping participants think about emotions. The main novel interventions used in CREST focus on: emotion awareness, emotion regulation, emotion processing skills, promoting micro skills in social communication and self-regulation/self-awareness.

CREST was initially designed in an individual format to offer support to patients in the inpatient treatment programme who are physically and medically compromised and find it difficult to engage in psychological treatment (Money *et al.*, 2011a; Davies *et al.*, 2012). Our approach in developing this clinical intervention was based on extensive input from patients, clinicians and parents (see our qualitative study of the focus groups: Kyriacou *et al.*, 2009) and recent findings from experimental studies (e.g. Russell *et al.*, 2009; Castro *et al.*, 2010; Davies *et al.*, 2010; Oldershaw *et al.*, 2011b; Harrison *et al.*, 2010, 2011, 2014; Hambrook *et al.*, 2012; Tchanturia *et al.*, 2013, 2014, 2015; Fonville *et al.*, 2014; Rhind *et al.*, 2014).

In our qualitative study (Kyriacou *et al.*, 2009), we asked patients, parents and clinicians to help us identify the areas of difficulty in people with anorexia. We carefully analysed all responses for overlapping themes and it became apparent that the main difficulties named by all parties were in recognising and regulating one's own emotions. In experimental studies, our results show that patients with anorexia are reasonably capable at recognising simple emotional stimuli (faces with basic emotions), unlike the deficits noted in other psychological disorders (Davies, 2011 PhD thesis). However, when presented with more complex emotional stimuli, patients in the acute state of illness tend to find it hard to read emotions from images of eyes (Russell *et al.*, 2009) or from film clips (Oldershaw *et al.*, 2011a) in which the social context is presented. We also found that expressing positive emotions is highly problematic in both adult and adolescent patients with anorexia nervosa (AN) (e.g. Davies *et al.*, 2010; Rhind *et al.*, 2014). Finally, in one study, we found patients with anorexia exhibited lower emotional intelligence (EQ) relative to IQ compared to a group of non-eating disorder females (matched for age and IQ), meaning that it was hard for patients to find solutions in socially challenging scenarios and other EQ tasks (for more details see Hambrook *et al.*, 2012). We felt that it was important to tailor and pilot a psychological intervention capturing some of the findings based on this new research evidence.

We designed a manual for an individual format of therapy aiming to improve recognition and expression of emotions, which was evaluated using qualitative feedback from patients (Money *et al.*, 2011a). Overall, the qualitative feedback was very positive, but it also highlighted some areas for improvement. For example, patients suggested that the tasks involving recognition of emotional faces were too simple and they did not learn anything new as a result. On revision, we removed the exercises which the majority of patients did not find helpful (e.g. recognising other people's facial expressions in a social context and 'cold' cognitive exercises). In the revised version, we also expanded on the exercises that patients said were the most helpful parts of the original manual (e.g. emotion vocabulary development, recognising and doing positive things, and improving communication skills). In addition, we incorporated more recent research findings, such as the lower emotional intelligence relative to high IQ (Hambrook *et al.*, 2012) in groups of AN patients, poor facial expressions of positive emotions (Davies *et al.*, 2010, 2013; Rhind *et al.*, 2014; Tchanturia *et al.*, in press), limited vocabulary for describing positive emotions (Deborde *et al.*, 2006), difficulty in expressing positive emotions (Tchanturia *et al.*, 2015), social anhedonia (Tchanturia *et al.*, 2012, 2015; Harrison *et al.*, 2014), extreme difficulties in private and social leisure activities (Tchanturia *et al.*, 2013) and poor coping with socially frustrating situations (Harrison *et al.*, 2011).

Five recent studies have revealed that CREST is perceived as helpful by patients and that it may produce improvements in emotion processing skills (Money *et al.*, 2011a, 2011b; Davies *et al.*, 2013; Tchanturia *et al.*, 2014; 2015). Most of the evaluation and development was carried out in the individual format of CREST, which is delivered over ten sessions. Currently, we are delivering and evaluating the benefits of the group format of CREST in inpatient and day care settings. We have outlined a five-session group protocol, but as demonstrated in Table 5.1, patients' feedback suggests that they would like to extend the number of sessions. As such, at the end of the chapter we have provided a number of additional exercises which could be incorporated for additional sessions. In developing the group format, we used the same principle as for the individual CREST manual, using simple, concrete and engaging exercises. For example, role plays and exercises that require actions (e.g. picking emotion labels out of a jar, finding a useful motto from the calendar of positive emotions, picking a ball from a bag full of balls with emotion expressions and commenting on it). We have observed that this style of 'doing vs discussing' encourages more interaction and also helps in modelling a confident, relaxed communication style. We try to begin sessions with specific experiential exercises to ensure that group members can start by 'doing' things and then have opportunity to 'discuss and think' about what the take-home messages could be. Furthermore, we try to give homework based on psycho-education and experiential material (e.g. watching a 'YouTube' clip about body language, doing online tests of positivity ratio and practising positive logbook writing.

Table 5.1 CREST – Thinking about Emotions Group Therapy, some qualitative feedback from the participants in the inpatient ward. These ideas and feedback have helped us to tailor this group format further before testing it formally in a manualised Randomised Control Treatment study

Date group commenced	What did you enjoy most about the sessions?	How can we improve the sessions?
November 2009	• Releasing our feelings, listening to others' experiences, their symptoms etc.	
March 2010	• Hearing other people's views. • I enjoyed listening to everyone's thoughts about the certain emotion. How we all think differently. • The openness and detail spoken about. • Sharing thoughts, feelings, ideas. • Listening to other people's perspectives of these emotions. • Discussions about how to accept feelings.	• I would have liked a bit longer to have time to discuss all suggested emotions. • Perhaps learning how to identify emotions more and how to use new knowledge. • Maybe more practical ideas for coping strategies. • Provide more tools to encourage positive emotions and avoid negative ones. • More practical strategies for encouraging positive emotions and coping with negative emotions.
May 2010	• Sharing. • Sharing ideas, thoughts, experiences. Learning alternative ways of thinking about and viewing situations, events and experiences. • Analysing emotions, hearing other people's experiences with emotions.	• Mixed emotions would be good to explore. • Encourage others to attend and share experiences. Maybe suggest further resources – books, etc. – to develop themes in own time. • Give more tools to encourage positive emotions.
July 2010	• Sharing experiences, learning how emotions are communicating something to us. All emotions are valid and valuable – no 'good' or 'bad' feelings. • Learning about positive emotions and trying to appreciate not only the good in other people but also in yourself. That it is OK to feel and recognise negative emotions. • Finding out about different emotions – none are good or bad. Learning different ways of expressing emotions. • How things were open for discussion.	• I think this group was a definite improvement on previous 'emotions' group. • Less group tasks of just considering emotions – I didn't identify with how other people saw emotions and wanted to deal with them.

Date		
October 2010	• Sharing with others. New ways of thinking about and experiencing emotions – the way all emotions are valid and are a way to communicate our needs. There are no 'right' or 'wrong' emotions. Very insightful. • Felt safe space to share things.	• Think it is just right. • Not allow people to point, refuse to participate.
March 2012	• They were very interactive. • Interactive, friendly, open, nice facilitators. • Interactive tasks – emotional thermometer. • Looking in detail at specific emotions of anger and anxiety – the different levels of intensity, body symptoms. • The practical activities. • It opened my eyes to others' emotions and behaviours that follow.	• More focus on how to let positive emotions in, not just on how difficult it is. • As I have done the group before, more variety and new content. • More practical activities as I enjoyed those the most. • More practical activities.
November 2012	• The sessions really got me thinking about how to notice my emotions and deal with them. They made me feel a bit more positive about my recovery. • Exploring different emotions and learning about them and why we feel them. • Being able to openly speak about emotions (good and bad) and learn new thinking styles. • Discussing with patients.	• Encourage more practical activities. • Just wasn't for me.
February 2013	• Open discussions, thinking about positive memories. • The scales applied to each emotion.	• More discussions and patient involvement. • Less on positive emotion.
August 2013	• The last session interaction. • Thought provoking and informative.	• More interaction.

The optimal number of participants in the group is 8–10, with two facilitators (one from the psychology team and the other from the multidisciplinary team, or a trainee). A flipchart, pens and paper will be needed for all sessions. We also use audio-visual equipment when possible and specific materials to facilitate discussion (e.g. coloured balls with basic emotional expression words, emotional word lists, and cards).

Before starting the group we administer self-report questionnaires to all participants: the Toronto Alexithymia Scale (TAS-20), which measures alexithymia; the Revised Social Anhedonia Scale (RSAS), which measures social anhedonia; and the Motivational Ruler (MR), which measures perceived importance and ability to change. The same measures are re-administered at the end of the group run, after the last session. We plan to publish this ongoing research in the peer review journals; here we focus on the treatment protocol and patient feedback. It is not possible to provide all hand-outs from our clinical in-house manual – which we keep reviewing – but we have included some in the appendix and have attempted to describe the ideas throughout this chapter protocol.

Session 1: The power of positive emotions

Introduction

Welcome the group members and start by generating a list of ground rules and expectations. These rules typically include: 'avoid being late or missing sessions', 'confidentiality', 'respect', 'one person speaks at a time' and 'everyone contributes'. Explain to the participants that we are aiming to evaluate the group format and that in the last session, in addition to the self-report questionnaires, they will be asked to complete a short feedback questionnaire which takes less than ten minutes to help us improve upon the content of the group. We introduce the format of the group and provide a brief description of what will be covered within the sessions.

We introduce the first session by engaging the group in a discussion about the importance and power of positive emotions. For example, do group participants attend more to positive or negative stimuli? We incorporate background information from the field of positive psychology, highlighting the power of positive thinking for the group attendees. For example, positive psychology experts Barbara Fredrikson (1998, 2001, 2009), Martin Seligman and Mihaly Csikszentmihalyi (2000), Sonia Lyubomirsky and Kristin Layous (2013) and others have found that people who have a higher positivity ratio tend to live longer, happier lives and are healthier both physically and psychologically.

We also explore with the group the benefits of the 'half full/half empty' glass metaphor.

In addition, the 'positivity self-test' (see: http://www.positivityratio.com/single.php) is a brief measure developed by Barbara Fredrikson that can be completed and scored in the session itself, providing a useful tool to engage the group in a discussion about their own tendency (or lack of) towards positivity.

Exercise 1: Discussion around the experience of positive emotions

The following are possible questions that can be posed to the group with a mind-map of the answers written on the flipchart:

- How do we define positive emotions?
- Where and when do we experience positive emotions?
- Is there anything difficult about experiencing positive emotions?
- Why are positive emotions important?
- How do our positive emotions affect what we do?

Experiential task

This exercise can be extended by developing a collage associated with a positive emotional state – pictures, colours, animals, nature, motivational words/phrases, experiences, people, pets, inspirational figures.

Therapist tip

- Hand-outs with a list of emotion words can be distributed in order to help with some of these discussion topics (see appendix).

Exercise 2: Emotions and our body

Present a diagram of the body on the flipchart. Ask the question: How is positive emotion experienced in the body? The aim is to help patients explore the sensations associated with positivity to help with emotion identification. Explore within this the physical reasons why it may be harder to recognise and attend to positive emotions versus negative emotions.

Therapist tips

- Remind the group that negative emotions are not 'bad', they are just signalling something about our internal and/or external environment that requires our attention.
- It can be helpful to consider how different emotions can be experienced within the body in a similar way, such as excitement and fear.

Exercise 3: The language of positive emotions

On the flipchart ask the group to generate a range of emotion words, with the aim of developing greater awareness around the vocabulary of positive emotions. Then ask the group to choose one of these emotion words and try to recall a memory associated with this. Explore how this felt in the body, how this emotion was communicated to the self and to others, as well as the associated body language and facial expression.

Therapist tips

- We recommend that the participants have a notebook or journal to keep a record of the work they are doing in CREST and to collate the information they are given.
- We always ask the group for feedback and endeavour to incorporate their ideas into future groups to foster patient ownership over the group.

Inter-session work

1. Introduce the concept of the 'Portfolio of Positive Emotions' and encourage the group participants to start engaging with one of these for homework.
2. The 'three good things' exercise aims to address the bias patients so often have towards focusing on negative experiences (see appendix).

Session 2: Introduction to emotional experience

Introduction

This session aims to start exploring the range of emotional experience. The focus is general, rather than our own personal experience of emotions.

Homework review

We explore any barriers to engaging with the homework tasks and consider any additional support group participants may require, to act as a reminder between sessions. We continue by explaining that the remainder of the group will focus more on negative emotions and how to manage them, in order to more readily attain a positive emotional state.

Therapist tip

- It is our experience that inter-session tasks are often not completed. In an effort to model and be collaborative, group facilitators also engage in all 'homework' tasks and there is a dedicated space at the beginning of all sessions to review the group's experience of completing the exercises.

Exercise 1: Discussion

The following questions are posed to the group to develop a joint understanding of difficulties experienced in emotional processing, with answers written on the flipchart forming the basis of group discussion.

- How able are you to identify and label what you feel?
- What strategies do people use to manage or tolerate difficult emotions?
- What happens if we avoid emotions?

Therapist tips

- Explain that many of us at different times have difficulty in accurately identifying what we are feeling and that we can all struggle in tolerating and managing certain emotions, both positive and negative.
- Reinforce with the group that when we describe emotions as being 'negative', this does not mean that they are wrong or bad; rather they are 'negative' in the sense that they can be uncomfortable and painful for people to experience. Emphasise that all emotions are valid and important signals worth listening to.
- Highlight that effective management of our emotions involves an awareness, acceptance and understanding of them. It should be clarified that the focus of this group is not to provide strategies to eliminate emotions; instead it is to explore and change your relationship with and response to your emotions. Explain that we cannot always control our emotions, but the way we behave and respond to them can either help or hinder us.
- Make clear that refusing to accept our emotions or avoiding them can amplify these feelings and contribute to the experience of emotions being negative and undesirable. Ask the group if they have any other thoughts or ideas about the importance of identifying, tolerating and managing emotions.

Exercise 2: Vignette

Read or write on the flipchart the following case vignette:

> Jo is 27 and lives with her partner. They have a close relationship and have been together for three years. Jo works as a secretary in a busy office. Her boss puts lots of pressure on her to meet deadlines and often piles on the work. Jo often stays late at work, not getting home until about 9pm on some nights. She is feeling stressed and low but avoids dealing with the situation.
>
> At the same time Jo is also involved in helping to plan her friend's wedding which takes up a lot of her free time. This leads to Jo feeling more stressed, tired and irritable as she does not have any time to herself or with her partner.
>
> Rather than try to acknowledge and deal with how she is feeling she ignores it and carries on.

What might be the difficulties for Jo if she continues to avoid her emotions?
Prompts for facilitators during discussion might be:

- With regards to work, do you think she is more or less efficient?
- Consider her relationships: might she be snapping at people or arguing with them more often?
- Consider her feelings about herself. Might she feel bad about herself for not standing up to people and beat herself up about it? Do you think Jo feels taken for granted?

Therapist tips

- Explain that there is a difference between emotional *pain* which is a part of human life, such as grief after losing a loved one or disappointment at not getting the exam result you hoped for, and emotional *suffering* which comes about from the avoidance of or an unwillingness to accept and respond adaptively to a negative emotion. Mention here that emotional suffering is an aspect we will be targeting in the coming weeks.
- Throughout check if there are any questions and encourage the group members to identify any possible questions they have about emotions that could be addressed over the coming weeks.

Exercise 3: Challenging beliefs

Introduce the idea that the negative beliefs we have about emotions impact on our ability to respond to and manage them effectively. Write the following beliefs on a flipchart:

- Negative emotions are bad.
- It is not acceptable to have a negative feeling.
- Having emotions is a sign of weakness.
- Emotions are not important.
- If I really think about and acknowledge how I feel, I will lose control.

Ask if anyone identifies with any of these beliefs. Discuss in the group how these beliefs impact on our response to emotions. Next introduce some facts about emotions by giving the 'Reasons for Emotions' hand-out and work through this as a group.

Exercise 4: Simple pleasures toolkit

We typically generate a list of simple pleasures, with the purpose of enabling access to positive emotional experiences. You can provide hand-outs of those developed in previous groups to aid this process (see appendix).

Therapist tip

- We always try to end the group by returning to positive emotional experiences. For example, ask the participants to think of a good experience they have had during the day. It can be as seemingly inconsequential as it needs to be. For example, it could be somebody smiling at them when they felt low.

Inter-session work

- Introduce the 'List of Personal Strengths' exercise and encourage the group to continue working through the 'Portfolio of Positive Emotions' exercises (see appendix).
- Ask the participants to bring a photo/picture which elicits positive emotions for them to next week's group.

Session 3: How do we identify emotions?

Introduction

This session will focus on how we identify our emotions. We explain that sometimes people struggle to identify how they feel, discussing whether the group can relate to this and explore their thoughts about what makes identifying emotions difficult. Next, we explain that we will be looking at a number of emotions and clues to help identify when we are experiencing them.

The emotions discussed could include: anger, sadness, anxiety, guilt and happiness.

Homework review

- Ask for feedback on the experience of completing the 'Portfolio of Positive Emotions'.

Exercise 1: Emotion word map

The group agrees which emotion they would like to consider first. This is written on the flipchart and a list of associated emotion words are generated. The aim of this is to increase participants' vocabulary for describing emotions and to highlight that emotions vary in strength and intensity.

Therapist tip

- Incorporating the emotion word list (see appendix) can be useful to support this process if group participants are struggling.

Exercise 2: Exploring the experience of emotions

Next on the flipchart write and discuss:

- How do people know they are feeling this emotion?
  E.g. anger.
- How does the body feel?
  E.g. tense, racing heartbeat.
- What kind of thoughts are you having?
  E.g. everyone's against me, no-one listens or understands.
- How are you behaving?
  E.g. started shouting, pacing up and down, hurting myself.
- What was the situation or event which prompted this emotion?
  E.g. being challenged, not feeling listened to.
- How do people currently manage this emotion? What makes it difficult?
  E.g. self-harming, withdrawing. Not wanting to upset people; it will get out of control.

Therapist tips

- Complete the above exercise several times considering different emotions, always ending on a positive emotion.
- Bring the focus of the discussion back to positive emotions by asking the participants to share the photos/pictures they have brought with them.

Inter-session work

1. Distribute the 'Identifying Emotions' worksheet and ask participants to start using it to record their emotions. Explain to them that a good time to complete this record is when they notice a change in mood; although they may not initially recognise what the emotion is, completing the record may help. Suggest that it may also be helpful to start a feelings diary.
2. Ask the participants to write a letter of gratitude or a list of things for which they are grateful. Alternatively, suggest that they generate a list of emotion words associated with the word 'grateful'. Remind them to bring their work to next week's session.

Session 4: Emotion expression and emotion suppression

Introduction

This session explores the advantages and disadvantages of expressing and suppressing emotions.

Homework review

- How did people find the emotions worksheet?
- What did they notice about the emotions they experienced?
- Did the exercises help with identifying feelings?

Therapist tip

- We often start the group with a brief interactive task to engage the participants. For example, we encourage participants to pick coloured balls with faces of basic emotions (sad, happy, angry, surprise, etc.) out of a bag at random and relate to the material covered in the previous session by identifying what this emotion is, how it feels and what is its function.

Exercise 1: Discussion

Ask the group which emotion they would like to think about first (e.g. anger, guilt, sadness or anxiety). On the flipchart, list the advantages and disadvantages of both expressing and suppressing this emotion and discuss these. Repeat this exercise again for a different emotion if there is time.

Therapist tip

- Discuss as a group that sometimes in the short term people suppress or avoid emotion, as it provides relief, but often the long-term consequences are emotion intensification or not getting what you need. Elicit the participants' thoughts and views about this.

Exercise 2: The emotion continuum

This exercise aims to introduce to patients that emotions vary in strength and intensity. Similar to when we looked at words to describe an emotion, this exercise will encourage participants to think about and identify varying levels of emotions within themselves. The rationale behind this exercise is that if we have a better understanding of the language of emotions, then we are in a better position to express our emotions accurately and get the right support or help in return as others will have a clearer understanding of what it is that we are feeling. Furthermore, if our emotions vary in intensity then our physiological response and behaviour will also vary, which provides us with more information regarding how we are feeling. If we can be aware of the emotion, the physical sensations and how we are behaving, then we are in a better position to manage emotions more effectively and catch them before they become overwhelming.

Start by explaining that sometimes people experience emotions as all or nothing; such that they either feel nothing or feel overwhelmed. Introduce to the group that emotions are in fact on a continuum and they vary in intensity. For example 'fury' and 'irritation' may be on the same continuum but they have very different levels of emotional intensity. Suggest that irritation may be an easier emotion to manage than fury. Ask the group if they can identify with this. Materials needed:

*   Emotion word cards that describe varying levels of anxiety or anger.
*   Descriptions of physiological sensations associated with increasing emotion.
*   Descriptions of behaviour changes.

Ask the group to place the emotion cards on the floor in order of intensity, from the least intense to the most intense. Next ask the group to place the descriptions of associated physiological sensations and behaviours next to the varying levels of emotion. Then ask each group participant to think about the final point on this continuum at which they feel that they could manage the emotion before it overwhelms them and they either feel out of control or they block or avoid the emotion: 'Is this the point at which you need to do something about the emotion before it continues to escalate and you then feel unable to manage it?'

Ask the group to come up with ideas around what other group members would do at the emotion continuum points that they have placed themselves on to manage or express the emotion. Generate a list of strategies on the flipchart.

Therapist tips

Use the following pointers to facilitate the discussion:

*   If you find yourself easily overwhelmed by an emotion would it help to look out for sensations in your body? This may give you clues to how you are feeling and help you to manage the feeling before it becomes overwhelming.

    For example: If someone is getting angry they may notice that their shoulders are tensing and their heart rate is increasing. At this point the person may be able to take themselves away from the situation to cool off.

*   Would it help to look out for certain behaviours as these may also give you a clue to how you are feeling and give you an opportunity to do something before the emotion feels out of control?

    For example: If someone is getting angry they may notice that they start to fidget or pace around. At this point the person may be able to say a few key words to themselves or use a relaxation exercise to calm the feelings of anger down.

- Spend five minutes reflecting on the session and bringing it together. Finish on a positive note by asking if anyone is willing to share their homework letter of gratitude/list of things/emotion words.

Inter-session work

1. The 'Emotion Thermometer' hand-out: ask the participants to complete this during the week for an emotion they struggle with.
2. The 'Ways to Manage Difficult Emotions' hand-out: explain that this has a number of simple and useful ideas to help with managing difficult emotions. Ask people to choose and practise a technique over the week.
3. Ask patients to try 'Getting into the Flow' (see appendix, p. 96) which involves engaging fully in small pleasures, preferably with someone else.

Session 5: Emotions and needs

Introduction

Introduce this session as one that will be looking at the needs that emotions communicate to the self and others. Highlight that emotions are important signals worth listening to as they are communicating that we may need something and can guide how we and others should respond to this need.

Homework review

- If the group would benefit, explore the emotion thermometer with another emotion.
- Check the participants' progress with ongoing positive emotional work.
- Reflect on the 'Getting into the flow' exercise.

Exercise 1: Vignette

Read the case vignette and ask the group the accompanying questions, noting the answers on the flipchart. The aim of this exercise is to encourage people to start thinking about the needs that emotions communicate, the impact that ignoring them can have, and ways to communicate needs.

> Sarah has been invited to her friend's birthday party on a Friday night. The plan is to meet in a restaurant at 7pm, have dinner and then go for drinks. Sarah really wants to see her friend but is very anxious about meeting people in public for dinner and is worried about talking to her friend about this. Sarah worries about this all week and on the night texts her friend

saying that she has a headache and cannot go out. Sarah has now cancelled on her friend a couple of times.

Points for discussion:

- How does Sarah feel after cancelling?
- What is she thinking?
- What does or did she need?
- What was the outcome for Sarah? How about her friend? (Does she feel better or worse?)
- Are there any other ways that she could have handled this situation bearing in mind her needs? What are they?

Exercise 2: Making emotions work for you

On the flipchart list a number of emotions and discuss as a group which needs these emotions are communicating. Also discuss how people can respond to the emotion based on the need it is communicating.

Flipchart example:

- When I feel **sad** I need .... (e.g. comfort/reassurance).
  When I feel this emotion I will respond to it by .... (e.g. phoning a friend/family member, doing something that will cheer me up).
- When I feel **angry** I need .... (e.g. someone to listen to me, time out).
  When I feel this emotion I will respond to it by .... (e.g. taking myself away from the situation and dealing with it later, talking to someone and not bottling it up).
- When I feel **anxious** I need .... (e.g. to face the fear, reassurance).
  When I feel this emotion I will respond to it by .... (e.g. reminding myself that I can cope with this as I've been able to overcome anxiety before, speak with someone).

To end the group

Finally, spend time recapping the material discussed in the group and reiterating the importance of eliciting and attending to positive emotions, as well as the importance of thinking about the needs emotions are communicating.

Complete the self-report questionnaires which were also administered before the first session, in addition to the patient satisfaction questionnaire.

We use the following self-report questionnaires:

The Revised Social Anhedonia Scale (RSAS; Chapman *et al.*, 1976) assesses the reduced ability to experience social pleasure (previously reported in an eating disorder (ED) population; Tchanturia *et al.*, 2012, 2015).

The Toronto Alexithymia Scale (TAS-20; Bagby *et al.*, 1994) is the most widely used measure of alexithymia, loading onto three sub-scales: difficulty describing feelings, difficulty identifying feelings, and externally oriented thinking (reported in relation to CREST in Tchanturia *et al.*, 2014, 2015).

The Motivational Ruler (MR; Miller and Rollnick, 2002) is used for all groups in order to compare motivational changes both within and between the groups. A Likert scale of 0–10 measures self-reported importance and ability to change.

In general we find that self-report measures improve more with ten-session individual format (Tchanturia *et al.*, 2015), and short five-session group intervention does not produce such impressive changes (Tchanturia *et al.*, 2014). Having said that, reflecting on patient feedback we think that the group format of CREST helps to consolidate awareness of emotional and social difficulties and helps patients to practise some of the skills, for example communicating, expressing their needs and simply being with other people in a safe contained therapeutic environment. We have collected patients' feedback from CREST groups and present this in Table 5.1 to illustrate themes which emerged from this evaluation.

As it can be seen from this synthesis of the patient feedback the CREST group has many aspects which patients are finding useful and good suggestions and ideas on how to develop this work further. At present we are developing more materials and practical tasks to address the suggestions and we are looking forward to doing more work to consolidate the format of this group.

APPENDIX WITH SOME EXAMPLES OF HAND-OUTS: (SUITABLE FOR BOTH INDIVIDUAL AND GROUP SESSIONS)

Emotion word list

Abandoned, Abrasive, Accommodating, Adored, Affectionate, Afraid, Aggressive, Agreeable, Awkward, Alienated, Altruistic, Amused, Angry, Annoyed, Anxious, Avoidant

Betrayed, Bitter, Blessed, Bored, Bothered, Brave, Bursting, Blue, Belittled, Bad, Brilliant, Blamed, Blissful, Beautiful

Calm, Careless, Caring, Celebrating, Charming, Cheerful, Cherishing, Cold-blooded, Comfortable, Compassion, Competitive, Confused, Cool, Creative, Crucified, Crushed, Cheated, Controlled

Defensive, Delicate, Delighted, Depressed, Desirable, Discontented, Disgust, Distracted, Dull

Eager, Earnest, Easy, Enjoying, Enthusiastic, Exited, Euphoric, Energised, Elated, Effective, Energetic, Empowered, Empathic, Edgy, Embarrassed, Envious

Fascinated, Fear, Frustrated, Funny, Furious, Fearless, Fortunate, Fragile, Fidgety, Fulfilled

Giggly, Glad, Glee, Gloomy, Grateful, Guilty, Gentle

Happy, Hectic, Hilarious, Hopeful, Horrific, Humorous, Hurt, Heroic, Helpful, Hostile, Heartless, Hateful

Impressed, Impulsive, Inflexible, Insensitive, Inspired, Interested, Intimidated, Irritated, Incensed, Infuriated, Irate, Intelligent, Influential

Jealous, Jittery, Jolly, Jubilant, Joyful, Jumpy

Lively, Lonely, Lost, Loved, Lovely

Mad, Manic, Melancholic, Merry, Mindful, Miserable, Moved

Nervous, Numb

Optimistic, Overwhelmed, Out-of-control

Passionate, Passive, Panicky, Pleased, Proud, Petrified, Peaceful, Positive, Paralysed, Powerful, Pissed-off

Reckless, Refreshed, Romantic, Restless, Resistant, Ruthless, Resigned, Rejected, Receptive, Relaxed, Revitalised, Refreshed

Safe, Satisfied, Scared, Secure, Seduced, Selfish, Sentimental, Shamed, Shy, Strong, Self-reliant, Serene, Soothed, Sympathetic, Surprised, Shocked, Stressed

Tolerant, Tranquil, Troubled, Twitchy, Thrilled, Talented, Tender, Terrified, Tense, Threatened, Tentative, Tolerated

Uncomfortable, Unhappy, Understood, Unpopular

Victimised, Vulnerable, Vigorous, Vivacious, Vehement, Vindictive, Violent

Warm, Worried, Worthless, Wise, Worthy, Wild, Wanted

Homework

The purpose of this homework is to assist the participant in increasing positive experiences in their life. The homework is something which the participant can continue to do in their lives and is not just a one-off piece of work. With the participant, decide which of the following exercises they would like to do for homework.

Portfolio of positive emotions

The aim is for the participant to collect positive images, metaphors, anecdotes and mottos, which they will log in their book. The portfolio helps in the process of shifting attention towards aspects of life that make them feel more positive.

Bank of positive experiences

The bank of positive experiences (see worksheet on p. 92) is useful in helping the participant recognise that, even when they are feeling particularly negative, there are and have been positive experiences which will recur.

Three good things

This is based on Martin Seligman's positive thinking research (e.g. 'Authentic Happiness'). The idea is that if you can think about and reflect on positive things regularly, it can move you into a more positive mind state. The three good things exercise is especially useful for those who have a bias towards negative emotions, as it highlights that even when 'having a bad day', there can be positives within this. Thus, participants can be made more aware of their negative bias and also see that emotions can and do fluctuate, but that sometimes we may fail to pay attention to the positives.

Ask the participant to think of a good experience that has happened during the day. It can be as seemingly inconsequential as it needs to be. For example, it could be somebody smiling at them when they felt low. As they become more accustomed to finding one good thing it can be expanded up to three good things.

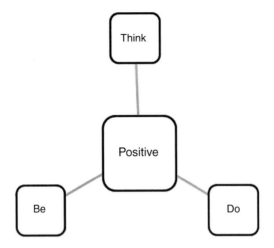

Figure 5.1 Think, be, do positive things

Bank of positive experiences

Finding ways of keeping hold of positive emotions is crucial. One way is a 'bank system' using the log book below. You may experience more positive experiences than you think…

In the session

Day	Positive action or experience	New or unusual?	Tick each time that you revisit the positive feeling it gave you

Reflect on homework:

Ask the participant to discuss what they did for homework and to reflect on what they noticed and learnt. Encourage them to continue to practise noticing when they have positive emotions and experiences.

Aim

1. To recognise and identify positives in everyday situations and in ourselves.
2. To provide the participant with a range of strategies that encourages them to notice and amplify positives, shifting from a tendency to focus on negatives.

Therapist tip: We found it useful to explain that positive people automatically look for positives in their environment and hold on to these, amplifying them and remembering them after the event. The participant needs to *learn* how to do this. The tasks and exercises help to shift focus onto the positives as well as showing what it feels like so we know what we are aiming for.

Instructions

Discuss the positive psychology experiments/interventions described below with the participants. Explore which ones would be easier, which would be most helpful, which ones would they like to try? Use the taster tasks to break up the discussion.

The following text provides background information and supporting evidence from the positive psychology literature. Please use your own judgement as to whether it would be beneficial for your particular participants to share the scientific basis for the exercise in this session.

Positive Psychology: pleasure from being with people and positive thinking

For many years, clinical and experimental psychologists have studied negative emotions such as anger, sadness, fear and disgust. All of these emotions are vitally important for survival, but positive emotions are as important and psychologists have begun to focus more on understanding and appreciating the power of positive emotions.

This work has been collected together under the field of Positive Psychology, a branch of psychology which focuses on strengths, resources, resilience, optimism and hope, rather than a deficit model of human experience. The most notable proponents of this field of psychology have been Martin Seligman, Mihaly Csikszentmihalyi and Barbara Fredrickson. For example, a simple experiment in which you are asked to remember something that made you feel happy during the past month is an easy and effective way of positively influencing mood. Mood relates to free-floating or objectless experience that is long-lasting and occupies the background consciousness, whereas emotions focus on a specific event (past, present or future), are shorter in duration and the individual experiencing the emotion tends to be acutely aware of it at the time.

Based on many years of laboratory experiments, Professor Barbara Fredrickson (2001) developed her Broaden and Build theory of positive emotions. In summary, her work demonstrates that positive emotions broaden our thought-action repertoires, they can undo, or counteract negative emotions and they build resilience (Fredrickson, 2001, 2009). More specifically, the broadening effect of positive emotions relates to their capacity to open up our minds which helps us to 'think outside the box', giving a bigger picture view of our current situation, enabling us to become more creative at finding solutions.

Several experiments have shown that dwelling on positive emotions enhances performance in verbal creativity tasks. More specifically, the building effect relates to the capacity of positive emotions to build personal resources which can be accessed now or in the future. These include intellectual resources such as problem solving and openness to new learning, physical resources such as cardiovascular health and coordination, social resources such as the ability to maintain relationships and make new social connections, and psychological resources such as resilience, optimism, our sense of identity and our drive to achieve personal goals. As we develop these resources, they generate more positive emotional experiences and these positive emotions continue to build the resources further in an upward spiral. Some new evidence is emerging that demonstrates that positive emotions have the potential to build religious and spiritual resources as well as the other personal resources highlighted in the literature above.

Fredrickson's work has led to the development of a list of ten important positive emotions. These are: joy, gratitude, serenity, interest, hope, pride, amusement, inspiration, awe and love (Fredrickson, 2009). Enhancing our experiences of these emotions can lead to greater psychological (and physical) well-being. Through CREST we would like to encourage thinking about and noticing positive emotions: 'Think, be, do positive things…'

Empirical/experimental research shows that we can improve well-being by:

writing letters of gratitude, counting blessings, performing kind acts, cultivating strengths, visualising an ideal future, meditating (Lyubomirsky and Layous, 2013).

Exercises

1.   Being mindful of positive experiences

Try just 'being' in your environment and notice its effect on your mood. This means trying to pay attention, non-judgementally, and purposely to your current surroundings. If you have ever tried mindfulness before, you can use your experience of learning how to do this. Research shows that being present in your environment helps you to focus your attention on what's around you, rather than ruminating, and this can lead to a positive emotional experience.

You could try paying attention to positive events/items/experiences during the day by keeping a positive event diary. At the end of each day, write down three positive things (no matter how small) that you saw, experienced, thought about or planned that day.

Figure 5.2 Positive emotions

We have learnt that when we're feeling depressed, it is difficult, if not impossible, to see the positives in life. However, with practice, by keeping a positive log, over time, you will train yourself to see more of the positives in life.

TASTER TASK… Ask the participant to think of three good things that have happened to them in the last 24 hours. How does it feel to explore this?

We know that people can often have a glass 'half empty' approach, but there is lots of evidence to suggest that people who see the glass as 'half full' have healthier, happier, more successful, balanced lives and the positive event log is one way to practise experiencing the 'glass half full' approach to life.

The service users in our unit have developed a toolbox of simple pleasures and positive resources to remind them what they have available to them when they are experiencing negative emotions or negative mood states.

These include: smiles, personal treats (massage/facial/nails), reading a book, watching old films, losing yourself in London, walking in the park (or lake, river or on the beach), watching ballet/dance, spicy food, candles, crafts, writing a wish list for travels, being with positive people, visiting museums, looking at photos, bathing, writing a diary, having a conversation, standing on grass with bare feet, people watching, card making, knitting, music playing or listening, company with people/animals, making jewellery (or pottery, posters, art or glass painting) and having a five-minute time out.

This list was generated by the group and individuals are free to add their own ideas and resources to their own copy of this simple pleasures toolbox and they are encouraged to share new ideas with the group. Having these positive strengths and activities written down is one way to access positive strengths and emotional states when mood is so low that your problem-solving skills are reduced.

2.   Being with others

Spending time with others is an excellent way to boost positive emotions. This works especially well if you are sharing interesting and novel activities. This might mean you need to try a new hobby or go along to an event that you wouldn't normally try in order to share the experience with others there.

3.   Favourite person exercise

Simply look at a picture of your favourite person, pet or place. It has been found that simply looking at our favourite person produces enhanced immune function, improved mood states, improved experience of positive emotion and a feeling of invigoration.

TASTER TASK... Ask the participant which photograph or image they would choose and ask if they could bring this to the next session.

4.   Getting into the flow
Do activities that are high in these dimensions: Activities that...

- are structured and have clear goals and immediate feedback;
- have a balance of challenges and skills;
- absorb your full attention;
- make you lose track of time, requiring complete concentration where everything else but the activity is irrelevant at that moment in time;
- give you a sense of control;
- make you want to do the activity again just for the sake of doing it (not for any material reward it might give);
- provoke curiosity in life.

By participating in an activity that offers you many of the above factors, you will achieve 'flow'. This has been described by the positive psychologist, Mihaly Csikszentmihalyi (2002) as: the intense experiential involvement in moment to moment activity which can be either physical or mental. Attention is fully invested in the task at hand and the person functions at their fullest capacity. This is an experience where you start to do something and you become so lost in it that you lose track of time and become completely absorbed in the task. It is different to persisting with something to get it perfect. Rather, it is about the positive experience of 'being in the zone', and the research shows that activities which are most likely to lead to the experience of flow include: sports, dance, creative arts, sex, socialising, studying, listening to music, reading and working. Activities that prevent the experience of flow from occurring include housework, watching TV and being alone, and these experiences were more likely to produce emotional states of apathy and boredom (Csikszentmihalyi, 2002).

5.   Optimal positive to negative emotions ratio

This experiment encourages people to look for a balance of three positive emotions/experiences/interactions to one negative emotion/experience/interaction.

TASTER TASK… Complete the online calculator on Fredrickson's website: http://www.positivityratio.com **together. You could come back to this in a later session to see if the positivity ratio has changed.**

Fredrickson and Losada (2005) initially looked at the performance of 60 business teams and explored the ratio of positive to negative interactions. The research showed that those with the best balance of positive to negative emotions had three positives to every one negative. Fredrickson and Losada concluded that this ratio offers the optimal balance for 'human flourishing'. Therefore, if you train yourself to notice more positive emotions/experiences/interactions in life, then you will achieve a better emotional balance and improved well-being.

Homework example

The purpose of this homework is to put into practice the strategies discussed in session. With the participant, decide which of the tasks they would like to do for homework. Also, remind them that their homework from last week (Portfolio of Positive Emotions/ Bank of Positive Experiences) is ongoing and can be continued alongside the new tasks.

Instructions

Choose one or two of the strategies we have talked about today and experiment with introducing them into each day.

1. **Being mindful of positive experiences** *(can be integrated into log book/ bank)*
2. **Being with others**
3. **Favourite person exercise**
4. **Savouring**
5. **Getting into the flow**
6. **Optimal positive to negative emotions ratio** *(list three good things each day)*

'Managing the negative to get to the positive'

The strategies explored in this session should be encouraged throughout the remaining CREST sessions, fitting in with the objective of 'managing the negative to get to the positive'.

If the participant finds a strategy that works for them, encourage them to keep this going and integrate it into their weekly routine. If they do not find a strategy useful, prompt them to return to the list of positive psychology exercises and try a different one.

How could you experiment with introducing some of these strategies into your daily life? Which one seems possible to start with? How could you begin to use it each day?

1. Direct and clear communication skills
2. 'I' messages
3. Simple pleasures toolkit
4. Pay it forward quotes
5. Three good things
6. Letter of gratitude
7. Positive body language

Therapist tip: See appendix for materials for additional exercises that aim to elicit positive emotions including writing a letter of gratitude, a list of quotes and hand-out for the 'three good things' exercise.

Simple pleasures toolkit

This toolkit was developed collaboratively with therapists and patients involved in the CREST group. We found it useful to generate ideas in the CREST sessions and to add them to this list in order to develop it further.

- winning an eBay bid;
- positive connections with others;
- putting fresh sheets on the bed;
- sunny days;
- exploring London;
- contact with friends;
- writing to family, knowing they will value it;
- getting letters;
- jewellery making;
- cup of coffee when you are cold;
- music;
- electric blanket;
- yoga;
- being active/outdoors;
- first signs of spring/smell of blossom;
- flowers;
- getting your hair/nails done;
- pampering: reflexology/massage/facial;
- making others happy;
- laughter;
- shopping;
- playing games;
- singing;
- random walks;
- watching old films;
- warm clothing;
- art/writing;
- sand/grass between your toes;
- having a hot bath;
- smiling at strangers;
- lighting a scented candle;
- knitting;
- gardening;
- spending time with your pets;
- putting on slippers;
- using nice cream/perfume;
- photography;
- massage;
- feeling the breeze;
- watching your favourite TV show.

Pay it forward quotes

Sail beyond the horizon; fly higher than you ever thought possible; magnify your existence by helping others; be kind to people and animals of all shapes and sizes; be true to what you value most; shine your light on the world; and be the person you were born to be.

Blake Beattie

I hope the fruits of my labour are ripe for many generations to come.

Donovan Nichols

They say don't believe your own hype, but if you don't why would anyone else? To be great you have to believe you can do great things.

Charley Johnson

Be the change you want to see in the world.

Ghandi

A life lived for others, is the only life worth living.

Albert Einstein

If you can't feed a hundred people, then just feed one.

Mother Teresa

The only time you should look down at someone, is when you are helping them up.

Jesse Jackson

If you have much, give your wealth; if you have little, give your heart.

Anonymous

You may be only one person in this world, but to one person at one time, you are the world.

Anonymous

An untruth kept in the heart, is a burden which weighs down the soul.

Blake Beattie

There is no such thing as can't.

Christopher Reeve

There are two way to live your life. One as though nothing is a miracle, the other as though everything is a miracle.

Albert Einstein

I have a dream.

Martin Luther King Jr

Every man dies, not every man really lives.

William Wallace

Three good things

Each day fill in one or more of the following with a positive:
Today I appreciate
....
....
Today I value
....
....
Today I felt positive when
....
....
Today I appreciate
....
....
Today I value
....
....
Today I felt positive when
....
....
Today I appreciate
....
....
Today I value
....
....
Today I felt positive when
....
....

Letter of gratitude

Taking time to think about what and who you are grateful for having in your life can encourage positive emotions.

First, make a list of people who have had a positive impact on you and for whom you are really grateful.

I am grateful for _____

because _____

I am grateful for _____

because _____

I am grateful for _____

because _____

Second, choose one of these people to write a letter of gratitude to, explaining how they have had a positive impact on you and why you are grateful to them. As you write the letter, try to really engage with the feelings of gratitude and thanks.

Once you are done, send this letter to the person, or even better, visit them and read it aloud. However, if you are not comfortable doing this, just the act of writing the letter should have a positive effect.

Positive body language

Politics-body language – http://www.youtube.com/watch?v=dW9ztSUGY_Q.

Body language with Alan Pease – http://www.youtube.com/watch?v=Aw36-ByXuMw.

Amy Cuddy: Your body language shapes who you are http://www.ted.com/talks/amy_cuddy_your_body_language_shapes_who_you_are.html.

We found watching these film clips together and discussing them as a group provides useful information for the patients; increasing awareness of the importance of their body, face and voice in communication and giving an opportunity to set up behavioural experiments exploring positive communication with peers, staff, families and broader social networks of people.

Acknowledgement

Kate Tchanturia would like to acknowledge the Swiss Anorexia Foundation for funding.

References

Bagby, R. M., Parker, J. D. A. and Taylor, G. J. (1994) The twenty item Toronto Alexithymia Scale I Item selection and cross-validation of the factor structure. *J Psychosom Res*, 38: 23–32.

Castro, L., Davies, H., Hale, L., Surguladze, S. and Tchanturia, K. (2010) Facial affect recognition in anorexia nervosa: Is obsessionality a missing piece of the puzzle? *Australian and New Zealand Journal of Psychiatry*, 44(12): 1118–1125.

Chapman, L. J., Chapman, J. P. and Roulin, M. L. (1976) Scales for physical and social anhedonia. *J Abnorm Psychol*, 85: 374–382.

Csikszentmihalyi, M. (2002) *Flow: The Psychology of Happiness: The Classic Work on How to Achieve Happiness*. London: Random House.

Davies, H. (2011) An investigation of emotion expression in eating disorders, PhD Thesis, King's College London.

Davies, H., Schmidt, U., Stahl, D. and Tchanturia, K. (2010) Evoked facial emotional expression and emotional experience in people with anorexia nervosa. *International Journal of Eating Disorders*, 44: 531–539.

Davies, H., Fox, J., Naumann, U., Treasure, J., Schmidt, U. and Tchanturia, K. (2012) Cognitive remediation and emotion skills training (CREST) for anorexia nervosa: An observational study using neuropsychological outcomes. *European Eating Disorders Review*, 20(3): 211–217.

Davies, H., Schmidt, U. and Tchanturia, K. (2013) Emotional facial expression in women recovered from anorexia nervosa. *Journal of Biobehavioral Medicine, Psychiatry special issue 'Treatment resistance in eating disorders' BMC Psychiatry*, 13(1): 2917.

Deborde, A. S., Berthoz, S., Godart, N., Perdereau, F., Corcos, M. and Jeammet, P. (2006) Relations between alexithymia and anhedonia: A study in eating disordered and control subjects. *L'Encephale*, 32(1 Pt 1): 83–91.

Fonville, L., Giampietro, V., Surguladze, S., Williams, S. and Tchanturia, K. (2014) Increased BOLD signal in the fusiform gyrus during implicit emotion processing in anorexia nervosa. *NeuroImage: Clinical*: 266–273.

Fredrickson, B. L. (1998) What good are positive emotions? *Review of General Psychology: Journal of Division 1, of the American Psychological Association*, (3): 300–319.

Fredrickson, B. L. (2001) The role of positive emotions in positive psychology: The broaden-and-build theory of positive emotions. *The American Psychologist*, 56(3): 218–226.

Fredrickson, B. L. (2009) *Positivity: Groundbreaking Research to Release Your Inner Optimistic and Thrive*. Oxford: Oneworld.

Fredrickson, B. L. and Losada, M. F. (2005) Positive affect and the complex dynamics of human flourishing. *Am Psychol.*, 60(7): 678–686.

Hambrook, D., Brown, G. and Tchanturia, K. (2012) Emotional intelligence in anorexia nervosa: Is anxiety a missing piece of the puzzle? *Psychiatry Research*, 200(1): 12–19.

Harrison, A., Sullivan, S., Tchanturia, K. and Treasure, J. (2010) Emotional functioning in eating disorders: Attentional bias, emotion recognition and emotion regulation. *Psychological Medicine*, 40: 1887–1897.

Harrison, A., Genders, R., Davies, H. and Tchanturia, K. (2011) Experimental measurement of the regulation of anger and aggression in women with anorexia nervosa. *Clinical Psychology Psychotherapy*, 18(6): 445–452.

Harrison, A., Mountford, V. and Tchanturia, K. (2014) Social anhedonia and work and social functioning in the acute and recovered phases of eating disorders. *Psychiatry Research*, 218: 187–194.

Kyriacou, O., Easter, A. and Tchanturia, K. (2009) Comparing views of patients, parents and clinicians on emotions in anorexia: A qualitative study. *Journal of Health Psychology*, 14: 843–854.

Lyubomirsky, S. and Layous, K. (2013) How do simple positive activities increase well-being? *Current Directions in Psychological Science*, 22(1): 57–62.

Money, C., Genders, B., Treasure, J., Schmidt, U. and Tchanturia, K. (2011a) A brief emotion focused intervention for in-patients with anorexia nervosa: A qualitative study. *Journal of Health Psychology*, 16: 947–958.

Money, C., Davies, H. and Tchanturia, K. (2011b) A case study introducing Cognitive Remediation & Emotion Skills Training (CREST) for anorexia nervosa in-patient care. *Clinical Case Studies*, 10: 110–121.

Oldershaw, A., Hambrook, D., Stahl, D., Tchanturia, K., Treasure, J. and Schmidt, U. (2011a) The socio-emotional processing stream in anorexia nervosa. *Neuroscience and Biobehavioural Reviews*, 35: 970–988.

Oldershaw, A., Treasure, J., Hambrook, D., Tchanturia, K. and Schmidt, U. (2011b) Is anorexia nervosa a version of autism spectrum disorders? *European Eating Disorder Review*, 19: 462–474.

Rhind, S., Mandy, W., Treasure, J. and Tchanturia, K. (2014) An exploratory study of evoked facial affect in adolescents with anorexia nervosa. *Psychiatry Research*, 220(1–2): 711–715.

Rollnick, S., Miller, W. R. and Butler, C. C. (2008). *Motivational Interviewing in Health Care: Helping Patients Change Behavior*. New York: Guilford.

Russell, T., Schmidt, U. and Tchanturia, K. (2009) Aspects of social cognition in anorexia nervosa: Affective and cognitive theory of mind. *Psychiatry Research*, 15: 181–185.

Seligman, M. E. and Csikszentmihalyi, M. (2000) Positive psychology: An introduction. *The American Psychologist*, 55(1): 5–14.

Tchanturia, K., Davies, H., Harrison, A., Fox, J., Treasure, J. and Schmidt, U. (2012) Altered social hedonic processing in eating disorders. *International Journal of Eating Disorders*, 45(8): 962–969.

Tchanturia, K., Hambrook, D., Curtis, H., Jones, T., Lounes, N., Fenn, K., Keys, A., Stivenson, L. and Davies, H. (2013) Work and social adjustment in patients with anorexia nervosa. *Comprehensive Psychiatry*, 54(1): 41–45.

Tchanturia, K., Doris, E. and Fleming, C. (2014) Effectiveness of Cognitive Remediation and Emotion Skills Training (CREST) for anorexia nervosa in group format: A naturalistic pilot study. *European Eating Disorders Review*, 22(3): 200–205.

Tchanturia, K., Marin Dapelo, M., Hambrook, D. and Harrison, A. (2015) Why study positive emotions in the context of eating disorders? *Current Psychiatry Reports*, 17(1): 537.

Tchanturia, K., Doris, E., Mountford, V. and Fleming, C. (in press) Cognitive Remediation and Emotion Skills Training (CREST) for anorexia nervosa in individual format: Self-reported outcomes. *BMC Psychiatry*.

Chapter 6

Perfectionism short format group for inpatients

Samantha Lloyd, Caroline Fleming and Kate Tchanturia

It was in the 1970s that Bruch first alluded to the perfectionist nature of Anorexia Nervosa (AN) in her characterisation of a typical AN patient as meeting 'every parent and teacher's idea of perfection' (Bruch, 1978). In line with clinical observations of the highly perfectionistic and rigid AN patient, models of eating disorders have since posited perfectionism as both a risk and maintaining factor (Fairburn *et al.*, 2003a; Schmidt and Treasure, 2006). In support of the association between perfectionism and AN, there exists a robust evidence base for elevated perfectionism in patients with AN in comparison to individuals without eating disorders (Bardone-Cone *et al.*, 2007; Egan *et al.*, 2011) and some evidence that perfectionism is higher in eating disorders relative to other disorders (Bardone-Cone *et al.*, 2007). There is also evidence of perfectionism being elevated in first degree relatives of AN patients (Jacobs *et al.*, 2009; Woodside *et al.*, 2002).

Some studies have shown perfectionism to be associated with poorer prognosis and attrition from treatment in AN (Bizeul *et al.*, 2001; Sutandar-Pinnock *et al.*, 2003; Woodside *et al.*, 2002). Although the means by which perfectionism impacts upon outcome are not clear, it has been suggested that the all or nothing thinking style and perceived failures associated with perfectionism may make the setting of appropriate treatment goals difficult and that perfectionistic traits may prevent the self-disclosure needed to establish a strong therapeutic alliance (Goldner *et al.*, 2002). Some support for this theory comes from a study carried out by Zuroff *et al.* (2000) into the outcome of depression following treatment, where it was found that the relationship between perfectionism and poorer treatment response was mediated by the impact upon the therapeutic alliance.

Although recognition of the important role of perfectionism in eating disorders is evident in the targeting of this trait within enhanced cognitive behavioural interventions (Fairburn *et al.*, 2003), the evidence base for interventions specifically targeting perfectionism in AN is extremely limited. A recent systematic review and meta-analysis carried out by our group (Lloyd *et al.*, 2014a) found some evidence that a cognitive behavioural approach is efficacious in reducing perfectionism in adults with clinically significant perfectionism and/or psychiatric disorders associated with perfectionism. Interestingly, only one of the studies targeted perfectionism in individuals with eating disorders, with no studies of perfectionism interventions for patients with AN identified. Steele and Wade (2008) reported on an intervention aimed at targeting perfectionism and bulimic behaviours, comprising eight sessions of guided self-help-based cognitive behavioural therapy. Although significant change was not found on the Frost Multi-Dimensional Perfectionism Scale (FMPS; Frost *et al.*, 1990) Concern over Mistakes subscale during the intervention, significant change was identified at six-month follow-up compared with pre-intervention, with a large effect size achieved. Change in perfectionism was not found for the cognitive behavioral therapy (CBT) for bulimia nervosa (BN) or placebo groups. Although no significant differences were found between groups on other symptoms, in the CBT for perfectionism group significant decreases were also observed for bulimic symptoms.

There is similarly limited evidence for group interventions targeting perfectionism, with only one of the eight identified studies using a group format intervention. Steele *et al.* (2013) compared eight sessions of group CBT for perfectionism with psycho-education in adults with clinically significant perfectionism and/or a range of clinical disorders including depression, social phobia, panic disorder, generalised anxiety disorder and obsessive compulsive disorder. It was found that in the CBT for perfectionism group there were significant changes of large effect size in perfectionism and negative affect between baseline and post-treatment, with these changes maintained at three-month follow-up.

Our group recently reported pilot data on the efficacy of the perfectionism group intervention which we deliver on the inpatient ward (Lloyd *et al.*, 2014b). In this chapter we present the group protocol in detail and include additional audit data which we collect routinely in order to evaluate the effectiveness of the group. We also present recommended outcome measures for evaluating perfectionism groups for AN.

Outline of the perfectionism group

The overall aim of the 'Living with Perfectionism' group-based intervention is to increase awareness of the negative impact of perfectionism through exploration of striving for perfection versus excellence, identification and reduction of perfectionist behaviours and challenging perfectionist thinking. The group consists of six weekly sessions which are each one hour long.

The group is always delivered by two facilitators, with at least one facilitator a psychologist. One of the reasons for this is that within the group interventions important issues are dealt with in terms of group dynamics. The second facilitator is typically a trainee clinical or counselling psychologist or psychology assistant, although other members of the multidisciplinary team such as nurses and occupational therapists can co-facilitate groups. Group content is discussed and planned in supervision sessions, where any necessary changes are made to the programme.

Because of the inpatient setting, as with other groups on the ward, the group is open to new patients for the first two weeks. After this time it is closed to new members. Like with any other group work in the inpatient programme we find that a short format works well with the patients so as to create the opportunity for patients to attend most groups during their admission to the ward. In the past the principal author facilitated longer format groups (e.g. 12-week programmes). This proved difficult to manage as a closed group because newly admitted patients had to wait a long time in order to join the group, with some patients discharged before the end of the group. This resulted in small group numbers. The short format groups in general are mainly based upon psycho-education and offer a 'taster' of the content and ways in which this problem can be addressed psychologically.

An overview of the group programme is presented both in the ward introduction pack and in the ward community groups (which take place twice a week). The facilitator or other members of the clinical team remind the patients when the 'Living with Perfectionism' group is taking place and that they have to sign up if they would like to attend. We inform patients that our brief groups are designed as workshops to provide psycho-education, awareness about symptoms, personality features, cognitive styles and emotional processing that contribute to the maintenance of the disorder. We also highlight that this group is based upon a cognitive behavioural model of perfectionism developed by Shafran and colleagues (Shafran *et al.*, 2002).

We have found it very useful to utilise a combination of the different CBT-based perfectionism materials available. It was very stimulating for the clinical team to have two important study days to inspire the development of the 'Living with Perfectionism' group materials. Dr Roz Shafran kindly accepted an invitation from the principal author of this chapter (KT) and conducted a workshop on working with perfectionism; shortly after which Dr Anthea Fursland delivered training in 'CBT for perfectionism'. Additionally, KT attended Dr Melanie Fennell's training and used *Overcoming Low Self-Esteem* (Fennell, 2009) as a foundation for this brief format group. Many of the worksheets and activities provided for the patients are taken from the Centre for Clinical Intervention's (CCI) 'Perfectionism in Perspective' module (http://www.cci.health.wa.gov.au; Fursland *et al.*, 2009), with work from Shafran *et al.* (2010) also being highly influential to the development of the group content.

Content of the group

To provide a brief introduction, a key aspect of the group content is the presentation and exploration of the cycle of perfectionism which is introduced in Session 2. Each of the subsequent sessions explores and challenges aspects of this cycle in greater depth, with the final session focusing on shifting towards the more attainable 'cycle of appropriate self standards'. With regards to homework, the goal is for group members to be able to work behaviourally towards reducing perfectionism while also challenging perfectionist rules and assumptions, an approach suggested as especially useful by Shafran and colleagues. An overview of the group is presented below, with reference to the materials used within each group session.

Session 1

As with all of our group interventions, the first session begins with the establishment of general ground rules collaboratively between facilitators and group members. This is followed by an exploration of hopes, expectations and concerns about engaging with this group in particular. Our experience in facilitating the perfectionism group has highlighted heterogeneity in individuals' relationships with perfectionism. Because of this, particular attention is given to the fact that everybody's relationship to perfectionism will be different, along with an awareness of the competitiveness with others which perfectionism may engender and which may influence the group.

A drawing exercise is used at the beginning of the group in which individuals are asked to work in pairs to draw a tree, a house and a person in a short space of time (this projective method is used as an interactive tool and experiential exercise in order to facilitate discussion based on the observations group participants make while engaging with the task). Group members are asked for feedback on their experiences of carrying out the task 'imperfectly' in a short space of time and how they approached and engaged with the task. This exercise also serves as an icebreaker which prompts discussion early on in the session, as well as illustrating with a simple task any anxieties or concerns which arise in relation to perfectionism.

A second exercise involves asking group members to generate a mind map exploring ideas about what perfectionism is and highlighting both positive and negative aspects of perfectionism. This is followed by psycho-education of definitions based on research and theory and further exploration of the costs and benefits of being a perfectionist (as set out in Chapter 1 in *Overcoming Perfectionism* by Shafran *et al.* (2010). We find mind maps to be a very useful tool in our clinical work. We originally adapted this tool from educational psychology to use within our cognitive remediation therapy (CRT) groups (see Chapter 3). This tool was later embedded in the perfectionism group as it allows patients to draw out very specific elements of perfectionism, as well as to think about the bigger picture impact of perfectionism in everyday life. We find that many of our group attendees like to take away mind maps generated from different psychology-based groups and individual work to keep in their recovery folders. They are useful tools for the patients to later reflect upon learning from the groups. We encourage patients to do so and when they attend their individual therapy sessions – including outside of our service or in outpatient treatment with another therapist – they can use them as the basis for further therapeutic work if this is deemed important and meaningful.

The group continues with an explanation of the fundamental aim of the group, which is to support group members in learning to reduce their perfectionism to a more manageable level. Finally, the group members engage in an exercise that aims to raise awareness of the ways in which their perfectionism affects them negatively, and small changes which they can start to work towards.

Through discussion of the exercises, facilitators notice and discuss similarities and differences in perfectionist thinking and behaviours across different individuals. This enables a discussion highlighting that each individual's relationship with perfectionism is unique and therefore how they use this group will be individual to them, their perfectionism and what they want to target. As mentioned, this seems particularly important to verify as participants have fed back that, from the initial session, they can engage in negative social comparisons, i.e. 'I am not a good enough perfectionist in comparison with others'. Homework for the first session is for each group member to notice, observe and monitor their perfectionism in an area they have identified as being most active, paying particular attention to the costs and benefits of attempting to achieve perfection in this area.

Materials used: CCI 'Perfectionism in Perspective' Module 1, pp. 2–7 (http://www.cci.health.wa.gov.au).

Session 2

Session 2 starts with a check-in and provides an opportunity for individuals to provide feedback from the previous homework. This session explores three areas:

1. How perfectionism develops.
2. Thinking styles associated with perfectionism.
3. What maintains perfectionism – modified from *Overcoming Perfectionism*, Chapter 3 (Shafran *et al.*, 2010).

First, a brief overview is provided which is structured around the way in which perfectionism can be both learned and a personality trait. This is used to generate a group discussion on the ways in which perfectionism can be learned both directly and indirectly, as well as interacting with a perfectionist temperament. We explore messages which members may have received during their development, within the home environment and from school and society more generally, as well as more self-oriented perfectionism stemming from personality traits.

Second, through consideration of the thinking styles associated with perfectionism, namely biased attention and biased interpretation, we explore how people with perfectionism can develop rules for living and personal standards which are unhelpful. Third, through psycho-education regarding rules and assumptions, the group is encouraged to explore unhelpful rules and assumptions that may be contributing to the maintenance of their perfectionism (incorporating understanding from *Overcoming Perfectionism*, Chapter 5, Shafran *et al.*, 2010). Finally, we explore a model of perfectionism (Figure 6.1) and the importance we attribute to the concept of reasonable doing.

This model of perfectionism informs the group intervention and is explained to and discussed with the patients. It was developed based upon the CCI model of perfectionism and Dr Roz Shafran's work on perfectionism, as a framework for

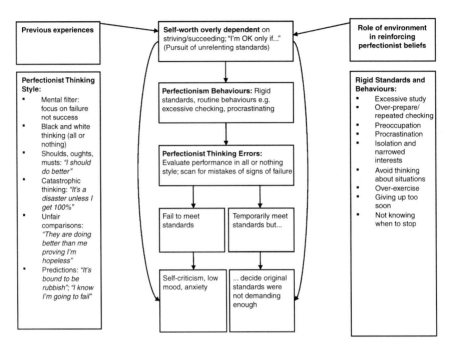

Figure 6.1 Model of perfectionism

the aspects of perfectionism we cover in the group. The model is explored in depth in this session and is developed and referred to throughout the rest of the sessions.

For homework, group members are asked to try out being a 'reasonable doer' in the area where their perfectionism is most active, paying particular attention to thoughts and feelings which arise when attempting this.

Materials used: CCI 'Perfectionism in Perspective', Module 2, pp. 2–4, Module 3, p. 7 (http://www.cci.health.wa.gov.au); *Overcoming Perfectionism*, Chapters 3, 5 (Shafran *et al.*, 2010).

Session 3

At the beginning of the session, we invite group members to reflect on their home-work and whether they were able to manage 'reasonable doing', exploring their experiences of attempting to tone down the volume of their perfectionism and, if not, the barriers to being able to engage with working towards change. This is particularly important to explore as this session focuses on a consideration of perfectionist behaviours and how to begin the process of changing some of these behaviours.

The first exercise focuses on an exploration of over doing and under doing and what might be more reasonable and manageable goals which could be set.

Additionally, consideration is given to any obstacles which individuals may face in attempting to adapt their perfectionism and reduce perfectionist behaviours. From a theoretical basis the group chooses one behaviour which has been identified and a discussion is facilitated in which the group identifies how a goal for change could be set and broken down into small steps.

The second exercise involves group members individually identifying a goal to work on and constructing a reasonable plan to reduce one perfectionist behaviour. The group members are encouraged to feed back to the wider group so that they can support each other in working on their goal during the forthcoming week.

Materials used: CCI 'Perfectionism in Perspective', Module 4, p. 7, Module 5, p.4 http://www.cci.health.wa.gov.au; *Overcoming Perfectionism*, Chapter 7 (Shafran *et al.*, 2010).

Session 4

The group starts with a reflection on the homework, encouraging group members to share what they have discovered. Homework for the following week is set at the start of the session, which is for group members to identify an area where they typically 'under do'. This may be as a result of perfectionism-related procrastination, because of neglecting enjoyable activities due to a lack of time because of striving in other areas, or because of not allowing oneself to engage in an activity purely for pleasure. Guidance is given on how group members can get started with this.

This session focuses on thinking styles and rules associated with perfectionism which may have become more evident as group members start to try to change their behaviours. The aim of the session is to work towards the identification of more helpful rules.

The group engages with an exercise which enables individuals to start questioning and challenging unhelpful, perfectionist rules and move towards developing more realistic and useful rules in day to day life. To make this as interactive as possible, each group member is provided with one or two questions on cards which are numbered 1–12 and on which are questions aimed at challenging perfectionism. The group picks an unhelpful rule or assumption from a list. The group facilitator then rolls two dice and asks the person holding the card with the number on to read out the associated question. The group is asked to discuss the evidence for the unhelpful belief using these questions. The process continues until enough challenging questions have been posed to help to identify a more helpful rule.

The group are then provided with a visual representation of the cycle of perfectionism and asked to fill out the parts of the model for themselves, identifying beliefs, rules, behaviours and thinking styles that are contributing to the maintenance of their perfectionism.

For homework, alongside challenging their perfectionist behaviours, group members are encouraged to use the types of challenging questions discussed in this session to assess whether the thoughts which arise from behaving differently are flexible, balanced and realistic.

Materials used: CCI 'Perfectionism in Perspective', Module 7, p. 3 (http://www.cci.health.wa.gov.au); *Overcoming Perfectionism*, Chapters 7.4, 7.7 (Shafran *et al.*, 2010).

Session 5

The session starts with feedback from the homework. This session focuses on the links between perfectionism and the over-evaluation of the importance of achievement in relation to self-worth. Group facilitators provide psycho-educational materials as a basis for group members to explore how this impacts upon them personally. We consider how judging self-worth solely based on meeting exacting standards impacts negatively on self-esteem, and move on to focus upon how self-worth can be recognised, acknowledged and appreciated in other aspects of life (as highlighted in *Overcoming Perfectionism*, Chapter 8, Shafran *et al.*, (2010)). Based upon Fennell's work, we also take a bigger picture perspective regarding how to enhance self-acceptance through managing perfectionism more effectively.

The first exercise asks individuals to think about how they judge their own self-worth by completing a mind map exploring aspects of their life which influence their self-esteem. Group members are invited to share what they have identified or learned about themselves. This leads to a group discussion exploring the differences between striving for perfection and striving for excellence and highlighting the energy, futility and despondency produced by attempting to achieve perfection.

The next exercise explores compassionate affirmations, encouraging participants to write down specific non-perfectionist affirmations which they may find helpful for themselves. In the final exercise we ask the patients to complete a 'compassionate self-worth' mind map, exploring what could make up their self-worth if it was not dominated by the need to be perfect. For homework, alongside continuing to work towards their goals, group members are encouraged to value their imperfections.

Materials used: CCI 'Perfectionism in Perspective', Module 8, p. 2 (http://www.cci.health.wa.gov.au); http://www.getselfhelp.co.uk; *Overcoming Perfectionism*, Chapter 8 (Shafran *et al.*, 2010); *Overcoming Low Self-Esteem* (Fennell, 2009).

Session 6

At the beginning of the final session there is the opportunity for group members to report back on and review their homework.

An overview of the five sessions is provided:

1. What is perfectionism, costs and benefits.
2. How did I become a perfectionist – direct and indirect learning, temperament, the model of perfectionism.

3. Managing perfectionism, adapting perfectionist behaviours.
4. What maintains perfectionism and challenging perfectionist thinking, adjusting unhelpful rules and assumptions.
5. Re-evaluating the importance of achievement, the pursuit of excellence versus perfection.

The group then explores the adaptive model of appropriate self-standards which is compared with the perfectionism model shown in Figure 6.1. Discussion and reflection regarding thoughts and observations about the new model are encouraged, centring on the following areas:

*   how group members would like to manage their perfectionism in future;
*   which parts of the model people think are the easiest for them to adapt;
*   what else their self-worth could be based upon;
*   which behaviours they could reduce;
*   which new thinking styles could be practised.

The group is finally asked to reflect on the six sessions as a whole, what they have learned and how they are planning to take this learning forward.

Recommended outcome measures

As with all group interventions, ongoing evaluation is carried out using outcome measures completed prior to and following the group. Numerous self-report perfectionism measures exist and a discussion and critique of the most appropriate measures is complex and beyond the scope of this book. However, we use the following outcome measures to evaluate the perfectionism group:

Frost Multi-Dimensional Perfectionism Scale (FMPS) (Frost et al.*, 1990).* This widely used measure assesses the following aspects of a multi-dimensional concept of perfectionism: concern over mistakes, personal standards, doubts about actions, parental criticism, parental expectation and organisation (not included in total score).

Clinical Perfectionism Questionnaire (CPQ). This self-report measure is based upon the cognitive behavioural model of clinical perfectionism proposed by Shafran *et al.* (2002). The scale assesses the core components of clinical perfectionism: the tendency to set high goals and standards and the negative consequences which not meeting these goals have, for example upon feelings of self-worth (Riley *et al.*, 2007). We have more recently started to use the CPQ alongside the FMPS and have found it to be ideal for the purpose of assessing group outcomes, due to the short length (12 items) and sensitivity to the effects of treatment (Riley *et al.*, 2007; Steele *et al.*, 2013).

Motivational ruler (Miller and Rollnick, 2002). A Likert scale which measures an individual's perceived importance to change and ability to change on a scale from one to ten. Higher scores indicate greater importance and ability. This measure is used with all group interventions on our inpatient ward.

Patient satisfaction questionnaire. The questionnaire has been designed specifically for this group and includes both quantitative and qualitative questions, such as the perceived helpfulness of the group and what the patient feels they have gained from the group. Quantitative questions use a Likert rating format, ranging from one to five.

Both the FMPS and motivational ruler are completed by group members prior to and at the end of the group. The patient satisfaction questionnaire is completed at the end of the group.

Results of our pilot study

Using this data, our small pilot study (Lloyd *et al.*, 2014a) found significant changes of moderate effect size for perfectionism – as measured by the FMPS total score and Concern over Mistakes, Doubts about Actions and Personal Standards subscales. These changes were found to be independent of changes in Body Mass Index. This data has since been extended and results are shown below for pre- and post-intervention scores for 28 patients completing the perfectionism group. Since introducing the CPQ as a routine measure pre and post-group, we have also found significant change in clinical perfectionism following the group. Figures 6.2 and 6.3 show change in perfectionism on the FMPS and CPQ. These results are promising and support the effectiveness of targeting perfectionism in AN using a short format group intervention.

Continuous evaluation of the feedback from patients attending the group has been invaluable in helping us to further develop the group. Through qualitative

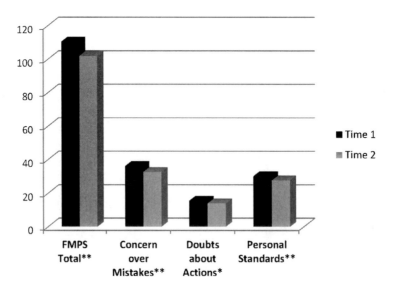

Figure 6.2 Changes in FMPS score following the 'Living with Perfectionism' group (N = 28)
Notes: * Change significant at p = 0.05. ** Change significant at p = 0.01.

CPQ

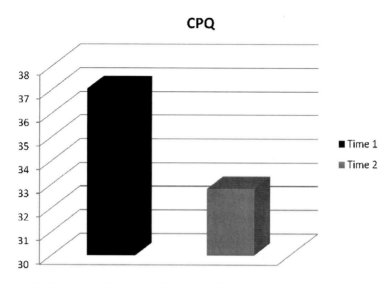

Figure 6.3 Changes in CPQ score following the 'Living with Perfectionism' group (N = 16)
Note: Change significant at p = 0.01.

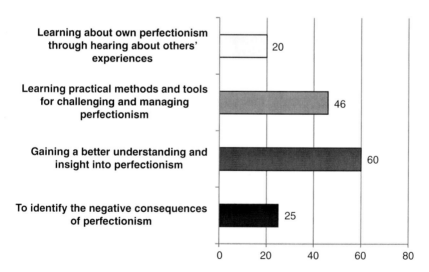

Figure 6.4 Responses to the question 'What did you learn from attending the group?'
Numbers refer to proportion of patients endorsing each theme (N = 28).

feedback we have discovered what patients feel they have gained by attending the group, as well as suggestions for improvements. We responded to feedback on wanting more practical activities and examples and increased interaction in the group by using specific exercises done in pairs and small groups which are useful

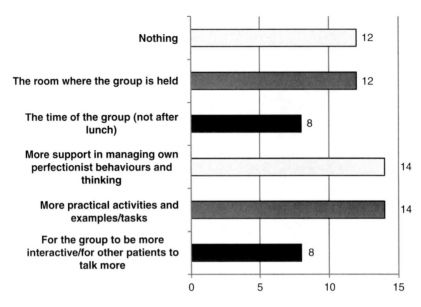

Figure 6.5 Responses to the question 'What would you change about the group?' Numbers refer to proportion of patients endorsing each theme (N = 28).

for group dynamics and provide opportunities for more experience based learning (e.g. producing a drawing of a tree, house and person; mind maps). Figures 6.4 and 6.5 show themes from our qualitative data derived using the method described by Braun and Clarke (2006).

As with all groups in the brief group intervention programme, we try to make talking based groups as action based as possible because we are well aware of the thinking styles of our patients in the severe malnourished phase. We therefore focus on concrete exercises rather than extensive discussions, using as much visual and concrete material as possible.

The first (SL) and principal (KT) authors are currently conducting empirical and experimental research into perfectionism in AN, with the aim of translating this into clinical work. We hope that this will make the group more useful for patients, as well as addressing the qualitative feedback we have received for this group.

References

Bardone-Cone, Anna M., Wonderlich, Stephen A., Frost, Randy O., Bulik, Cynthia M., Mitchell, James E., Uppala, Saritha and Simonich, Heather. (2007). Perfectionism and eating disorders: Current status and future directions. *Clinical Psychology Review*, 27(3), 384–405.

Bizeul, C., Sadowsky, N. and Rigaud, Daniel. (2001). The prognostic value of initial EDI scores in anorexia nervosa patients: A prospective follow-up study of 5–10 years. *European Psychiatry*, 16(4), 232–238.

Braun, Virginia and Clarke, Victoria. (2006). Using thematic analysis in psychology. *Qualitative Research in Psychology*, 3(2), 77–101.

Bruch, Hilde. (1978). *The Golden Cage* (p. 59), Cambridge, MA: Harvard University Press.

Centre for Clinical Interventions. (2002). Overcoming Perfectionism, http://www.cci .health.wa.gov.au/.

Egan, Sarah J., Wade, Tracey D. and Shafran, Roz. (2011). Perfectionism as a transdiagnostic process: A clinical review. *Clinical Psychology Review*, 31(2), 203–212.

Fairburn, Christopher G., Cooper, Zafra and Shafran, Roz. (2003). Cognitive behaviour therapy for eating disorders: A 'transdiagnostic' theory and treatment. *Behaviour Research and Therapy*, 41(5), 509–528.

Fennell, Melanie. (2009). *Overcoming Low Self-Esteem*, UK: Constable & Robinson.

Frost, Randy O., Marten, Patricia, Lahart, Cathleen and Rosenblate, Robin. (1990). The dimensions of perfectionism. *Cognitive Therapy and Research*, 14(5), 449–468.

Fursland, A., Raykos, B. and Steele, A. (2009). *Perfectionism in Perspective*. Perth, Western Australia: Centre for Clinical Interventions.

Goldner, Elliot M., Cockell, Sarah J. and Srikameswaran, Suja. (2002). Perfectionism and eating disorders. In G. L. Flett and P. L. Hewitt (Eds), *Perfectionism: Theory, Research, and Treatment* (pp. 319–340), Washington, DC: American Psychological Association.

Jacobs, M. Joy, Roesch, S., Wonderlich, Stephen A., Crosby, Ross, Thornton, Laura, Wilfley, Denise E., … Fichter, Manfred M. (2009). Anorexia nervosa trios: Behavioral profiles of individuals with anorexia nervosa and their parents. *Psychological Medicine*, 39(3), 451–461.

Lloyd, Samantha, Fleming, Caroline, Schmidt, Ulrike and Tchanturia, Kate. (2014b). Targeting perfectionism in anorexia nervosa using a group-based cognitive behavioural approach: A pilot study. *European Eating Disorders Review*, 22(5), 366–372.

Lloyd, Samantha, Schmidt, Ulrike, Khondoker, Mizanur and Tchanturia, Kate. (2014a). Can psychological interventions reduce perfectionism? A systematic review and meta-analysis. *Behavioural and Cognitive Psychotherapy*, 1–27. doi: 10.1017/ S1352465814000162.

Miller, W. R. and Rollnick, S. (2002). *Motivational Interviewing: Preparing People for Change*, New York: Guilford Press.

Riley, Caroline, Lee, Michelle, Cooper, Zafra, Fairburn, Christopher G. and Shafran, Roz. (2007). A randomised controlled trial of cognitive-behaviour therapy for clinical perfectionism: A preliminary study. *Behaviour Research and Therapy*, 45(9), 2221–2231.

Schmidt, Ulrike and Treasure, Janet. (2006). Anorexia nervosa: Valued and visible. A cognitive-interpersonal maintenance model and its implications for research and practice. *British Journal of Clinical Psychology*, 45(3), 343–366.

Shafran, Roz, Cooper, Zafra and Fairburn, Christopher G. (2002). Clinical perfectionism: A cognitive–behavioural analysis. *Behaviour Research and Therapy*, 40(7), 773–791.

Shafran, Roz, Egan, Sarah and Wade, Tracey. (2010). *Overcoming Perfectionism: A Self-Help Guide Using Cognitive Behavioral Techniques*, London: Robinson.

Steele, Anna L. and Wade, Tracey D. (2008). A randomised trial investigating guided self-help to reduce perfectionism and its impact on bulimia nervosa: A pilot study. *Behaviour Research and Therapy*, 46(12), 1316–1323.

Steele, Anna L., Waite, Sue, Egan, Sarah J., Finnigan, Janelle, Handley, Alicia and Wade, Tracey D. (2013). Psycho-education and group cognitive-behavioural therapy for clinical perfectionism: A case-series evaluation. *Behavioural and Cognitive Psychotherapy*, 41(2), 129–143.

Sutandar-Pinnock, Kalam, Woodside, D. Blake, Carter, Jacqueline C., Olmsted, Marion P. and Kaplan, Allan S. (2003). Perfectionism in anorexia nervosa: A 6–24-month follow-up study. *International Journal of Eating Disorders*, 33(2), 225–229.

Woodside, D. Blake, Bulik, Cynthia M., Halmi, Katherine A., Fichter, Manfred M., Kaplan, Allan, Berrettini, Wade H., ... Klump, Kelly. (2002). Personality, perfectionism, and attitudes toward eating in parents of individuals with eating disorders. *International Journal of Eating Disorders*, 31(3), 290–299.

Zuroff, David C., Blatt, Sidney J., Sotsky, Stuart M., Krupnick, Janice L., Martin, Daniel J., Sanislow III, Charles A. and Simmens, Sam. (2000). Relation of therapeutic alliance and perfectionism to outcome in brief outpatient treatment of depression. *Journal of Consulting and Clinical Psychology*, 68(1), 114.

Chapter 7

Single session groups

Suzi Doyle

For individuals with anorexia nervosa, particular times of the year are especially difficult, due to characteristics of the disorder such as rigid rules and obsessive rituals (Schmidt and Treasure, 2006). For instance, as the festive season approaches, a representative proportion of residents of the inpatient ward frequently express feelings of anxiety and a resolute intent to avoid any celebrations. The anticipation of increased requirement for social interaction exacerbates the sense of isolation that is a feature of anorexia nervosa (Tchanturia *et al.*, 2012). The expectations and perceived or real pressure to have a wonderful time magnify the disabling impact of anhedonia and difficulties in emotional expression experienced by many eating disordered individuals (Davies *et al.*, 2010; Davies *et al.*, 2012; Tchanturia *et al.*, 2012). At these times, there is a need for support of a specific nature, for individuals who experience occasions such as Christmas and New Year as threatening, alienating and anxiety-provoking.

We have developed protocols for single session groups, to support patients receiving the treatment in the inpatient ward. Each group runs for between 45 minutes and one hour and is advertised as a 'pop-up' group, in reference to the trend for short-term use of available premises for unique, creative and engaging projects. Since these groups have been recently implemented, refinement of the protocols is ongoing. The protocols we have included in this chapter are entitled:

- Distress Tolerance group;
- Christmas is Coming;
- New Year's Eve group.

Notably, some of the content presented in the single session groups is also covered within other groups which span several weeks. For instance, we also run a longer version of the Distress Tolerance group, which comprises six weekly sessions. These multiple session groups are closed to new members after the initial two sessions, with the result that patients admitted thereafter are required to wait until a new group begins. One advantage of the single session groups is that they are available to all patients who wish to attend at the time. When a group has been arranged, it is announced in the weekly community group meeting and patients are warmly invited to come along. Posters may also be placed on the ward as reminders, with the aim of encouraging patients, some of whom tend to avoid group situations, to attend.

Pop-up groups are run according to a common set of guiding principles, underpinned by the primary aims of engaging patients in a shared endeavour to increase awareness of difficulties they may be experiencing, to reduce the sense of defectiveness, and to develop more effective coping strategies which individuals can feel motivated to implement. To this end, the groups are both psycho-educational and exploratory, in many instances employing a cognitive behavioural therapy (CBT) framework for addressing challenges and developing positive alternatives. We find that it is important for facilitators to take a curious and interested stance, encouraging the group to engage actively in the exercises and warmly affirming individual or collective contributions. To encourage active participation and increase learning, each group is designed to be interactive. Owing to the time-limited nature of single session groups, completion of the protocol requires a fairly vigorous pace, which ideally does not compromise the depth of reflections elicited or group members' sense that their contributions are valued.

The groups are facilitated by a psychologist, who always has a co-facilitator who may be a trainee psychologist or a member of the multi-disciplinary team, such as an occupational therapist or nurse. A standard format for beginning and ending of groups provides a familiar and predictable frame for supporting individuals who may find attending a group to be a challenging experience. After welcoming group members, the facilitators invite them to:

- check in by sharing their hopes, fears and expectations for the group;
- suggest boundaries for the group, such as honouring confidentiality of material shared.

Before ending the group, members are invited to:

- provide feedback, which may be verbal or written;
- share one thing they gained from attending the group.

Informal feedback provided by patients has indicated that the short duration of the pop-up groups is experienced as an advantage in that individuals are not required to commit to a series of sessions. Instead, there is the opportunity to benefit from a brief, digestible intervention, where group members can gain from hearing other perspectives and are encouraged to contribute their own ideas in a social setting. While we have not conducted formal outcome assessment, responses by individuals attending the single session groups suggest that patients have generally found the process of participating and the exchange of perspectives helpful. Some of their written comments are included here:

'... found it more beneficial than initially expected'

'… appreciated hearing suggestions from other group members'
'… putting suggestions into action will be difficult'

These comments carry a sense of authenticity and are indicative of positive engagement with the group and the material presented.

Positive responses to these groups have led to the development of further pop-up group protocols, which have been well-received during summer time for instance, when holidays disrupt the normal timetable of longer group programmes. While topics for the groups have generally been determined by staff, patients have been invited to suggest topics that they would find helpful. As a result of this collaborative approach to identifying groups that are considered to be beneficial, we have run further pop-up groups, including:

- Assertiveness and saying 'no';
- Worry group (which spanned two sessions).

Appreciation of the benefits of pop-up groups for patients must be balanced with consideration of the resources involved in developing and delivering the protocols. To address this issue, we have found it helpful to build up a series of protocols which may be shared and enhanced. With this aim, therefore, the original three single session group protocols are included in this chapter, as 'living' documents that may be modified according to current requirements of the patient group and developments in our understanding of the psychology of eating disorders.

DISTRESS TOLERANCE GROUP PROTOCOL

Aspects of the material used in the development of this protocol have been based on the methods described by the Centre for Clinical Interventions (http://www.cci.health.wa.gov.au), a specialist public mental health service based in Western Australia. Many of their resources are based on the principles of Cognitive-Behavioural (Leahy *et al.*, 2011) and Mindfulness-based Therapies (Linehan, 1993).

Aims of the group

- To explore the meaning and impact of distress intolerance.
- To identify unhelpful ways of dealing with distress.
- To increase distress tolerance by exploring and practising healthy adaptive ways of managing distress.

What is distress intolerance?

Distress is part of life and we cannot avoid experiencing it at times. There are many different definitions of distress intolerance. What we mean by distress intolerance is a perceived inability to fully experience unpleasant, aversive or uncomfortable emotions, and is accompanied by a desperate need to escape the uncomfortable emotions (Centre for Clinical Interventions, 2012).

Difficulties tolerating distress are often linked to a fear of experiencing negative emotion. Often distress intolerance centres on high intensity emotional experiences, that is, when the emotion is 'hot', strong and powerful.

However, it could also occur for lower intensity emotions (e.g. nervousness about an upcoming medical examination, sadness when remembering a past relationship break-up). It is not the intensity of the emotion itself, but how much you fear it, how unpleasant it feels to you, how unbearable it seems, and how much you want to get away from it, that determines whether you are intolerant of distress.

Invite group members to name hot emotions and triggering situations.

The continuum of distress tolerance

Ask group members to provide examples of the impact of different styles of dealing with distress (e.g. someone who is extremely tolerant of distress may remain in an unhealthy environment without taking steps to reduce risk). Points on the continuum include:

*   extremely intolerant of distress;
*   healthy distress tolerance;
*   extremely tolerant of distress.

Invite group to consider their own position on the continuum.

Escape methods/unhelpful coping mechanisms

Our escape methods are usually automatic habits we quickly jump to when we feel distressed, hence the decision not to go down this path sometimes slips past us. By being more aware of triggers, warning signs and our distress, we can choose to take a different path of doing the opposite action.

Invite group to contribute unhelpful ways in which people might attempt to avoid distress, identifying impact – emotional and physical (e.g. alcohol, drugs, binge eating, self-harm, avoidance, shoplifting).

We can think about two approaches to improving distress tolerance, and how it would be helpful to balance the two.

Accepting distress mindfully

Accepting negative emotions mindfully is important in the first instance, to allow you then to consider calmly how to alleviate distress. This involves allowing and experiencing feelings. Many people feel as though intense feelings come out of the blue – this can be because they are not aware of the thoughts, feelings and sensations they are experiencing. By being more mindful, it is possible to be less reactive and impulsive. It can help to visualise the hot emotion as growing in intensity until it peaks, and then gradually subsiding, as a wave does.

Flipchart showing the 'what' and 'how' of mindfulness:

What – Observing (what do I notice? Does my mind wander?)

Describing (what types of thoughts, emotions, body sensations?)

Participating (can I participate fully, or do I become self-conscious?)

How – Being non-judgemental (can I keep an open mind?)

Focusing on one thing at a time

Doing what is effective (can I get on with the activity, without needing to do it perfectly?)

Mindfulness exercise – using play dough, consider:

- What are you experiencing? (thoughts, feelings, sensations)
- Can you accept the experience without judging/controlling?
- Can you focus on the play dough, bringing your attention gently back when your mind wanders?

Invite discussion on mindfulness, asking group members to share ideas that have been helpful to them.

Distress improvement activities

Once we have accepted negative emotions, we are better placed to work on improving our emotional experience. This can be through activities that are either about being actively involved in the moment (i.e. activating), or that give a sense of being soothed and nurtured (i.e. soothing).

Some people find it helpful to put together a distress tolerance kit bag. Once we have identified some of the activities, it will give ideas for people to create their own personalised distress tolerance bags.

Flipchart with columns for Activate and Soothe.

Generate ideas for both activating and self-soothing activities, which will be printed off and distributed to group members for planning their distress tolerance kit bags.

The hand-outs from this group may utilise the following table, which has been adapted from Module 3: Improving Distress (Centre for Clinical Interventions, 2012).

MY ACTIVITIES FOR DISTRESS IMPROVEMENT

Activating	Soothing
Call a friend	Listen to relaxing music
Games	Relaxation tape
Create art/needlework	Slow breathing
Favourite movie/book	Look at beautiful art or scenery
Listen to inspiring music	Favourite perfume
Shopping	Do something pampering
	Smile!

'CHRISTMAS IS COMING' GROUP PROTOCOL

Aspects of the material used in this group have been developed using information and guidelines which were provided prior to the Christmas period by the charity, b-eat, on their website, http://www.b-eat.co.uk.

Aims of the group

- To gain a shared view of the challenges people face over the festive season.
- To explore and understand negative patterns of thinking, feeling and behaving.
- To engage in strategies for normalising the difficulties and increasing a balanced perspective.
- To support the development of a toolbox comprising coping strategies.

Christmas and eating disorders – are they incompatible?

The general expectation is that people will have a wonderful time at Christmas or during the festive season. Yet for many people, Christmas can be difficult, and this is particularly so for people affected by eating disorders. Stimuli and triggers are found in abundance.

Show flipchart with the following: (or invite patients to contribute from their own experience):

There is food everywhere
People are loud and insensitive
There is food everywhere
Parties seem to go on for days
There is food everywhere
Everyone else seems happy
There is food everywhere
Everyone wants you to be happy
There is food everywhere
Everyone is watching you (or so it seems)
There is food everywhere …

Challenging environment – a vicious cycle

With the pressure to eat and be merry, people who do not feel joyful, including those with eating disorders, may feel the discrepancy even more intensely. Changes in the environment during the holidays can exacerbate the discomfort:

Non-food-related pressures

Financial burden
Everything seems to close down

Family stresses more obvious
Finding yourself isolated

Food-related pressures

Being overwhelmed by food and conversations about food
Focus on plenty
Fear foods
Unusual meal plans and times
Festive foods
Alcohol

This can give rise to a vicious cycle where thoughts about the situation are mixed with feelings of anxiety, hopelessness and loneliness. Distressed emotional states tend to worsen eating disorder behaviours, and these unhelpful behaviours in turn generate further negative thoughts and emotions.

Show flipchart with a vicious cycle diagram and invite group to add their own examples:

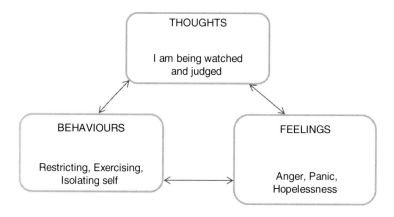

Putting our understanding to positive use

While it may not be possible to change much about the situation itself, there are options for influencing how we feel during the festive season through developing more effective strategies, using our understanding of the patterns of thinking, feeling and behaviour that we have just explored.

It can be helpful to remember that others find Christmas overwhelming at the best of times. In the past, b-eat (the national eating disorders charity), who recognise the challenging nature of the disruption to routines, have provided a Christmas survival guide on their website. Looking at some of the ways that others have made Christmas more manageable, we can see that this involves being realistic and flexible, planning ahead and keeping a bigger picture perspective.

We can now look at some of these strategies.

Gaining perspective – seeing the bigger picture

A good way of helping put the festive season in perspective is to draw a line down the middle of a large piece of paper and divide it into 12 months/52 weeks/365 days (whichever you feel like). Then highlight the bit which is Christmas. Suddenly it looks very small and perhaps more manageable.

Use flipchart to show 12 lines for months of the year and highlight the few days in December and January that represent Christmas. Invite comments from the group.

Gaining perspective – realistic expectations

It is realistic and some people find it helpful to acknowledge ahead of time that there will be moments when you feel out of control. In fact, you might even prepare yourself by assuming that you'll feel this way at least five, or ten, or twenty times during the holiday season. When you feel out of control, you can count it as one of those expected times.

Explore the idea of creating a customised calendar showing the days of the Christmas period, with space to mark the expected times of distress.

Help others to support you

While it can feel as though you have to deal with stresses on your own, perhaps with some advance thought it may be possible to think of people – or perhaps one person – who understands how you feel and would be supportive. Here are some ideas for getting ready for the social challenges at Christmas:

- Talk with a trusted person about your fears and concerns, so that they can understand what might be hard and then discuss what might help.
- Decide in advance 'where your exits are' and where your support persons are, so that when you need to, you can get away and get connected with someone supportive.
- Consider choosing someone you trust to be your 'reality check' with food, to help you serve up your portions.

Invite group members to generate any other ideas that they have found helpful.

Getting ready for the holidays – your Christmas toolbox

Now that we have shared some ideas about the challenges ahead over the festive season, we can work together to identify ways that people have coped with these difficulties. It might not be possible to change the situation, but being prepared can enable people to take some helpful measures as alternatives to less healthy ones.

It is important to say that not all of these strategies will be suitable for all people. The aim is to find a few that seem 'right', for you.

Introduce next exercise as a way of matching up helpful coping strategies with problems. Hand out a strategy card (see below) to each group member, each card having a strategy printed on it.

Offer hand-outs to group members, with two blank columns – left hand column for Problems and right hand column for Strategies. Invite everyone to share problems experienced at Christmas time and use strategy cards to enter suggested coping mechanisms in right hand column of their hand-outs.

Strategy card for Christmas is Coming group (one items per card)

1. Focus on what you would **like** to do, rather than putting all your energy into trying to prevent something.
2. Try to keep to your regular routine or a manageable pattern.
3. Take a holiday from self-imposed criticism and perfectionism.
4. Leave time for relaxation, reflection and enjoying simple things.
5. Stay connected – plan in advance if possible, to ensure you don't isolate yourself.
6. Enlist family/friends' support to plan activities that are about being together without focus on food – games, movies, puzzles, music, for instance.
7. Plan and discuss your meals in advance.
8. Don't be afraid to experiment, e.g. swap mealtimes around.
9. Other people's talk about diet and fatness is not aimed at you. Ask your family and friends to be sensitive with these comments.
10. If you feel pressured, don't be afraid to say NO.
11. Two days of Christmas are not worth sabotaging your meal plan for.
12. If you choose to drink alcohol, don't substitute this for food.
13. Stay connected – share your thoughts and feelings.
14. Don't starve yourself in anticipation of eating more later on – this may lead to stress or binging later.
15. Remember Christmas doesn't go on forever – it will surely go faster than you think.
16. Keep it simple, stay focused on recovery, and enjoy!

NEW YEAR'S EVE GROUP PROTOCOL

Aims of the group

- To explore the meaning and impact of finishing one year and beginning another.
- To reflect on the tradition of making New Year's resolutions.
- To consider whether and how individuals would like to make changes.
- To explore the potential benefits of an alternative approach which involves letting go of a behaviour pattern to achieve benefits, e.g. relief from self-imposed pressure or stress.

Goodbye 2015 (or the previous year)

What does it mean to say goodbye to the previous year?

Use flipchart with mind map to record contributions from the group.

Note for therapist: It is important to assess at this point whether this discussion leads to consideration of New Year's resolutions, before deciding whether to progress to the next section. If group members express strong opposition to the idea of resolutions (as we have discovered may be the case), the remainder of the session can be used to explore the ongoing challenges and goals that are meaningful to them, as well as resources that they can recognise and sources of support.

New Year's resolutions

Consider the statistics for keeping New Year's resolutions – what percentage are kept? (somewhere between 8 and 12 per cent).

Invite group members to contribute their views of people's aims in making resolutions, for example:

- to become a better person;
- a sense of duty;
- an obligation.

How do resolutions make us feel? What do they set up? Invite discussion.

An alternative view

As an alternative to introducing another 'should' or 'must not', we could consider the possibility of letting go of an obligation or accepting an aspect of ourselves. Shall we explore a different emphasis?

Generate ideas which are written onto flipchart, for example:

- giving myself permission to make mistakes in some areas;
- accept my work/efforts when good enough, even when it's less than perfect;
- no more checking emails after 10pm.

Discuss obstacles to your plan to let go, for example:

- expectations of family and friends;
- breaking a habit or routine;
- negative emotions, particularly guilt.

Strategies for keeping resolutions

By understanding how people struggle to stay true to their resolutions, we may be able to develop strategies for maintaining positive changes. Here are some ideas.

Invite the group to contribute examples related to the following guidelines, which may be provided in hand-out form:

- Planning helps. It is best not to wait until the last minute – instead, plan ahead of New Year's Day. Decide on your change goals: establish clear objectives for what you want to change, how you will go about this and the outcome you want to achieve.
- Be realistic. Unattainable goals are often the enemy of achievable resolutions. Change one **small** thing at a time.
- Measure your successes – how will you know whether you are maintaining the changes? Stay motivated by measuring how far you've come each week. This will help you realise how small changes can make a big difference.
- Develop a support network. Friends, family and colleagues can all help you. Talk to people you trust about what you're planning to do and tell them how they can help.
- Environment: Create an environment (i.e. people, surroundings and activities) that support and encourage your efforts.
- Pinpoint obstacles: Specify what baggage, habits, emotions and environment there are that may make things difficult.
- Identify best practices: Explore how others have successfully made changes in the area you would like to change.
- Action steps: Describe the specific steps you will take to counter your old baggage, habits, fears and environment, and pursue your change goals.
- Forks in the road: Recognise that you have choices in which road you can take and can choose the most conducive road toward positive change.
- Reward yourself, in healthy ways, e.g. ... generate suggestions from the group.
- If you do slip up, don't despair! Learn from the setback: what situations made you slip? Don't obsess over small setbacks – they are a normal part of the process of change. Start fresh the next day. Don't give up!

Maintaining positive change

Invite the group to consider the Three P's and add their own suggestions:

- **P**ersistence means we must maintain our determination to achieve our goals consistently.
- **P**erseverance refers to our ability to respond positively to setbacks we will surely experience in the change process.
- **P**atience is important, given that change takes time and that if we maintain our commitment, we will make the changes we want.

References

Centre for Clinical Interventions. (2012). Facing Your Feelings. Available at http://www.cci.health.wa.gov.au/.

Davies, H., Schmidt, U., Stahl, D. and Tchanturia, K. (2010). Evoked facial emotional expression and emotional experience in people with anorexia nervosa. *International Journal of Eating Disorders*, 44: 531–539.

Davies, H., Schmidt, U., Swan, N. and Tchanturia, K. (2012). Verbal expression and emotion regulation in anorexia and bulimia nervosa. *European Eating Disorders Review*, 20(6): 476–483.

Leahy, R. L., Tirch, D. and Napolitano, L. A. (2011). *Emotion Regulation In Psychotherapy: A Practitioner's Guide*. New York: The Guilford Press.

Linehan, M. M. (1993). *Cognitive-Behavioral Treatment of Borderline Personality Disorder*. New York: The Guilford Press.

Schmidt, U. and Treasure, J. (2006). Anorexia nervosa: Valued and visible. A cognitive-interpersonal maintenance model and its implications for research and practice. *British Journal of Clinical Psychology*, 45: 343–366.

Tchanturia, K., Davies, H., Harrison, A., Fox, J., Treasure, J. and Schmidt, U. (2012). Altered social hedonic processing in eating disorders. *International Journal of Eating Disorders*, 45(8): 962–969.

Chapter 8

An introduction to compassion group for eating disorders

Jane Evans

With thanks to Ken Goss for his useful support and input.

Introduction

Compassion focused therapy (CFT) is a transdiagnostic approach which has been developed to help people who struggle with issues around shame and self-criticism (Gilbert, 2009; Gilbert and Irons, 2005), both of which are difficulties which have been found to be common in individuals with eating disorders (Allan and Goss, 2011; Goss and Allan, 2009). Kelly *et al.* (2013) found, within a specialist eating disorders service, that lower self-compassion and higher fear of self-compassion were associated with more shame and higher eating disorder pathology. They also found that those with low compassion and high fear of compassion had significantly poorer outcomes.

The aims of CFT are to help people to build up a more compassionate way of being with themselves and with others. As will be explained in more detail later in this chapter, much of the work is based on evolutionary theory and the three circles model, which proposes that we have three affect regulation systems: the threat based system, the drive based system and the soothing-affiliative system (Gilbert, 2009, 2010). CFT aims to help people to strengthen their soothing-affiliative system, which is often underdeveloped. It is likely that individuals with eating disorders have a heightened threat system and often move into the achievement system as a means of managing threat, e.g. 'If I lose weight, then I'll feel better'.

Gale *et al.* (2014) demonstrated that CFT could be beneficial when introduced into a treatment programme for individuals with eating disorders. There is also an evidence base developing for group based CFT across both community groups and inpatient units, and for individuals with varying presenting problems (e.g. Gilbert and Proctor, 2006; Heriot-Maitland *et al.*, 2014; Judge *et al.*, 2012).

There is a strong rationale for providing CFT in a group, given that this may help increase a sense of affiliation, which is in keeping with the model. Within eating disorders inpatient services, given the nature of the disorder, it is common for issues around competition and comparisons to arise, which can at times be unhelpful for recovery (see Vandereycken, 2011). Patients may compete to be the thinnest or the illest, in order to gain status. If we consider this from the perspective of social rank theory (Gilbert, 1992, 2000; Price and Sloman, 1987), then we can see how difficulties can arise. Those at the top of the social ladder may feel in a position whereby holding on to the anorexia is necessary to maintain their social rank. Those who find themselves within that environment at a lower social rank, may experience more shame, anxiety and depression (Gilbert, 2000), and unfortunately their means of coping with these feelings may be through the use of eating disorder behaviours and cognitions. Thus, the interaction of the environment and nature of the eating disorder could serve to keep individuals trapped within their illness, wherever in the social rankings they find themselves. Conducting this work within a group setting provides the opportunity for group members to develop feelings of compassion towards themselves and others which may help to alleviate some of these unhelpful dynamics which can occur within inpatient and day care settings. Dynamics such as these have commonly been observed within the services that I have worked in. Self-criticism, shame and difficulties in demonstrating self-compassion were also commonly observed. In accordance with Kelly et al.'s (2013) findings, such difficulties appeared to be creating obstacles to recovery. A typical phrase that I would hear in my work with these clients was 'I don't deserve to recover'. Such beliefs can, understandably, create a barrier to patients feeling able to fully utilise the treatment offered to them. It was due to such observations that the idea to develop a compassion group came about.

Overview and aims of the group

The group described in this chapter is not designed as a stand-alone treatment for eating disorders. For a stand-alone group based outpatient CFT treatment for eating disorders see Goss and Allan (2014). Their treatment programme targets specific eating disorder behaviours directly from a compassion focused perspective; however, as this group was embedded within a comprehensive inpatient or day patient programme, work targeting the eating disorder behaviours was conducted elsewhere, and therefore this was not addressed within the group. The settings where the group has been conducted have utilised different models of therapy within their group and individual treatment programmes, such as cognitive behavioural therapy (CBT) and cognitive analytic therapy. The group was designed in a way which could be integrated within these programmes. Weight restoration, physical monitoring and risk were managed elsewhere.

The group was designed as a seven session group. Each weekly group lasting for 60 minutes. This is a much shorter duration than a comprehensive CFT programme would be. Although it would have been preferable to deliver a CFT group over a longer duration of weeks, given the changing nature of an inpatient and/or day patient setting, with patients frequently being admitted and discharged, it was decided that a short term introductory group, that could be repeated frequently, would enable patients to benefit most from the group. Given these time limitations, this meant that the aims of the group were to provide psychoeducation on compassion and introduce a number of strategies to the group that would enable them to begin to work on developing self-compassion. Given the high levels of fear and concerns regarding self-compassion, which had been observed with the group, it was hoped that group members would be more able to develop an openness to the idea of being self-compassionate.

The group was developed to be interactive in style, involving psychoeducation, group discussions, group and pair exercises, alongside mindfulness and imagery exercises. Homework was set at each session and reviewed each week. We found it helpful to have two facilitators for the group, so that while one is leading the group material, the other facilitator can be focusing on the group members and any issues/needs which may arise, as is the case in the other short format group exercises described in previous chapters (Flexibility, Chapter 3; CREST, Chapter 5; Perfectionism, Chapter 6).

Considerations for the group

Although the group was fairly structured in nature, it was important to be flexible. At times, group members became distressed, and this was managed by the facilitators responding with compassion, in order to model this. As the group progressed, this role was handed over to the group themselves. As facilitators, our general stance was to try to model compassion; being warm, understanding and non-judgemental. The CFT model tells us that it is understandable that given each individual's evolutionary history, combined with their unique experiences, that they have found themselves in their current position, having managed in a way which made sense, even if now their ways of coping serve to cause them harm. Given this, as facilitators, we held the position that 'it is not your fault'. This is important in helping group members to begin to challenge the position, which is so often held by our patients, that they are to blame for their eating disorder.

It was also the case that group members with difficulties with flashbacks and dissociation sometimes found the mindfulness and imagery exercises triggering. Therefore one of the facilitators would have a pre-group meeting with them and plan what they could do to manage this within the group setting and how the facilitators could support them if they were to experience a flashback or dissociation within the group.

The group programme is outlined below. This is not intended as a protocol for how the group should be conducted, as at this stage we do not have the outcomes to support that, but as a description of how our group was conducted. This is followed by some reflections upon the process.

Session 1

1. Introductions and group contract

The group begins with a round of introductions, beginning with the facilitators and then moving around the group members (unless, of course all members are known to each other). Following on from introductions a discussion is had around group rules/group contract/group boundaries, whatever you wish to call it.

Issues to consider:

I feel that the term 'group rules' can sometimes sit a little uncomfortably with the tone that is being aimed for within a compassion focused group. It is important to encourage group members to generate the contract for themselves and to gen-erate discussion around what they feel is important in order for it to feel like a safe and comfortable environment in which to share. The topics which are useful to suggest for discussion, if they are not generated by the group members them-selves, are: confidentiality, attendance, punctuality, respect. Within the environ-ment of an inpatient setting, it is important to think through the issue of group membership. There is a dilemma in whether to have a closed group, in which members may feel safer to share, but yet there is the risk of group membership reducing significantly as a result of discharges, etc., or an open group where group membership may change from one week to another, resulting in a slightly less settled group, but one that is more likely to maintain its numbers. I think that the decision around how to manage this can be thought about in relation to the individual setting and group. I have tended towards asking the group members themselves how they would like to manage it. Punctuality is also an important topic to discuss. The majority of sessions will begin with a mindfulness or relax-ation exercise, therefore it is not helpful for the group to be interrupted by late arrivers during this time. There will be occasions where it is unavoidable that people will be late, but it is worth considering a system around this that will be least disruptive to the group as possible.

2. Introduction of group

Discussion: Moving on to ask the group what their thoughts are on why the topic of self-compassion might be relevant in an eating disorders setting. The idea is to generate group discussion around their own experience of being self-compassionate or, more likely, of being self-critical and to consider how this is related to their eating disorder. The group are informed that individuals with eating disorders have been found through research to be highly self-critical and low in self-compassion and that this is likely to impact upon eating disorders symptoms. The purpose of providing this information is to normalise their experi-ences and to help them develop some understanding of their difficulties and how these might relate to self-criticism and lack of self-compassion.

3. What is compassion and how compassionate are you?

Discussion: Ask the group to brainstorm the meaning of compassion, marking this up on a flipchart. This usually generates words such as empathy, kindness, understanding, acceptance and warmth.

> *Exercise:*
> *Ask the group to consider how compassionate they are to others and how compassionate they are to themselves. Ask each member to rate themselves from 0–10 and to each mark themselves up, using their initials, on a continuum on the flipchart, having one sliding scale for compassion towards the self and another for compassion towards others.*

It is typical to see a distribution such as that in Figure 8.1. This can then be used to generate a discussion around why it might be that they are more compassionate to others than themselves. This discussion can begin to identify people's beliefs about the meaning of being compassionate to themselves. It is common to hear statements such as 'It is too self-indulgent to show compassion to myself', 'If I was too self-compassionate, I wouldn't achieve anything'. It is useful to encourage the group to challenge each other's viewpoints and to note the often common case of 'one rule for me and one rule for everybody else', in that often group members will believe that it is good for everyone else in the group to be compassionate to themselves, but not for them. This discussion can start to generate a process of group members demonstrating compassion to others within the group.

4. The affect regulation systems – the three circles model

Gilbert (2009, 2010) presented the three circles model, which proposes that there are three different affect regulation systems evolved for different functions. This idea is presented to group members alongside Figure 8.2, to provide a further understanding of the model and a rationale for them to work on their self-compassion.

Compassion to others

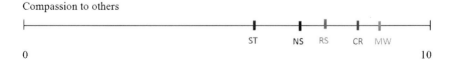

Compassion to self

Figure 8.1 Comparison of compassion to selves and others scale

Figure 8.2 Three types of affect regulation system
Source: Gilbert (2009), reprinted with permission from Constable & Robinson Ltd.

The threat and self-protection system is associated with emotions such as fear, anger and disgust. These emotions drive us to respond to the threat through means of fight, flight or freeze. It is important to point out to the group that threat can be triggered by either external or internal stimuli. An individual with a very self-attacking internal voice can be perpetually caught in the threat system. It is useful to introduce Goss and Allan's (2014) adaptation of the three circles model for eating disorders. They suggest that for individuals with eating disorders, the threat system can be triggered by stimuli related to size, shape, weight and eating control. They also suggest that the positive emotions associated with the drive system may often relate to eating disorder behaviours such as weight loss, or resisting hunger, such as pride and a sense of achievement. It is likely that individuals will also relate to other behaviours related to the drive system as a means of managing threat, such as academic achievement.

Discussion: Does this fit with the group's own experiences? Can they give examples? What disadvantages do they think there might be to such a strategy?

It is useful to prompt individuals to identify the shortlived nature of the drive based system as a means of managing threat.

This then is followed by an introduction to the soothing and affiliative system and its importance. This is the system that is connected with compassion. It allows us to develop a sense of safety and connectedness. It also allows us to be soothed by either ourselves or by others.

Discussion: How well do people think that they manage to self-soothe and allow themselves to be soothed by others? How do they think this compares as a strategy compared to the drive system?

Goss and Allan (2014) also propose that food can be linked in with the soothing system as it is something that we often see as comforting and often brings people together. It can be useful to introduce some exploration of the group's thoughts on the relationship between food and self-soothing/affiliation. This is likely to vary greatly from one individual to another and the relationship that they currently have with food; for example, somebody who binge eats may more readily see this connection than someone who only restricts.

The idea is introduced that these systems are like muscles, and it might be that for many of them, they have an over-developed threat system muscle and drive system muscle and an under-developed soothing system muscle. We can see the exercises that will be introduced through the group as being similar to having physiotherapy to help improve the strength of the undeveloped muscle.

5. Mindfulness of breath exercise

The session ends with an introduction to mindfulness and a short mindfulness exercise. Each session following this will begin with either a mindfulness exercise or a relaxation/imagery exercise.

Discussion: The group are invited to share any experiences that they have of using mindfulness and their understanding of it, along with how they have found it in the past. If the group do not volunteer the following ideas then it is useful for the group facilitator to introduce the following points:

- Mindfulness is about learning to pay attention to the present moment.
- Mindfulness is about taking an accepting non-judgemental stance towards our thoughts, feelings and bodily sensations.

It is also useful to ask the group how they think that this might be linked to compassion. It is important to state that the purpose of mindfulness is not to activate the self-soothing mode; however, the themes of non-judgement and acceptance of our experiences are important components of demonstrating compassion towards ourselves. It is often the case that mindfulness may be about sitting with difficult emotions and tolerating these, while developing the position of an observer of these emotions.

Issues to consider:
Experience from the group has shown that many of the patients, particularly the very unwell patients, find mindfulness practice very difficult. I believe that this might be partly due to starvation effects which result in the mind being busy with thoughts of food which can be particularly difficult for individuals to let go of. These difficulties seemed to be intensified if the practice was done directly before or after a meal time, so this should be taken into consideration when planning a group. Mindfulness of bodily sensations can also cause distress due to the often complex relationships individuals with anorexia nervosa may have with their bodies. Furthermore, mindfulness of emotions can also create difficulties, given the often flattened affect created by the anorexia, or the desire

to avoid emotions may create some resistance to the idea. In the face of these obstacles that are likely to be encountered, it is important to acknowledge that it might be difficult for people prior to carrying out the exercise and to give them permission not to strive to do it 'perfectly' as is so often the drive for these individuals, but that it is something to be practised and to experience. I also give group members the option to open their eyes and just sit quietly if they find the exercise too distressing, although encourage them to try and sit with it.

Exercise:
For this first mindfulness exercise, a short three minute mindfulness of breath exercise is conducted.

Discussion: After completing the mindfulness exercise, group members are asked to share their experiences. Normalise any struggles that they may have faced and encourage practice outside of the group. For any group members who had particular difficulties, explore what the struggles were, and ask other group members if they could offer any guidance around what might be helpful. Asking the group to support each other throughout this process is a helpful way of encouraging compassion and affiliation between the group members.

It can be useful to spend a few minutes linking mindfulness with self-compassion through the shared principle of acceptance of emotional experience.

Homework:

- Complete self-compassion scale (Neff, 2003).
- Complete the forms of self-criticising/attacking and self-reassuring scale (FSCRS) (Gilbert *et al.*, 2004).
- Practise the mindfulness of breath exercise for a few minutes each day.

The group are asked if they have any thoughts or questions that they would like to share before we finish this week's group.

Session 2

1. Mindfulness of breath exercise

Exercise:
Commence the group with a further mindfulness of breath exercise. This can be extended to five minutes.

Discussion: Ask the group to share their reflections and to consider how this week's exercise compared to last week's exercise. Also, check in around how their mindfulness practice outside of the group has been going and encourage them around the importance of practice.

2. Homework and review

Group members are asked if they have any feedback or questions related to the questionnaires that they completed. The questionnaires are collected by the group facilitators.

Table 8.1 The pros and cons of self-criticism and self-compassion

Self-criticism	
Pros	Cons
It makes me work harder	It makes me feel bad about myself
It stops me from becoming fat and lazy	Nothing ever feels good enough

Self-compassion	
Pros	Cons
It would help me to feel better about myself	I might get lazy
I wouldn't have to punish myself all the time	I don't deserve it

The group are asked if they have any thoughts or questions related to last week's session and are asked to re-cap what was covered if there are any new members joining the group.

3. Self-criticism vs self-compassion

For individuals with anorexia, self-criticism can often be, not only something which is very powerful, but often something which they believe to be functional. At this early stage of the group, it is not uncommon for individuals within the group to feel sceptical or even fearful of the prospect of self-compassion and what that might mean. It is therefore important to explore their often ambivalent feelings around showing themselves compassion, in order to help to develop the motivation to work at making changes.

Exercise:
On a flipchart ask the group to generate their pros and cons of being self-critical and their pros and cons of being self-compassionate (Table 8.1).

Discussion: Following this exercise, generate a group discussion around challenging their pros of self-criticism and cons of self-compassion (which are often fear based). Encourage those within the group who are more able to see the positives of self-compassion to share with those who find it more difficult, and generate examples from their own experiences of the consequences of having been self-compassionate rather than self-critical.

In order to help challenge the idea that their self-criticism helps them to perform better, it can be useful to ask group members to identify a teacher from school who they feel got the best work from them and to ask them to discuss this teacher's attributes, how they responded when they did well and how they responded when they made mistakes. Usually this generates responses whereby group members identify teachers who were compassionate and encouraging and would respond to mistakes by helping them to learn from them. It can also be useful to ask them to talk about how they responded to their teachers who were extremely strict and critical. This often elicits responses related to anxiety, which often hinders performance. This is a useful way of helping the group to use their own experiences to reflect upon how a more compassionate approach rather than a self-critical approach can maximise performance. It can often be useful at this point to talk a little about what compassion is not, which is letting themselves off the hook and not pushing themselves forward, in fact often quite the opposite, as a self-compassionate perspective often means facing difficulties and struggles in order to work towards future goals, which will enable them to live more fulfilled lives. Contrary to this, self-criticism can often get in the way of us achieving what we want in our lives as it can cause us to become fearful of the consequences of our actions, often causing us to freeze.

Exercise: in pairs
In order to try to build both self-compassion and compassion for each other, in this pair exercise they are asked to tell each other what they believe the obstacles to being self-compassionate are for themselves. Their partner will then respond with compassion around what they could do to try to overcome those obstacles. They are then to swap roles. They then feed back to the group, and think about what they could do in response to overcoming the obstacles over this coming week.

Homework:

•   Piece of writing: 'a day in the life of a more compassionate me'. To consider what would be different from the point of waking up to the point of going to bed.
•   Practise the mindfulness of breath exercise each day for approximately three minutes.

The group are asked if they have any thoughts that they would like to share or questions before we finish for this session.

Session 3

1. Mindfulness of thoughts exercise

This week's session begins with a slightly different mindfulness exercise. The mindfulness of thoughts exercise is conducted here, as much of this session's content relates to cognitions and the impact of these upon our emotions and behaviours. Therefore this exercise helps group members to begin to work on developing a different relationship with their thoughts in which they can learn to allow them to pass, rather than becoming entangled with them. Let group members know that if they are struggling with this exercise that it is okay to just bring themselves back to the mindfulness of breath exercise; however, encourage them to try the exercise even if it is difficult.

Exercise:
A five minute mindfulness of thoughts exercise is conducted. Examples of such exercises are seeing thoughts as clouds in the sky or leaves on a river floating by

Ask the group to reflect upon how they found the exercise.

2. Homework review and re-cap

Begin by asking if the group have any thoughts that they would wish to share regarding last week's group and ask for them to provide a re-cap for any group members who were not present last week or for whom this is their first group.

Ask the group to feed back their homework of a 'day in the life of a more compassionate me'. Ask them to reflect upon how it was to do the exercise.

Also, ask the group how they are managing with their individual obstacles to being compassionate. Given that the group is based in an in and day patient setting, you can ask group members to generate ideas for how they can offer support and encouragement to each other outside of the group sessions.

3. Distinguishing compassionate self-correction from self-criticism

Linking this back to last week's group, give group members the handout on self-correction versus self-criticism (see Gilbert, 2009).

Exercise:
In pairs discuss an example of when you made a mistake/error/did something hurtful towards someone. Discuss the following:

- *What did you think?*
- *What did you do?*
- *What were the consequences?*
- *How might you have responded differently, in terms of your thoughts and behaviours and what might have been the consequences?*

Feed back to the group.

4. Compassionate thought balancing

Compassionate thought balancing is introduced at this stage as a first step of getting them to engage with the idea of what compassionate responses to their self-critical thoughts might be. It is likely that group members may have some familiarity with the CBT model and the use of thought records, which hopefully means that this task is not too difficult. As mentioned earlier, it was common for group members to find it easier to be compassionate to others than to themselves and introducing the compassionate thought challenge, utilising the prompt of 'how would you respond to a friend?' could be very useful to help them to build on applying that compassion to themselves. Within a standard CFT approach, compassionate thought records would be introduced later, once the ability to activate the self-soothing system has been developed, so that thought challenging can take place within this affect system. Within this group, the aim is that group members will work towards achieving this, while starting from a point of familiarity.

When introducing the concept of compassionate thought challenging it can be useful to give a very brief introduction of the cognitive therapy model. A useful way to illustrate this can be to give an example of walking down a street and seeing a friend who you wave to but doesn't respond. Ask the group to generate what alternative thoughts and subsequent emotions they might experience.

The practice of cognitive therapy and thought challenging is then introduced. However, some of its limitations are then discussed regarding how although challenging a negative thought with a rational alternative may be believed on an intellectual level, for many people, it might be difficult to believe the thought on an emotional level. We can refer to this as the head heart lag. Therefore the work following on from here is about learning to think differently from an emotional perspective, hence the need to strengthen the ability to self-soothe, in order that we are able to generate responses within the self-soothing affect regulation system, rather than when we are within the threat system.

Compassionate thought balancing is then introduced to the group as a starting point, with the caveat that further work will be done in later groups to help them to strengthen their ability to move themselves into the self-soothing mode in which they are more likely to be able to effectively utilise the compassionate thought.

Exercise:
- *Hand out a compassionate thought balancing sheet (this can be as simple as two columns, one for self-critical thought and one for compassionate alternative thought).*
- *Ask for a volunteer to offer an example of a time this week when they have been particularly self-critical.*
- *Ask them to provide the group with the context of the situation and what the self-critical thoughts were and the emotions that this generated.*
- *Ask them to come up with an alternative compassionate thought. The alternative should be warm and kind in tone.*
- *Next, ask the group members to get into pairs and work through an occasion when they have been self-critical and to practise generating a kind and compassionate alternative thought.*
- *Feed back to the group.*

There are occasions when group members may misinterpret the message, from their self-critical stance, and believe that they are being told that their thoughts are wrong and faulty. It is important that we are giving them the message that it is understandable that they have developed their thinking styles in the way that they have, and that it is likely that these thinking styles and the behaviours linked to these (e.g. the eating disorder behaviours such as starvation, compulsive exercise, bingeing and vomiting) have served a self-protective function at some point; however, that it is likely that both the thinking and the behaviours have now become the difficulty in themselves. The message conveyed here and a stance which should be reflected throughout the group sessions is one of 'it is not your fault'; however, encouraging them to see that the responsibility for change lies with them.

Homework:

- To use the compassionate thought record over the week on occasions when they notice themselves being self-critical.
- To continue their mindfulness practice.

Finish by asking the group if they have any final thoughts or questions for the group before we finish.

Session 4

1. Mindfulness of emotions

Exercise:
This session begins with a mindfulness of emotions exercise. It can be useful to begin to extend the length of practice to 7–10 minutes. It can be useful to ask the group how long they would like to take for the mindfulness practice.

Discussion: Ask the group to reflect upon how they found the exercise.

2. Re-cap and homework

If new members have joined the group, or if members missed the group, the group are asked to provide a re-cap on the group itself and/or the last session. Group members are asked if they have any thoughts or questions following on from last week's session.

They are then asked to give feedback from their thought records. Each member is to provide one example of a self-critical thought and the compassionate alternative that was found. The group is encouraged to consider how compassionate they had been and support to be elicited from other group members in order to help individuals to generate more compassionate challenges, if they had struggled.

3. Acceptance of emotions

Discussion: Generate a discussion around why we have emotions. Ask the group what they believe the purpose of emotions to be. Brainstorm with the group their ideas about why we have emotions and draw these ideas up on the flipchart. Work towards generating the following ideas:

Emotions are there for the purpose of:

- communication with and (to influence) others;
- bonding within relationships;
- survival;
- preparing a person to act;
- communicating with ourselves.

Exercise:
- *In pairs identify a recent example of an emotion which you experienced.*
- *Identify what the function of that emotion was. Was it communicating with others, communicating with yourself or driving an action?*
- *Feed back to the group.*

Link acceptance of emotions to compassion and the development of the soothing mode. The aim is not to avoid our emotional states, but to listen to them and respond to them with acceptance. Emotions provide us with an indicator to our needs; if we do not listen to our emotions, than we are likely to ignore our needs, and we are also likely to use destructive behaviours such as eating disorder behaviours, self-harm, alcohol, etc. as a means of suppressing our emotional states.

4. Compassionate behaviours – to others and ourselves

Group exercise and discussion: Using the flipchart develop a list of compassionate behaviours that they can show to themselves and also a list of compassionate behaviours that they can do for others.

Individuals with anorexia often have a tendency towards self-sacrifice and subjugation. It is important that this is not confused with compassion for others, as the former are unhealthy patterns of interaction which often serve to reinforce their negative beliefs about themselves or other people. Generate a discussion around the difference between self-sacrifice and being compassionate to others. In order to help group members get in touch with feelings of compassion to others, the following imagery exercise can be used.

Exercise:
Sit comfortably and allow your eyes to close ... Allow your attention to rest on your breath ... bring to mind a person or animal who you experience genuine care and warmth towards ... Imagine yourself wanting to offer support and kindness to them ... imagine yourself slowly moving towards them ... Focus on your own compassionate self ... How does it feel in your body to experience genuine care and warmth towards another ... allow yourself to sit with that feeling for a few moments.

Ask the group to feed back how they found the exercise.

Homework:

• Hand out sheet on the function of emotions and ask group members to read this (see appendix 1).
• Continue mindfulness practice.
• To try to notice and listen to what their emotions are telling them.
• Each day try to do at least one compassionate thing for themselves and one compassionate thing for another person.

Session 5

1. Safe place imagery

Session 5 begins to draw on imagery to facilitate self-compassion and for this reason the group commences with an imagery exercise. This exercise is help-ful in that it is a way of practising the use of imagery in order to activate the self-soothing mode.

> **Exercise:**
> *Sit comfortably with your eyes closed … Begin by noticing your breath entering and leaving your body, and with each breath out, allow yourself to let go of any thoughts, concerns or worries that you entered the room with … with each breath out, allow yourself to let go of any tension that you are holding in your body … Now I would like you to begin to imagine your safe place … It might be a place that is real or imaginary, from the past or the present, you may be alone or with others … I want you to bring to your mind's eye, yourself in your safe place … What can you see? … What can you hear? … What can you smell? … How does the ground beneath you feel as you sit, stand or lie on it? … What is the temperature of your body? Can you feel the sun or the wind against your skin? … If you are with somebody where are they in relation to you? Are they touch-ing you? … It is okay to allow different images to float into your mind but then begin to allow it to settle on one. [After a minute] Now I would like you to bring your attention to how you feel in your safe place … Notice a feeling of being safe and calm … Notice how that feels within your body … Now I will leave you with your safe place image for a few minutes. [After 2 minutes] And when you are ready, gently open your eyes and bring your-self back to the room.*

Ask each member of the group if they would be happy to share how they found the exercise and also where their safe place was. By sharing their experiences, this facilitates connectedness within the group and also enables group members to hold information which can be potentially useful when offering support to each other outside of the groups.

2. Re-cap and homework

If new members have joined the group, or if members missed the group, the group are asked to provide a re-cap on the group itself and/or the last session. Group members are asked if they have any thoughts or questions following on from the last session.

Ask the group to feed back from their homework:

*   How did they get along with listening to their emotions and did they notice themselves acting differently in response to this?
*   How have they managed with doing one compassionate thing daily for themselves and others? Gently challenge any group members who have only been doing compassionate things for others and ask the group to provide support and guidance, link back to self-sacrifice discussion in the previous session.

3. The role of imagery in compassion

Following on from the safe place imagery, to introduce the idea of how useful imagery can be in developing self-compassion. Have Figure 8.3 on the flipchart to help to illustrate what is being discussed:

Discussion: Ask the group about their likely physiological and emotional responses to the reality of food when they are hungry (while acknowledging the complexity of this for them as individuals with eating disorders), winning something, and being bullied, and also about their likely responses to that being generated internally. Then move on to consider both externally generated and internally

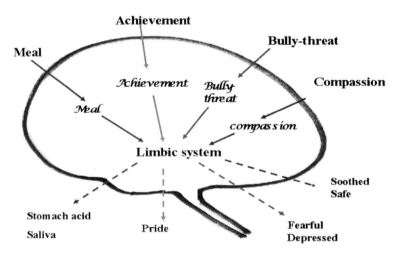

Figure 8.3 Interactions between our thoughts, images and our emotions
Source: Gilbert (2009), reprinted with permission from Constable & Robinson Ltd.

generated compassion. The response that you are looking to elicit is that both the external and internal events will generate a similar emotional and physiological response.

Given that our internal thoughts and images can be so powerful in eliciting an emotional and physiological response, this creates the rationale for using imagery in order to generate a sense of feeling soothed and nurtured and developing the self-soothing mode.

4. Compassionate others

Discussion: Linking back to the first session (you may want to return to the original brainstorm conducted with the group on what compassion means), generate a discussion around compassionate people or characters from books or film. Some possible ideas are Mother Teresa, Aslan from *The Lion, the Witch and the Wardrobe*; Gandalf from *The Lord of the Rings* or Dumbledore from *Harry Potter*. You can use film clips to portray this if possible or alternatively bring pictures or quotes from books that depict compassion.

Ideal nurturer

The group are now asked to begin to develop their own individual ideal nurturer. This exercise is drawn from Lee (2005).

I find that this exercise is more productive if done using the following imagery exercise within the session.

> *Exercise:*
> *Sit comfortably with your eyes closed … Begin by noticing your breath entering and leaving your body … Now I would like you to begin to generate your own ideal nurturer … They may have human features, yet will be without human failings … They are wise, strong and warm … They know everything about you and accept everything about you. Bring to mind an image of what they look like … Notice their facial expression, notice the look in their eyes … Try to bring to mind a smell which you associate with them … Notice the sound of their voice … What are they saying to you? … How do they provide you with comfort? Do they provide you with physical comfort? … Imagine yourself with them. How does it feel to allow yourself to receive their compassion? … I will leave you to play with your image for a few minutes. If nothing is arising, that is okay too, just sit with your breath or return to your safe place image.*

Give the group a few minutes to try to generate their image before asking them to open their eyes and return to the group. Ask group members to feed back how it was for them and what images they generated. It is useful to ask them to focus on a smell that they can have readily available (such as a perfume or a lip balm) that they can connect with their ideal nurturer and carry around with them, as this association smell can then act as a trigger to connect with their ideal nurturer image and more importantly the emotions connected to their self-soothing mode.

Homework:

- To continue with the development of their ideal nurturer image and to develop a piece of writing, picture or collage to illustrate them.
- Daily practice of bringing to mind their image of their ideal nurturer and connecting this with a smell and the feelings associated with being soothed.

End the group by asking for any final thoughts or questions.

Session 6

1. Compassionate colour

In this session we introduce another compassion imagery exercise (adapted from Gilbert, 2010).

> *Exercise:*
> *Sit comfortably and allow your eyes to close ... Now begin by gently guiding your attention to your breath ... letting your worries and concerns from outside of this room gently evaporate with each out breath ... Now imagine a colour that most closely depicts compassion for you. Allow yourself to see that colour, and slowly allow it to surround you like a light or a mist ... see the colour entering into your body or flowing through you ... See this colour as having wisdom and strength and kindness as it flows into you and around you...*

Leave them with this image for a few minutes before asking them to open their eyes. Ask for feedback on how they found the exercise.

2. Re-cap and homework feedback

Ask for any thoughts or questions from the last session and invite group members to re-cap for any members who missed the last group.

Discussion: Invite the group to feed back to the group their pictures, collages and writing about their perfect nurturer. Generate discussion within the group regarding how they found this exercise and how they have found the practice of using this image to help them to generate self-compassion and strengthen their self-soothing mode.

Introduce the next step with this work – to begin to use their ideal nurturer image in times of distress or when they are being self-critical and to see this as a signal to generate their image and the feeling of being soothed and then to imagine their ideal nurturer responding to their distress or self-criticism. The thought records can be used to help with this.

3. Compassionate letter writing

Compassionate letter writing is introduced as a useful way to develop a more compassionate stance towards their individual struggles. It can help them to face their emotional distress with acceptance, while also bringing compassion to their struggles. It can help them to focus on how to face and tackle their emotional difficulties.

Given that this is such an important exercise, the majority of the session is devoted to this task.

> *Exercise:*
>
> *Group members are given letter writing handouts (see appendices 2 and 3) and asked to choose one of the letters to write to themselves. They are asked to write either a compassionate letter to themselves or to their bodies (the second of these was developed by a previous colleague of mine, Dr Matthew Pugh). It can be helpful to give group members permission to find a space where they feel comfortable outside of the group room, where they can focus on the task and then to spend 30 minutes writing the letter before returning to the group room. Instruct them to spend a few minutes prior to starting the writing task to do some mindful breathing and to use whichever exercise they feel will be most helpful in allowing them to get in touch with their compassionate self. If they choose, they may also write the letter from their ideal nurturer to themselves.*
>
> *After 30 minutes group members are asked to feed back to the group and are invited to share any parts of their letter with the group that they would like to.*

Homework:

* To complete their letter if they have not already done so or to do the letter which they did not do in session.
* To practise whichever exercises they find the most useful to help them to get in touch with their compassionate self. Hand out the compassion practice diary and example sheet and ask them to complete this over the week (Gilbert, 2010).

Session 7

1. Mindfulness of emotions

> *Exercise:*
> *Repeat the mindfulness of emotions exercise from session 4.*

2. Re-cap and homework

Ask group members if they have any thoughts or comments regarding last week's session.

Ask the group members to get into pairs and to take it in turns to read the other person's letter to them. This can be a useful exercise as sometimes hearing it back can further enable them to get in touch with the emotion, rather than experiencing it as a pen and paper exercise. Ask them to feed back to the group how the process of writing the letter and hearing it read to them was.

Ask group members to feed back on how their compassion daily practice is going. Generate discussion about what people are finding most useful and most difficult.

3. Compassion blueprint

Given the short term nature of this group, it is important to think about how the group members will continue to take the practice forward. The group is seen as just an introduction, with the idea being that they take their practice forward to make real, sustainable changes.

See appendix 4 for compassion blueprint.

Exercise:
Ask group members to discuss each of the items in pairs in order to develop their own unique compassion blueprint. Once completed invite them to feed back to the group.

4. Compassion and self-criticism scales

Exercise:
Give out another copy of the self-compassion scale (Neff, 2003) and the forms of self-criticising/attacking and self-reassuring scale (FSCRS) (Gilbert et al., 2004) and ask them to complete them. Following this, give group members their scales from the initial session and ask them to reflect upon any changes and discuss with the group.

Return to the scales that they marked themselves in session 1 (see Figure 8.1), relating to compassion to others and compassion to themselves and ask them to re-mark themselves on the scales.

5. Saying goodbye

Each group member is invited to say goodbye to the group and to say how they hope to take their work on compassion forward. They are also asked to offer some words of compassion to the group member on their left and their hopes for how they might take the work forward.

Reflections and future directions

Given the time constraints, it was not possible to cover everything that I would have liked or in as much depth as I would have liked. The group therefore acted more as a taster of CFT for group members. Given the time limitations, it would have been ideal to have been able to commence with developing self-soothing techniques from the start. Unfortunately, when this was trialled in the first group, the levels of resistance that this was met with, due to the patients' levels of fear of compassion, resulted in individuals dropping out of the group. Due to this, the programme was redesigned in a way which focuses more heavily on psychoeducation, motivation and mindfulness in the first few sessions, which appeared to keep individuals more engaged and created a slow build up towards the more challenging exercises such as the letter writing and ideal nurturer exercises. Within the first session, it should be possible to judge how open the group are to developing compassion techniques; if it is felt that they are ready and willing to begin straight away, it might be preferable to leave out the mindfulness exercises and replace them with further compassionate imagery exercises, therefore providing the group with more experience of developing the self-soothing mode from the beginning.

For CFT to be optimally effective, it requires daily practice of the techniques. Within the context of an inpatient or day patient setting where patients have a full group programme alongside individual therapy and homework being set at a number of these, it is unrealistic to expect that this will occur. From my experience, within each group of approximately 6–10 patients, a few will feel that they really connect with the approach and have then tended to utilise the approach on a daily basis. This is not to say that these are the only patients who benefit, as I have found that even those who may not make use of the exercises outside of the group are often able to move from a position of feeling that they do not deserve compassion, or that their self-criticism serves an important function for them, to a place where they are more open to the idea of being self-compassionate or receiving compassion from others. It is possible that this shift may also enable patients to make better use of the treatment programme as a whole, if they are able to move away from a position where they may feel that they do not deserve the support. All of these reflections are unfortunately anecdotal as, at the current time, there are not any outcomes from the group. It has been conducted on four occasions and due to changes in the group membership from the start to completion, very limited outcome measures have been gathered. However, this is something which will continue to be worked on.

Feedback from group members has generally been positive, even for those who have struggled to put it into practice. Below are some examples of the feedback that the group has received.

One individual who really struggled with the idea of allowing herself to be compassionate at the beginning of the group left these comments:

> '*Engaging with compassion in a non-patronising way, with structure, that acknowledged the difficulty of it, meant I could take it on board and work within the group.*
>
> *I have been able to develop a compassionate voice for myself, which helps me to manage in difficult situations.*'

Another individual who struggles with obsessive compulsive disorder (OCD) alongside her anorexia and does significant amounts of reassurance seeking from staff and family members around her food and exercise, in an attempt to manage her anxiety, was able to begin regularly practising the imagery techniques and gave the following feedback:

> '*The imagery exercises help me to self-soothe before seeking external reassurance. I can therefore reduce my anxieties around food and exercise rather than rely upon others.*'

Despite the constraints and limitations of implementing a group such as this within an inpatient or day patient setting, it appears to be a useful group for individuals with severe eating disorders. Further work is needed to measure the effectiveness of the group.

APPENDIX I

The function of emotions

Emotions play a significant role in our daily lives, but why do we have emotions? Emotions act as a form of communication with others and with ourselves and can motivate our behaviour. Therefore, understanding our emotions can help us to better understand ourselves, other people and our behaviours.

Emotions help us to communicate with others

Facial expressions are an innate part of our emotions, we were born with them. Facial expressions communicate messages without words. Research has demonstrated strong evidence for the universal facial expressions of seven emotions – anger, contempt, disgust, fear, joy, sadness and surprise. Across all different cultures the same facial expressions are associated with each of these emotions. These facial expressions can communicate a message quicker than any words, and we react automatically to these communications. If our verbal and non-verbal messages do not match, then we are likely to cause confusion and create difficulties in our communications with others. The expression of our positive emotions enables us to bond with others. The expression of our negative emotions enables us to elicit support when we are sad and to make people aware of our displeasure at their actions when we are angry.

Emotions prepare us to act

Powerful emotions often motivate behaviours which are necessary for our survival. The fight or flight response is triggered in response to emotions such as anger and fear. It alerts us to danger and prepares us to run away or to fight, through the production of adrenaline. The responding action is often an automatic and immediate response. These automatic action responses are necessary for survival.

Other actions driven by our emotions might be the drive to search for something which is lost in response to the sadness or to drive us to achieve something again following the positive experience of the joy we felt at that achievement.

Emotions help us to communicate with ourselves

Emotions can be triggered by external or internal events (e.g. a thought). These emotional reactions then act as a signal. By recognising an emotion, labelling the emotion, and noticing what the action urge is, we can begin to make sense of our emotions. By listening to our emotions, we can begin to use them to help us to understand ourselves and to understand what our needs are.

If we choose to avoid our emotions, it is likely that we will struggle to understand what our needs are, struggle to communicate our needs to others and therefore will be unlikely to get our needs met.

APPENDIX 2

Compassionate letter to self

Write a letter to yourself from you or from your ideal nurturer. The letter should identify the difficulties and distress which you experience and provide care, kindness, wisdom and understanding to these difficulties. The letter should demonstrate the following:

- It expresses concern and genuine caring.
- It is sensitive to your distress and needs.
- It is sympathetic and responds emotionally to your distress.
- It helps you to face your feelings and become more tolerant of them.
- It helps you become more understanding and reflective of your feelings, difficulties and dilemmas.
- It is non-judgemental/non-condemning.
- It displays a genuine sense of warmth, understanding and care.
- It helps you think about the behaviour you may need to adopt in order to get better.

The point of this letter is *not* just to focus on difficult feelings but to help you reflect on your feelings and thoughts, be open with them, and develop a compassionate and balanced way of working with them. The letter should not offer advice or tell you what you should or shouldn't do. It is not the advice you need, but the support to act on it.

APPENDIX 3

Compassionate letter to your body

Write a compassionate letter from yourself, to your body. The letter should identify the struggles that you have had with your body over time and convey understanding towards yourself for those difficulties and the unintended consequences that they have had and also forgiveness and acceptance of your body. The letter should demonstrate the following:

- A recognition of the strengths that your body possesses and what it enables you to do.
- Understanding towards yourself for why the imperfections of your body feel so distressing for you.
- Forgiveness towards your body for not being perfect.
- Acknowledgement of the mistakes that you have made in how you have treated your body.
- Understanding towards why you have made these mistakes.
- Expressing your intention to accept your body as it is meant to be and to take care of it and meet its needs.

The letter should demonstrate warmth and kindness to both yourself and your body. While important to acknowledge the mistakes that you may have made, it is important that you do this with understanding and not blame or criticism.

Adapted from original exercise developed by Matthew Pugh (unpublished).

APPENDIX 4

My compassion blueprint

My self-critical voice tends to say...

....

....

....

....

....

My self-critical voice makes me feel ....

....

....

....

....

....

....

My self-critical voice impacts on my life in the following ways ....

....

....

....

....

....

....

The following strategies/imagery techniques help me to get in touch with a more compassionate way of being with myself ....

....

....

....

....

....

If I was more compassionate to myself, I would say ....

....

....

....

....

....

If I was more compassionate to myself, I would feel ....

....

....

....

....

....

....

If I was more compassionate to myself, it would impact positively on my life in the following ways ....

....

....

....

....

....

....

....

References

Allan, S. and Goss, K. (2011). Shame and pride in eating disorders. In Fox, J. and Goss, K. (eds), *Eating and its disorders* (pp. 139–153). Chichester, UK: Wiley-Blackwell.

Gale, C., Gilbert, P., Read, N. and Goss, K. (2014). An evaluation of the impact of introducing compassion focused therapy to a standard treatment programme for people with eating disorders. *Clinical Psychology and Psychotherapy*, 21, 1–12.

Gilbert, P. (1992). *Depression: The Evolution of Powerlessness*. Hove, UK: Erlbaum.

Gilbert, P. (2000). The relationship of shame, social anxiety and depression: The role of the evaluation of social rank. *Clinical Psychology and Psychotherapy*, 7, 174–189.

Gilbert, P. (2009). *The Compassionate Mind*. London: Constable & Robinson Ltd.

Gilbert, P. (2010). *Compassion Focused Therapy: Distinctive Features*. London: Routledge.

Gilbert, P. and Irons, C. (2005). Focused therapies and compassionate mind training for shame and self-attacking. In Gilbert, P. (ed.), *Compassion: Conceptualisations, Research and Use in Psychotherapy* (pp. 263–325). London: Routledge.

Gilbert, P. and Proctor, S. (2006). Compassionate mind training for people with high shame and self-criticism: Overview and pilot study of a group therapy approach. *Clinical Psychology and Psychotherapy*, 13, 353–379.

Gilbert, P., Clark, M., Hempel, S., Miles, J. N. V. and Irons, C. (2004). Criticising and reassuring oneself: An exploration of forms, styles and reasons in female students. *British Journal of Clinical Psychology*, 43, 31–50.

Goss, K. and Allan, S. (2009). Shame and pride in eating disorders. *Clinical Psychology and Psychotherapy*, 16, 303–316.

Goss, K. and Allan, S. (2014). The development and application of compassion-focused therapy for eating disorders (CFT-E). *British Journal of Clinical Psychology*, 53, 62–77.

Heriot-Maitland, C., Vidal, J. B., Ball, S. and Irons, C. (2014). Compassionate-focused therapy group approach for acute inpatients: Feasibility, initial pilot outcome data, and recommendations. *British Journal of Clinical Psychology*, 53, 78–94.

Judge, L., Cleghorn, A., McEwan, K. and Gilbert, P. (2012). An exploration of group-based compassion focused therapy for a heterogeneous range of clients presenting to a community mental health team. *International Journal of Cognitive Therapy*, 5(4), 420–429.

Kelly, A. C., Carter, J. C., Zuroff, D. C. and Borain, S. (2013). Self-compassion and fear of self-compassion interact to predict response to eating disorders treatment: A preliminary investigation. *Psychotherapy Research*, 23(3), 252–264.

Lee, D. A. (2005). The perfect nurturer: A model to develop a compassionate mind within the context of cognitive therapy. In Gilbert, P. (ed.), *Compassion: Conceptualisations, Research and Use in Psychotherapy* (pp. 326–351). New York: Routledge.

Neff, K. D. (2003). Development and validation of a scale to measure self-compassion. *Self and Identity*, 2, 223–250.

Price, J. S. and Sloman, L. (1987). Depression as yielding behavior: An animal model based on Schjelderup-Ebbe's pecking order. *Ethology and Sociobiology*, 8(1), 85–98.

Vandereycken, W. (2011). Can eating disorders become 'contagious' in group therapy and specialized inpatient care? *European Eating Disorders Review*, 19(4), 289–295.

Chapter 9

BodyWise: a low intensity group to address body image disturbance

Victoria Mountford and Amy Brown

Background

In our clinical experience, the issue of body image is often something that elicits anxiety in both patients and staff. Patients have told us they worry that talking about their bodies will make them feel worse and the slow pace of change can be dispiriting. Staff comment that they feel ill equipped to address such issues and again experience concern that they will further distress the individual.

This group was developed in response to reflections by staff and patients on an inpatient eating disorder unit. At that time, the unit provided a body image group (known as Body Awareness Therapy 10; BAT-10) for patients who had restored their weight to within the healthy range, developed by the St George's Eating Disorder Service team (see Key *et al.*, 2002; Morgan *et al.*, 2013). This programme was fairly intensive, utilising mirror exposure and requiring homework. The patients requested a group that was of lower intensity and that they could join, regardless of their weight. Thus, BodyWise (Brown *et al.*, 2010) was developed over a number of years in consultation with patients and clinicians. BodyWise aims to provide a structured and safe space for individuals to begin to voice and explore their thoughts about their body image. The focus is on raising awareness, rather than active change.

In a study undertaken across three eating disorder services, patients who took part in BodyWise groups reported improvements in shape and weight concerns compared to a control group. Additionally they reported a decrease in body checking and an improvement in their body image related quality of life. They also felt more able to communicate their feelings regarding their body image (see Appendix). Further individuals rated the group as acceptable and helpful (Mountford *et al.*, 2015). Our clinical hypothesis, albeit untested as yet, is that it may be of benefit for patients to complete BodyWise, followed by BAT-10 when they have reached a healthy weight.

Although, to our knowledge, BodyWise has mainly been delivered in inpatient and day care settings, it may also be appropriate for outpatient settings. In addition, the manual has been adapted for use with adolescents with eating disorders on an inpatient ward and is currently under evaluation (Rosewall, 2014; personal communication).

Description of the group

BodyWise is an eight session, structured group with clear agendas for each session. It is designed for up to eight participants with two facilitators. Over the years in development, we have run the group with patients with anorexia nervosa only (as this is the diagnosis most frequently seen on our inpatient ward), and with a mixed group of patients with anorexia and bulimia nervosa. In this latter scenario, facilitators need to be mindful of potential similarities and differences between individuals. Each session is 'standalone'; however, following feedback and discussion from patients we run the group as closed after the second session, to promote consistency and trust.

The group may be facilitated by any member of the multidisciplinary team who has experience working in this area. In addition, it is important for facilitators to be reflective regarding their own body image and their attitudes to body image in general. We have, on occasions, been asked about this and find it is helpful to be transparent and thoughtful about our own beliefs or biases.

As described above, we developed the group for use in the early stages of treatment, often before individuals have attained a healthy weight. It is developed as low intensity, and we explain to patients that they will not be asked to talk directly about their *own* bodies, although should they wish to reflect on their own thoughts, feelings and behaviours they can do so. The group utilises a combination of methods, from small group or pair work to whole group work or watching short DVDs/ internet clips relevant to the topic. We often find that quieter members of the group are able to contribute during small group work, which increases their confidence to contribute later. Due to the low intensity nature of the group, most sessions do not have formalised homework, although patients are encouraged to reflect over the week. We have found that the level of functioning and thinking can vary tremendously between cohorts and therefore we tailor the group to the current cohort, if appropriate, suggesting added or optional homework ideas. On occasions, participants themselves may suggest trying something new or different for homework.

Eating disorder services tend to treat fewer males than females. Nevertheless, we have had male patients and male facilitators in the group. We are keen to foster inclusiveness and transparency. If there are males in the group, this is always addressed in the first session. We explore anxieties or questions on behalf of all participants and we have found this transparency provides a good starting point for the remainder of the group. Regardless of whether there are males in a particular group or not, we always try to ensure the material presented is gender balanced and to include discussion and reflection regarding males as well as females.

The group broadly draws on three models. These are cognitive behaviour therapy (see Bamford and Mountford, 2012; Fairburn, 2008; Waller *et al.*, 2007), cognitive remediation therapy (CRT) (e.g. Tchanturia *et al.*, 2013, 2014) and the work of Thomas Cash on body image (see Cash, 2008).

A core aim of the group is to raise awareness of biased thinking. This runs across many sessions with facilitators supporting participants to notice when this may be occurring. This is compatible with the goals of cognitive remediation therapy in supporting individuals to shift their focus from high detail to broader understandings and to increase flexibility in their thinking. We frequently refer to the following thinking biases which may commonly present in body image thoughts. Patients in our ward programme are already very familiar with common thinking styles in eating disorders and have been part of the CRT groups described in Chapter 2.

All or nothing thinking

All or nothing thinking involves thinking in extremes and missing the grey area in between. This is highly salient in body image, for example, 'Either I'm thin or I'm obese', neglecting to realise the broad band of healthy weight in between. We often highlight that in fact the body functions best within a natural weight range, which is somewhere between these two extremes.

Unfair to compare

This thinking bias leads individuals to pit themselves against their own personal ideals, media images of physical perfection or people they find good looking that they meet in everyday situations. Often the individual picks the 'best' part of the other to compare themselves against, neglecting the parts of others that may be less 'desirable'. We highlight that this links to **double standards** – having different rules for other people – and can lead to shame, envy and intimidation.

Magnifying glass

Many participants will recognise this bias, which involves focusing on what they do not like and minimising attributes that do not cause a problem. It leads to a very unbalanced view and means individuals may be judging themselves harshly, based on one or two aspects of their appearance. The magnifying glass also selectively focuses attention; for example, focusing on all the people one sees who are significantly underweight or significantly overweight and ignoring those who may be in a healthy weight range.

Emotional reasoning

Emotional reasoning involves taking one's emotions as an accurate reflection of what is happening. For example, 'I feel fat therefore I am fat', even when one is actually underweight. This bias can set up waves of criticism and distress.

Mind reading

Mind reading means assuming you know what others – strangers and friends or family – are thinking. In the case of body image, individuals are projecting their own negative thoughts about their body into the minds of others. It can lead to avoiding social situations and attributing difficulties to one's appearance rather than considering alternatives. Chapter 5 describes some work we do with patients on emotion skills in our ward and day care programmes.

Evaluation of the group

The group has been evaluated to provide support for its effectiveness (Mountford *et al.*, 2015); however, it can be valuable for patients to evaluate their own outcomes by completing measures in the first and last session. This can be done in a number of ways. For example, through the use of validated measures such as the Eating Disorders Examination Questionnaire (using the Shape and Weight Concern subscales; Fairburn and Beglin, 1994), the Physical Appearance State and Trait Anxiety Scale – Trait Version (Reed *et al.*, 1991) and Body Checking Questionnaire (Reas *et al.*, 2002). Alternatively, a simple visual analogue scale can be used. To specifically target whether the group helped participants to feel more able to discuss their body image we developed a short questionnaire – Body Image Questionnaire: Communication and Understanding (see the Appendix).

General session structure

All sessions follow a similar structure:

1. Welcome and check-in. Patients are welcomed to the group and the topic is introduced. All participants take part in a check-in, in which they are asked how they are feeling at the moment and if they had any thoughts or observations from the last session or over the week. If homework was agreed, it will be discussed here.
2. Topic. The main topic for the session will be outlined. There are likely to be two or three exercises to explore the topic. We try to end this section with a positive comment about what people can do differently.
3. Check-out. All participants are encouraged to check out, letting the group know how they are feeling and one thing they will take away from the day's session.

Session outlines

Below are the outlines for the eight sessions. We aim to be creative and incorporate new information as it becomes available to each session. Often, participants will have good examples that they direct us to, which are incorporated into future groups. Therefore in each outline we have attempted to give a guide to the session, without being overly prescriptive.

For all groups, a flipchart and pens will be required. For session 3, a laptop or computer and projector will be required.

Content of the group

Session 1: Introduction and what is body image?

The aim of this session is to welcome members and introduce the aims and boundaries of the group. A discussion of what body image is and how it affects members follows. It is important to explore patients' hopes and fears about the group. Sometimes patients have unrealistically high expectations about the group and can become angry and disappointed when these are inevitably not met. Equally, patients can feel very anxious that the group will make them feel worse by bringing to their attention an issue they usually try to avoid. Both these assumptions need sensitive exploring. We also emphasise that the group works best when members are able to contribute and share some of their own thoughts and experiences.

1. Welcome and check-in.
2. Introduce facilitators and group members.
3. Introduce the session plan and discuss aims:

   - To give a place for patients to discuss issues regarding their changing shape.
   - To provide psycho-education focusing on issues related to body image.
   - Outline the different session topics and explain it will be a mix of small group work, discussion and occasionally watching a DVD.

4. Develop shared group boundaries.
5. Ask how participants feel about starting the group and explore patients' hopes and fears.
   Emphasise that this group is not about 'fixing' their body image; it's about exploring it and understanding why it is so important.
6. What do I use my body for?
   [Small group discussions with flipcharts to write ideas and then feed back to whole group]

   - Day-to-day activities, e.g. running for a bus, dancing with my friends.
   - Life events, e.g. having children, sporting achievements.

   [After individual discussions each group feed back to facilitator who writes ideas on the flipchart]
   The aim of this exercise is to enable participants to explore and reflect on the multiple roles and skills of their body, rather than the overwhelming emphasis on their body based on shape and weight.
7. What is body image?
   [Each group to come up with a sentence or two defining body image]
   Very generally it is the beliefs and feelings about how we look physically and about how we think others see us. It can be described as our *relationship* with our body.

Probing questions:

- *Do you think we hold accurate images of our physical self? (Perceptual)*
- *How do we feel about our bodies? (Affective – not just what we see when we look in the mirror but what we feel when we think about our bodies)*
- *Is how other people view our bodies important? (Influence of others' beliefs, or what we think others think, on our body image)*
- *What thoughts do we have about our bodies? (Thoughts)*

[Feed back sentences; add any major missing points]

If not mentioned, we discuss body image investment – how important the individual views their body in terms of self-evaluation. This is a key theme that we come back to throughout the group.

8. How does my body image affect my life?

    Introduce the idea of body image affecting our thoughts, emotions and behaviours. This is a low key motivational exercise to help participants think about the way their body image has impacted upon life. Both positive and negative ways should be considered.

    [Whole group discussion]

    Have headings on the flipchart (thoughts, emotions and behaviours) and separate answers into the appropriate column:

    a) Thoughts: e.g. self-esteem, feelings of femininity.
    b) Emotions: e.g. anxiety about people seeing my body.
    c) Behaviours: e.g. daily grooming (such as wearing baggy clothes), effect on eating, avoidance, checking.

9. Body dissatisfaction is part of anorexia. It can be useful to share the points below with participants.

    - Body image disturbance is a diagnostic criterion for anorexia ('Disturbance in the way in which one's body weight or shape is experienced, undue influence of body weight or shape on self-evaluation, or persistent lack of recognition of the seriousness of the current low body weight'; DSM-5 (APA, 2013)). Therefore, we expect and understand patients will have this and that distress may increase as they gain weight. Feeling this way does not make an individual vain or shallow – it is part of the disorder.
    - It can be useful to share research evidence and clinical experience that body image disturbance can be one of the slowest aspects of anorexia to change, which can be scary and frustrating. It is likely that individuals will continue to feel distress for some months to come and this may be the case even when they have completed treatment.

10. Finally, it can be helpful to initiate a discussion about healthy body image. Do they know anyone with a more positive body image? How does someone with a more healthy body image think, feel and behave?

11. If you wish to evaluate the group using questionnaires, please give them now for participants to complete and return next week.

12. Check-out.

Session 2: What is normal?

This session aims to help patients reflect on the difference between normal and healthy and the all or nothing thinking style that they often apply to their weight and shape. Some facilitators have found that this session can be somewhat tricky and therefore we encourage you to ensure you feel confident prior to delivery.

1. Welcome and check-in.
2. Highlight the difference between healthy and normal weight:
    *   Healthy being a weight at which the body best functions with lowest health risk. Draw out a chart that highlights the different ranges of weight and reflect on the range of weights that fall within a healthy weight range.
    *   Normal being the actual average weight for people living in a certain population (e.g. average weight for women living in the UK). Demonstrate using a bell curve. Point out that the mean of the bell curve may (but not always) represent the middle of the healthy weight range, although this may become skewed if the overall population size increases or decreases. (See Figure 9.1.)
    *   The mean BMI in the UK is 26.9 kg/m^2 for women and 27.4 kg/m^2 for males across all ages (Moody, 2013) and prevalence for obesity is lowest in the 16–24 age group.
3. Introduce the idea of all or nothing thinking in relation to weight: 'fat or thin'. Refer back to the bell curve, helping to illustrate the wide variety of weights and body shapes, it is not dichotomous.
4. We discuss how weight and shape change with age.
    *   It is important to acknowledge that our bodies changes as we get older. A 16 year old's body will be significantly different to a 30 year old's body even if they stay in the same weight range.
    *   This is particularly important to consider if someone has been underweight for a long time as their body will have naturally changed. They can expect that when they reach a healthy weight, their body may be different (and larger) than previously.
5. Quiz focusing on normal and healthy weight.
    We recommend developing your own multiple choice quiz which will be timely and relevant. We regularly update ours, using reports (see the Reference list). Sample questions ask participants to estimate the number of working age women/men in the UK who are underweight/overweight and those who are satisfied/dissatisfied with their bodies and what the average size of a UK woman is.
    The aim of the quiz is to generate discussion amongst the group. We emphasise that the quiz is not about right or wrong answers, but about exploration and discussion. We find participants often acknowledge that they apply an all or nothing thinking style when in public areas – for example, tending to notice others who are either very thin or overweight. Equally, they may only

focus on people of a similar age and gender. We introduce this as a cognitive bias known as the magnifying glass or selective attention, explaining:

if something is important or salient to us, we are more likely to notice it in our environment. If you value being thin, you are more likely to notice and compare yourself to thin people, so your perception of how many thin people there are in public is skewed in that you think there are more thin people than there really is.

Participants are often surprised to discover the high levels of body image discontent amongst non-eating-disordered individuals.

We also ask questions based on research into young people and body image, for example exploring how many young people might worry about becoming overweight or believe they would 'be happier if they were thinner'. This opens a discussion regarding how early such fears or beliefs might develop. Often group participants know young people (e.g. younger siblings, their own children) and are able to link this discussion to their own observations. We introduce the quiz as follows:

People often struggle to know what is normal in terms of weight, shape and attitudes towards our bodies. We have devised a quiz which we hope will give some insight into what is normal and a chance to discuss any thoughts around this issue.

We ask participants to complete the quiz in small groups of 2–3.

6. Check-out.

Information for facilitators

What is the difference between normal and healthy?

WHAT IS A HEALTHY WEIGHT?

Healthy weight is the weight at which your body functions best with the lowest health risk. Draw a diagram to demonstrate to participants the range of different BMIs from BMI 17.5 up to BMI 30. Add in the healthy range (BMI 20–25). BMI 20–25 is normally about 10 kg so people can be different sizes but still healthy. Highlight the range across which people can fall into the healthy weight range using a normal distribution. Emphasise how the diagram reveals that it is unlikely that someone will jump from being underweight to overweight overnight.

WHAT IS A NORMAL WEIGHT?

*   Normal weight will be the average weight of the population. While there will always be variation in the general population, over time this has been gradually increasing.
*   Ask participants to guess the average BMI of women and plot 'guesses' on a graph.
*   The average BMI at the moment is 27 – compare to participants' estimates.

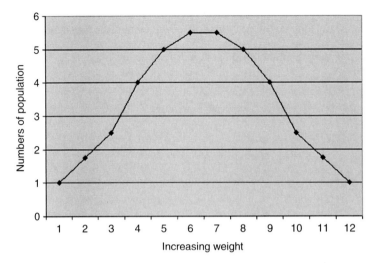

Figure 9.1 Bell curve to demonstrate normal distribution within a population

- Use the bell curve to highlight participants' all or nothing thinking – 'I'm either thin or I'm fat'.

Note to facilitators: The use of Body Mass Index is not without controversy and sometimes participants may raise this. We encourage a flexible approach, acknowledging the limitations, and stressing that is is a helpful guide, rather than rigid rule.

Session 3: Effects of media on body image

This session aims to consider how the media impacts on our body image and to encourage participants to critique the images we see and messages we are given. We emphasise at the start that we are not implying or stating that the media causes eating disorders. We are thinking more broadly about the impact of the media, on all people, whether or not they have an eating disorder. As facilitators, we keep an eye on the media as there are many interesting examples which can be flexibly incorporated into the group.

1. Welcome and check-in.
2. *What is the female/male beauty ideal as represented in the media?*
   [Ask to whole group]
   Female, e.g.:
   a) Extremely tall and thin.
   b) Small hips but a full bust.
   c) Large eyes, large lips and a small nose.
   Male, e.g.:
   a) Muscular – 'six pack'.

b)   Chiselled jaw, good head of hair.

c)   Tall.

Usually a very long list will form, and generally a participant will comment that the long list is unrealistic, if not impossible to achieve. The group can explore this, and the fact that most of us are likely to fall short in some way.

3.   *What are the sources of media?*

[Ask to whole group and write answers on flipchart].

Examples include TV, magazines, film, adverts, fashion industry, internet, music videos, Instagram, Facebook. It can be useful to reflect on how ubiquitous these influences are, even if we generally believe ourselves to be media literate. We also discuss the incongruent nature of these images; for example, a semi-naked body being used to advertise jewellery or a watch.

4.   Psycho-education on body image represented in the media.

For this section, we use pictures of famous individuals from a range of eras, representing a range of different body types, to start a discussion. We add in the following information. The body ideal as represented by the media has changed dramatically over time, as demonstrated by an icon of the 1950s and an icon today. Today's thin ideal is unrealistic for the majority of women. The body size of models is often more than 20 per cent underweight (exceeding the diagnostic criteria for anorexia nervosa of 15 per cent underweight). Numerous studies have shown that exposure to images of thin women can increase body dissatisfaction in women. Studies have shown that even very quick, flashed images can have a negative effect, so imagine what a lifetime of daily exposure can do to a woman's body esteem. It is not just teenagers and women who are vulnerable to media images. One study found that 5–8 year old girls reported lower body esteem and greater desire for a thinner body shape after being exposed to Barbie dolls (Dittmar *et al.*, 2006).

5.   Psycho-education on artificial beauty in the media.

Not only are females and males in the media represented by 'ideals', but many of the images have been digitally altered and do not represent accurately how the individuals really look. For example, females may have been airbrushed to appear thinner, while males may have added muscles. Again, pictures of famous people (before and after airbrushing) can be used. We also access short videos from the internet which show the ways in which photographs can be photoshopped. Using such videos can be very powerful. Participants often acknowledge that although they are aware of airbrushing, they underestimate the extent to which it is carried out.

6.   *Who benefits from the thin ideal and at what cost to us?*

[Ask to whole group and write answers on flipchart, who benefits on one side and what is the cost to us on the other]

Who benefits? E.g.:

•   fashion industry;

•   diet industry;

- cosmetic surgery industry;
- beauty industry;
- gyms.

What are the costs to us? E.g.:

- health (mental and physical);
- financial;
- self-esteem;
- time.

Initiate a discussion around the injustice of how these industries play a part in creating body dissatisfaction and make money out of providing a solution (however unhealthy, ineffective or dangerous to our health). How would people want to respond differently to this? How can individuals protect themselves from these messages? It can be helpful to finish with a short internet clip that promotes acceptance rather than criticism. For example, there are videos on YouTube promoting positive body self-esteem and how to manage body image concerns.

7.   Check-out.

Session 4: 'Feeling fat': what are we really saying?

The aim of this session is to explore what individuals mean when they say they 'feel fat', encouraging individuals to question this and to consider alternative meanings.

1.   Welcome and check-in.
2.   Today's session is going to be about 'feeling fat' and what we might actually be feeling when we say we feel fat. We'll then go on to discuss some more positive ways of talking to and about ourselves.
3.   Do people notice themselves saying or thinking that they 'feel fat'?
4.   Can we 'feel' fat?

- Technically, you cannot 'feel' fat, any more than you can feel square. The linguistically accurate phrase is 'I think I am fat'.
- We can feel emotions (e.g. I feel happy or I feel anxious) and we can feel physiological states (e.g. I feel tired or I feel thirsty).
- We cannot feel physical states (e.g. I feel I have blue eyes… I have blue eyes or even I think I have blue eyes).

5.   Telling ourselves that we feel fat can become so familiar that we take it for granted that we know what we mean when we say it.

It may be that we use it when we are feeling different emotions or physiological states; or we are unsure what we really are feeling; or it may be a way of describing negative emotions that we find difficult to express or put into words.

Identifying/finding out more about what 'feeling fat' means for you can help you manage the complex, intense and varied emotions associated with body image distress. What are we really saying when we say 'I feel fat'?

6. Draw on a flipchart 'I feel fat …'
    [Split into small groups and write answers on flipchart paper]

    • Identify as many feeling/descriptive words as possible that can be used instead of 'fat' and put on flipchart.

    E.g. bloated, full, lonely, guilty, shame, horrified, disgusted, etc.

    • The small groups feed back into the large group with the facilitator recording on the flipchart. Use a table with two columns headed 'Feeling' and 'Physiological State' and ask participants to identify which column the words should be assigned to.

    • Encourage group discussion around:

      'What are people saying when they say "I feel fat"?'

    If it does not come up in discussion encourage participants to consider this statement as a smokescreen which stops both themselves and other people understanding the underlying emotional experience. It also stops individuals being able to access help or support as the enquirer is diverted onto shape/ weight.

    Is it more about describing bodily sensations/feelings/thoughts? It may be helpful to separate and determine the difference between these. We know that the way we think, feel and behave towards our bodies all interlink and have an impact on each other, on our self-esteem and body image.

    Notice that it is easy to get into vicious circles:

    Feelings – Thoughts – Behaviours – Feelings – Thoughts, etc.

7. In the same way that negative thoughts, feelings and behaviours about our bodies interlink and impact on each other, so does positive self-talk and affirmations.

    Positive self-talk and affirmations can support emotional and physical health and promote the achievement of goals. They point us in positive directions, help us conquer the difficulties in life, and help us see others and ourselves more positively. As we highlight in Chapter 5 and Chapter 10 we use positive psychology research ideas in different groups to teach patients self-compassion.

    Group exercise:

    • Do people use any positive affirmations/self-talk? If so are they able to share them?

    • If not, get the group to identify/compile a list of affirmations. (It may be useful for facilitators to have suggestions handy to start the process.)

8. Homework:

    • Encourage patients to identify words that are relevant to themselves and to use these words instead of 'fat'. It may be that many of the words are relevant at the same time or in different environments/situations. Observe any situations over the week when they notice themselves 'feeling fat'.

- Pick or create positive affirmations to try over the next week. Encourage patients to use affirmations when and where possible.
9.   Check-out.

BodyWise session 4 homework

1.   Identify what you mean when you say 'I feel fat'. What are you really feeling?
2.   Identify some positive self-talk and affirmations that you can try out over the coming week. It may be useful to place them in strategic places/hot spots, e.g. mirror, table placemat, bed, cupboard, etc.

What I mean/feel when I say 'I feel fat':

-
-
-
-
-
-

Three affirmations I'm going to try over the next week:

1.
2.
3.

Session 5: Perception and self-defeating behaviours

This session encourages participants to explore the idea of distortion in how they see themselves. For many participants it can be a difficult session as it often challenges strongly held beliefs.

1.   Welcome and check-in.
2.   Do we see what is really there?
    - What is perception? It is not simply a physiological representation of what we are looking at, but the brain's interpretation of what we are looking at; which is based on past experiences and preconceptions. Perception alters what humans see, into a diluted version of reality. When people view something with a preconceived idea about it, they tend to take those preconceived ideas and see them whether or not they are there.
    - We tend to use optical illusions as a good way of demonstrating how prior knowledge or beliefs may distort what we see. This is often a good way of gently and with good humour establishing that our perception can be erroneous.

- The first illusion that we use is the Ebbinghaus Illusion (Roberts *et al.*, 2005). This illusion consists of a circle surrounded by smaller circles in one image and by larger circles in another image. We often ask participants which circle is larger – the viewer will often see the circle surrounded by smaller circles as larger, although they are exactly the same size. This opens a discussion into how the way the brain processes the surrounding visual cues (larger or smaller circles) can impact size perception. We link this to the way we look at our bodies – focusing down on the most disliked part is likely to 'increase' the size of the defect. This can be related to how we use mirrors – do we scrutinise the disliked part or do we conduct a quick 'once over' to get the overall impression of our appearance.
- The second illusion we use is the Checkerboard illusion (Adelson, 2005). This illusion consists of an image of light and dark squares. The area labelled A appears to be a darker colour than the area labelled B despite them being the same colour. This illusion demonstrates how we break down images using our prior knowledge (e.g. of the pattern of a checkerboard) to perceive the object in view. This can open a discussion on how prior knowledge or expectations may inform our view of our body.

3. Errors in perception can affect our body image:
Introduce the idea that our body image is different from our actual body and some behaviour (such as frequent checking) serves to reinforce distortions. You may use the example of looking down at oneself while sitting which generally makes one's thighs appear larger.

4. The research on body image distortion is mixed and underpinned by a variety of different methodologies. However, more recent research shows that people with and without eating disorders present with distortions in body image (e.g. Ferrer-García and Gutiérrez-Maldonado, 2008; Fuentes *et al.*, 2013) with individuals with eating disorders presenting with greater distortions. Often participants will contribute to this with an example of something they have seen on television that relates to this. We reflect that body image can change from one moment to the next and follow this up with the next exercise which explores factors that can trigger such variations.

5. What do you think makes people feel bigger or smaller?
[Group discussion – writing answers on a flipchart]

- low mood;
- eating high calorie foods;
- looking at magazines depicting thin images;
- comparing themselves to 'ideal' others;
- checking and scrutinising:
  - *Mirrors*: highly credible, but misleading, information about appearance. Illustrate by the example of catching sight of yourself in a reflection before you realise it is you, or some mirrors in shop changing rooms which show one in a very flattering light.

- *Body checking*: explore whether this increases or reduces anxiety and factors that may impact accuracy.
- We often use the example of having a spot; we may be very focused and concerned about it, yet other people will hardly notice it.

Sum up with: 'Body image can change greatly from day to day, hour to hour when the body stays pretty much the same. Body image is contextual rather than reliable information about our bodies': to illustrate ask patients to think about the last week, have there been times when your body image has been noticeably worse, but in fact your body has not changed?

6. We link these distortions to the idea of body image investment – suggesting that because body image may be relatively important to our patients, the more they are focusing on it, and the more distorted our perceptions become.

    Ask patients to reflect on how important weight and shape is to them. Does the level of importance they place on it affect their behaviour or perception? Can they remember a time when shape and weight was less important? How did they feel about their bodies then?

7. Self-defeating behaviours.

    So, in thinking about perception we have discussed some of the factors that may lead to changes in how one experiences one's size. We can call these self-defeating behaviours. One type of self-defeating behaviour is body checking which tends to increase anxiety and has been demonstrated not to be accurate. What other self-defeating behaviours impact our body image?

    Lead a discussion (writing the answers on the flipchart)

- E.g. body checking (feeling for bones), mirror checking, weighing, reassurance seeking, looking at old photos.
- Special attention to body checking behaviours and exercise.

    Highlight that some of these behaviours are considered favourably by society so it is important to consider when they become problematic. Encourage participants to consider how these behaviours may lead to reinforcing their perceptual distortion.

8. Encourage discussion around what participants could do differently in future.
9. Check-out.

Session 6: Body image and identity

For many group members, their low weight, anorexia or eating disorder has become tied up in their identity and it is hard to consider who they are without this. This session aims to encourage participants to reflect on who they are, independent of their bodies. Facilitators should hold in mind that for some participants who are in a pre-contemplation phase, the idea of considering anything positive about their identity is very challenging. For those with chronic histories, they may have very little sense of an identity aside from their eating disorder. For further information on the pie charts mentioned below, please see Waller *et al.* (2007).

1. Welcome and check-in.

2. For many people, their weight has become tangled up in their beliefs about who they are as a person. Indeed, some people may believe that they just need to get to their goal weight and then life can start or they will be happy. Today we will think about our identities and how these relate to our body image. First, we will think about all the aspects that might make up an individual's identity. In a group, ask participants to call out for facilitator to write on flipchart (e.g. gender, role, sexuality, culture, religion, interests, political beliefs, etc.).

3. Part of our identity stems from our roles and what we enjoy doing. What makes us feel good about ourselves? Ask participants to draw a large circle on a piece of paper. Explain that we are going to create a pie chart, where each slice of the pie represents part of their identity. Can they divide up the pie to represent proportionally how much each of these aspects form part of their identity right now? – e.g. mother, daughter, friend, pianist, anorexic/body focused, athlete, teacher, lawyer, student, part time waitress, film buff, theatre goer.

   • How do the divisions look?
   • Does the anorexic or body focused part dominate the pie?
   • What used to be on the pie chart before they got ill?
   • Have other group members learnt something new about someone in the group?
   • For patients who struggle to come up with ideas, facilitators can use closed prompts about interests, people in their lives, etc.

4. Encourage participants to consider how their weight/anorexia helps or hinders the other parts (e.g. 'weight takes away from my role as a daughter because now Mum worries about me all the time and we don't do the fun things we used to').

   • How much fun does life look at the moment?
   • How much does anorexia/eating disorder help/interfere with our other roles?

5. Ask group members to draw another pie chart, this time representing what they would like life to be like and how they would like to see their identity. Would there be new parts or parts from before that have been lost? Encourage reflection between the two charts. What steps can individuals take to get closer to this pie chart? Support individuals to develop manageable steps. For example, someone who wanted to start travelling could go to a language class or watch a foreign language DVD to develop language skills; someone who wants to become more creative could start to crochet.

6. Check-out.

Session 7: Learning to like my body – accepting change

In this session, psycho-education regarding changes in the body with weight gain is given and participants are encouraged to reflect on both physical and emotional changes they may undergo.

1. Welcome and check-in.
2. As part of restoring weight your body is likely to go through a number of changes; this session is for you to think about the changes you are likely to experience and to acknowledge all the functions your body does. Split the group up into two smaller groups and ask the participants to think about and identify:

    *   What did you/do you value about your anorectic/ED shape and size?

        *   E.g. being able to see/feel my bones, concave stomach, thighs not touching, no periods, no emotions, attention for looking unwell, etc.

    *   What didn't you/don't you like about your anorectic/ED shape, size, appearance?

        *   E.g. clothes not fitting properly, being cold all the time, people staring/looking at me, bones showing, thin/flat hair, lanugo hair, flaky/dry skin/nails, pressure sores, grey complexion, dark rings around the eyes, uncomfortable when sitting down, can't look in the mirror, etc.

    Ask the group to feed back to each other (write on flipchart) and discuss their responses.
3. Next, there is a discussion of 'What changes can you expect to happen as you restore weight?'
    It may be helpful to talk/think through the systems of the body:

    Circulatory system: normalising of blood results, blood pressure returning to normal, heart regains muscle and protective fat layer, heart normalises rhythm, healthier distribution of cells, e.g. white and red, reversal of anaemia.

    Lymphatic system: improves immunity to infection. There may be a discussion about the way anorexic patients do not appear to get colds – it is hypothesised that the body still gets ill but doesn't display any symptoms because it has no reserves to address the cold.

    Endocrine system: improved production and distribution of hormones that maintains homeostasis (equilibrium of the internal environment of the body), e.g. temperature of the body, sexual hormones produced and physical changes as a result, e.g. females: hips, breasts, periods, etc.; males: facial hair, hair under the arms and surrounding genitalia, deepening of voice, etc.

    Digestive system: normalising of digestive functioning, normalising of bowel movements, constipation and bloating common.

    Muscular system: initial storing of fat around trunk area, 9–12 months re-distribution of fat/weight and muscle, improvement in the muscles of the body increasing strength and energy.

    The skeleton: improvement in the worsening of osteoporosis/osteopenia.

    Brain: improved concentration, alertness, memory.

Group leaders may also want to bring attention to hair/eyes/skin tone/nails.

4. Group leaders to lead a discussion (write answers on flipchart):
    *   'Why/what is it that's daunting about these changes? What does it mean to you?'
    *   E.g. feels out of control, don't want bodily changes to happen, etc.

5. The final task of the session is to identify and appreciate the functions of the body, working up from the feet to the head. Provide groups with a flipchart-sized piece of paper with a simple body outline sketched on.

    'Your body is amazing. Work from the feet up to the head acknowledging all your body does for you.'

    [Split into smaller groups and come up with functions for as many parts of the body as possible] Some examples are given below, although often participants are able to generate many ideas themselves.

    Feet: enable me to move around/walk/dance/stand/balance, etc.
    Legs: walk around/run/skip/dance/balance/stand, they include the main weight bearing joints of the body, e.g. hips and knees.
    Buttocks: large muscles in the legs and bottom for strength and stability.
    Hips: widening of hips for childbearing/pregnancy and birth in women.
    Abdomen: a protective layer of fat and muscle to support and protect the vital internal organs.
    Shoulders and arms: for fine motor movements, e.g. writing, eating, etc.
    Breasts: feeding babies.
    Neck: stabilising and moving head.
    Brain: cognitive functioning, thinking, talking, planning, moving.
    Face: ears, mouth, nose, eyes (senses).

    Many participants find this a positive and uplifting exercise and become creative and thoughtful in considering functions.

6. Homework:
    *   If using questionnaires, ask participants to complete for final group next week.
    *   To act as a consolidation of the group, in this week's homework, participants are asked to 'Write a letter to a young girl. What would you want to tell her about body image? What are the important messages? How would you like her to feel about herself?' The aim of this letter is to encourage indirectly for patients to consider how they might treat themselves more kindly. It is a challenging homework and therefore it is important to consider all possible obstacles before finishing the group.

7. Check-out.

Session 8: Ending session

The final session aims to review the work covered and the process of the group and, if appropriate, for members to think about what they will take forward from the group.

1. Welcome and check-in.
2. In small or large groups, participants are to think about 'What do I want to take forward from this group?'
    - Encourage them to think about particular strategies they have found helpful.
    - Where will they access support?
3. If appropriate, review questionnaires. Emphasise that there might not be much change in body image dissatisfaction as the person is still gaining weight and the group has been about education rather than change.
4. Homework letters. Elicit the experience of writing the letters from participants. You may not have time to hear all the letters, but invite participants to share some or all of their letter. Participants describe this as a challenging homework so positive feedback is well received. Gently explore with the participants how they can apply some aspects of their letters to themselves.
5. Participants to complete feedback form and give feedback verbally, if wished.
6. Ending and goodbye. Thank participants for their contribution to the group over the weeks.

APPENDIX

Body Image Questionnaire: Communication and Understanding

Please read each of the following items and indicate the number that best reflects your agreement with the sentence:

1.   I feel able to talk about my body image

1	2	3	4	5
Definitely disagree	Mostly disagree	Neither agree nor disagree	Mostly agree	Definitely agree

2.   I have understanding about the general topic of body image

1	2	3	4	5
Definitely disagree	Mostly disagree	Neither agree nor disagree	Mostly agree	Definitely agree

3.   I am able to understand my own body image

1	2	3	4	5
Definitely disagree	Mostly disagree	Neither agree nor disagree	Mostly agree	Definitely agree

4.   I feel listened to about my body image

1	2	3	4	5
Definitely disagree	Mostly disagree	Neither agree nor disagree	Mostly agree	Definitely agree

5.   I am able to tolerate the anxiety I feel about my body image

1	2	3	4	5
Definitely disagree	Mostly disagree	Neither agree nor disagree	Mostly agree	Definitely agree

This measure was developed for use in the evaluation of BodyWise (Mountford *et al.*, 2015).

Recommended reading

Brownell, K. D. (1991). Dieting and the search for the perfect body: where physiology and culture collide. *Behavior Therapy*, 22, 1–12.

Waller, G., Cordery, H., Corstorphine, E., Hinrichsen, H., Lawson, R., Mountford, V. and Russell, K. (2007). *Cognitive Behaviour Therapy for the Eating Disorders: A Comprehensive Treatment Guide*. Cambridge: Cambridge University Press.

Waller, G., Mountford, V., Lawson, R., Gray, E., Cordery, H. and Hinrichsen, H. (2010). *Beating Your Eating Disorder: A Cognitive-Behavioural Self Help Guide for Adult Sufferers and their Carers*. Cambridge: Cambridge University Press.

References

Adelson, Edward H. (2005). *Checkershadow Illusion.* http://web.mit.edu/persci/people/adelson/checkershadow_illusion.html

American Psychiatric Association (APA). (2013). *Diagnostic and Statistical Manual of Mental Disorders* (5th edition). Washington, DC: American Psychiatric Association.

Bamford, B. and Mountford, V. A. (2012). Cognitive behavioural therapy for individuals with longstanding anorexia nervosa: Adaptations, clinician survival and system issues. *European Eating Disorders Review*, 20, 49–59.

Brown, A., Lamey, S. and Mountford, V. A. (2010). *BodyWise: A Psychoeducation Body Image Group*. (Unpublished).

Cash, T.F. (2008). *The Body Image Workbook*. Oakland, CA: New Harbinger Publications.

Dittmar, H., Halliwell, E. and Ive, S. (2006). Does Barbie make girls want to be thin? The effect of experimental exposure to images of dolls on the body image of 5- to 8-year-old girls. *Developmental Psychology*, 42, 283–292.

Fairburn, C. G. (2008). *Cognitive Behavior Therapy and Eating Disorders*. New York: The Guilford Press.

Fairburn, C. G. and Beglin, S. J. (1994). Assessment of eating disorders: Interview or self-report questionnaire? *International Journal of Eating Disorders*, 16, 349–351.

Ferrer-García, M. and Gutiérrez-Maldonado, J. (2008). Body Image Assessment Software: Psychometric data. *Behavior Research Methods*, 40, 394–407.

Fuentes, C. T., Longo, M. R. and Haggard, P. (2013). Body image distortions in healthy adults. *Acta Psychologica*, 144, 344–351.

Key, A., George, C. L., Beattie, D., Stammers, K., Lacey, H. and Waller, G. (2002). Body image treatment within an inpatient program for anorexia nervosa: The role of mirror exposure in the desensitization process. *International Journal of Eating Disorders*, 31, 185–190.

Moody, A. (2013). Adult anthropometric measures, overweight and obesity. Health Survey for England. http://www.hscic.gov.uk.

Morgan, J. F., Lazarova, S., Schelhase, M. and Saedi, S. (2013). 10 session body image therapy: Efficacy of a manualised body image therapy. *European Eating Disorder Review*, 22, 66–71.

Mountford, V. A., Brown, A., Bamford, B., Saiedi, S., Morgan, J. F. and Lacey J. H. (2015). BodyWise: Evaluating a body image group for patients with anorexia nervosa. *European Eating Disorders Review*, 23, 62–67.

Reas, D. L., Whisenhunt, B. L., Netemeyer, R. and Williamson, D. A. (2002). Development of the body checking questionnaire: A self-report measure of body checking behaviors. *International Journal of Eating Disorders*, 31, 324–333.

Reed, J. C., Thompson, J., Brannick, M. T. and Sacco, W. P. (1991). Development and validation of the Appearance State and Trait Anxiety Scale (PASTAS). *Journal of Anxiety Disorders*, 5, 323–332.

Roberts, B., Harris, M. G. and Yates, T. A. (2005). The roles of inducer size and distance in the Ebbinghaus illusion (Titchener circles). *Perception*, 34, 847–856.

Rosewall, J. (2014). Personal communication. 01/09/2014.

Tchanturia, K., Lloyd, S. and Lang, K. (2013). Cognitive remediation therapy for anorexia nervosa: Current evidence and future research directions. *International Journal of Eating Disorders*, 46, 492–495.

Tchanturia, K., Lounes, N. and Holttum, S. (2014). Cognitive remediation in anorexia nervosa and related conditions: A systematic review. *European Eating Disorders Review*, 22(6), 454–462.

Waller, G., Cordery, H., Corstorphine, E., Hinrichsen, H., Lawson, R., Mountford, V. and Russell, K. (2007). *Cognitive Behaviour Therapy for the Eating Disorders: A Comprehensive Treatment Guide*. Cambridge: Cambridge University Press.

Chapter 10

Recovery/discovery oriented group

Kate Tchanturia and Claire Baillie

One of our group members said she found it difficult to connect with the term of recovery, and discovery was working for her better; the beauty of the recovery group is that it can become the discovery group if this is what participants want to call it.

The egosyntonic nature of anorexia nervosa makes increasing and maintaining motivation to recover particularly difficult. As reported by Hay and co-authors (2012), despite the common focus on symptom reduction and the regular failure of this rationale to produce sustained recovery, eating disorder programmes need to look at identifying and minimising the personal and social impairment caused by living with an eating disorder.

In recent years there has been increasing interest in the field of eating disorders on wider definitions of recovery from more individualised perspectives (Turton *et al.*, 2011; Jenkins and Ogden, 2012) and how this affects engagement with treatment (Darcy *et al.*, 2010). There is clinical literature using the recovery star approach in the individual work with different groups of patients with mental health problems. It is considered a helpful tool to introduce in the mental health setting to promote the idea of holistic, person driven rather medical model driven recovery (Slade, 2009a, 2009b).

We decided to adopt the recovery star as a tool for the group work for our residential (step up and day care) programmes. These treatment programmes in our clinic provide support (meals, occupational therapy related to patients five days a week). There is minimal psychology input in the step up programme (only some of the groups). The resource allocation is becoming more problematic in the context of economic pressures on the National Health Service (NHS), therefore we offer psychology led groups to the patients in the residential programmes to give additional support and implement the recovery star approach in a group format.

Much of the ethos of the programme is epitomised in the recovery star model (McKeith and Burns, 2010). The recovery star considers ten domains of everyday life: (1) managing mental health, (2) relationships, (3) physical health and self-care, (4) addictive behaviour, (5) living skills, (6) responsibilities, (7) social networks, (8) identity and self-esteem, (9) work and (10) trust and hope. For each of these areas, the recovery star provides a 'ladder of change', which describes where each patient perceives they are for each outcome area. The patient and their keyworker can identify what level they are at for each area at the beginning of treatment, and revisit these areas in keyworker sessions and the recovery sessions to assess progress and discuss how each area contributes to their recovery.

While the recovery star has provided a useful tool supporting the general recovery based approach, the detailed nature of the individual ladders required adaptation in order to prevent patients becoming overwhelmed and therefore unable to rate themselves in any meaningful way. It was found to be more productive to explore, in the group setting, the various thoughts and feelings associated with each progressive stage, e.g. stuck, accepting help, believing, learning, self-reliance. Patients were then more able to identify where they were currently in different domains and therefore rate themselves on the recovery star.

We have highlighted the way we attempted to develop and modify the recovery star as a tool in working within the recovery oriented group and we hope clinicians and patients in our programme as well as outside of our clinic will find it helpful. Our evaluation of qualitative and quantitative outcomes is encouraging. We discuss available evidence at the end of this chapter.

The Maudsley residential programmes are part of the adult service, and the majority of the patients referred have a long history of illness (mean 7–8 years). The difference between these two residential programmes is that in day care most of the patients are signed up for full recovery (meaning healthy BMI 20–25, going eventually to full time jobs, a healthy lifestyle), and for better coping/adjustment in the community after hospitalization in the step up programme. Criteria for the day care programme are minimum BMI 16 and motivation to get better; in the step up programme (aimed at patients with a chronic course of illness) patients with BMI 14 are accepted (this decision is made in case by case clinical review meetings); the main aim of the step up programme is to support people to return to the community and function without hospitalisation, learning to use support available in the community. We are aware that a long duration of illness affects all aspects of patients' lives such as: work, relationships and leisure time. Treatment aims have often depended upon clinicians' definitions of recovery and current thinking is shifting to incorporate more fully patients' definitions of their recovery. This incorporates, on the one hand, more involvement of service users/patients in decisions about their care plan and on the other hand shifting from a medical recovery model to more flexible definitions of recovery, which has created new challenges both for people who have eating disorders and who treat eating disorders.

Interestingly, when we ask clinicians 'what is the strength of the step up programme?' the consensus is working flexibly with patients' definitions of recovery. When we ask them 'what is the main challenge?' the answer is absolutely the same. This reflects mixed responses to the notion of using a recovery approach in the wider literature, where, as well as significant positive responses, it also generates some anxiety in clinicians specifically with regard to risk, accountability and resources (Davidson *et al.*, 2006).

This chapter will bring together our work with patients who step down/out from the inpatient ward and are getting ready to return to the community. The majority of group members aim to minimise the harm and improve quality of life with gradual return to work and building up a network of social relationships. A pilot group utilising the format of the recovery star model will be discussed addressing a step wise approach to the main areas of life.

This approach is very much in line with the burgeoning 'recovery model' in mental health care, which advocates an individualised, holistic and strength focused approach to treatment and recovery. Further research in this area is warranted, particularly in relation to exploring social and occupational functioning, and exploring how functional impairment changes during the course of standard treatment of eating disorders.

Initial ideas for the recovery group based on the recovery star were continually adapted based on feedback and observation of which tools and approaches seemed most useful both in terms of achieving patient participation and addressing the key areas of difficulty of those recovering from an eating disorder. The first part of this chapter will set out the aims and objectives for the recovery group overall, then explore the structure of the foundation sessions; we will then focus on information about the open sessions, sharing ideas and tools that have been found to be useful from our pilot work. Finally, some outcome data will be reported and some thoughts for future work.

Recovery group protocol

Aim

To raise understanding of the recovery approach and the recovery star model.

Format

Fifteen session cycle with five foundation sessions followed by ten open sessions in the step up programme and four foundation sessions and four open sessions in the day care programme.

We have chosen to describe the step up group format to allow readers to see the outline of more sessions and adapt it for their own clinical needs.

Open sessions are designed to cover areas identified by the group members.

We decided on the number of sessions after piloting in several runs in the step up programme. For example, four foundation sessions were extended to five; we also modified the original recovery star manual to avoid too much attention to detail. With pilot work we have identified the importance of creative components in this group work. For example, creating a group product (recovery tree, positive message posters, Christmas card making, positive logbooks, collages, letters to the future; in the day care programme we developed a treasure box of positive messages, a box of emotional words, a toolbox for social interactions). We also found that after these foundation sessions it is more possible to share responsibility with the group members and be flexible in terms of choosing and delivering topics in the open sessions.

As the foundation sessions progress, it is important to identify particular areas of concern or interest amongst the group in order to set up plans for the open sessions (6–15). This allows time to 'prepare', meaning to find relevant materials, e.g. about social communication to share if the topic of the next session is communication skills (e.g. we successfully adapted the Rozenzweig frustration tolerance test in the social communication session based on research that the first author conducted for the reference Harrison *et al.*, 2011; a PowerPoint presentation can be found at http://www.katetchanturia.com). If the group is focusing on recovery stories the idea would be for everyone (patients and facilitators) to choose and bring a story they would like to share; if an invited speaker is coming all group members have to think in advance of the questions they would like to ask. This approach fosters collaboration and embeds the ethos of equality where patients, facilitators and invited speakers have both expert knowledge and human qualities therefore appreciate time to consider specific questions, needs and find relevant tools/information. Through experience of the group all members gain an appreciation that recovery is not a passive process but one that requires engagement from both sides. This creates more active discussion and role models the non-judgemental acceptance of individual responsibility for the group 'flow'.

This group has two facilitators, in most sessions one from the psychology team and one from the multidisciplinary team (it could be the occupational therapist or charge nurse who are trained and familiar with the protocol and thinking behind it). After establishing the protocol and running the group ten times different members of the clinical team take on the responsibility for running the group under supervision (KT).

The foundation sessions (sessions 1–5)

The main aim of these foundation sessions is to share information about the recovery ethos and the recovery star with the patients (we use the term 'patient' based on patient choice; having completed in-house exploration about how patients preferred to be referred), which helps to provide the wider context of treatment approaches and what this means for group members' personal recovery journeys.

Separating the understanding of the concept from the personal implications seems to reduce resistance and help recovery group members to identify what they can find useful. Exploration of pros and cons are invited in the first session with both facilitators and patients contributing ideas about the potential benefits and limitations of different approaches to treatment. Rather than resistance being 'worked with' by the professionals in the group it is discussed from a 'that's interesting, what would work better for you?' perspective. This validates the patients' experience, knowledge and opinion but also communicates an expectation that positive ideas and experiences are shared. In addition it demonstrates that participation is valued, therefore finding the current topic unhelpful does not mean an individual can opt out of the discussion. Good questions to explore might include:

- What do they want and need?
- What kind of relationship do they have/want with their treatment?
- What level of responsibility can they manage now and how do they want it to be?
- What are their strengths, what aspects of their lives do they take responsibility for and manage well?
- When can they take responsibility for their own recovery, when can they share it with carers/professionals and when do they need to hand it over?

These ideas encourage group participants to break down the notion of responsibility from a black and white either/or concept to a more fluid individual perspective. This can be quite frightening for some patients, particularly those who have recently been treated under the Mental Health Act or those who value the permission that handing over responsibility provides. If patients do not speak about these concerns in the group it may be important for the facilitator/s to name them as potential thoughts and feelings. This provides an invitation for openness and helps reduce any shame someone may be experiencing about feeling this way.

During the development process it was noted that group members had a great influence on the ongoing dynamic of the group towards both responsibility and recovery. At times the majority of the group were ready, willing and able to take back responsibility for themselves and their lives. During these phases the concept of the recovery approach was valued, and discussions enthusiastically explored how it could be applied to various aspects of life. At other times the predominant dynamic was fear of taking responsibility which showed itself in passivity and dismissiveness towards concepts being discussed both verbally and non-verbally. For example, repeatedly responding 'I don't know' or 'I have nothing to say', sitting curled up on a chair with head down or at times seating themselves outside of the group circle. Some of these shifts related to the slow open nature of the group where members could join and leave at any time resulting in significant changes in the membership of the group; however, it could also occur when the membership of the group was fairly stable.

As a facilitator it is important to expect these shifts and not become too enthusiastic or concerned by either. We found it helpful to consider with the group 'why now?', 'what has changed?' Various factors emerged from discussions of this kind during the development process ranging from individual (difficult news, family tensions, changes to accommodation, life stressors, not meeting expectations of self); external (like time of year, Christmas, New Year, start of academic year) or group factors (disagreements between members, anger, envy, feeling judged, criticised or idealised). The facilitators' role at these times is to encourage initial curiosity about what has happened then to support the group to be accepting of differences and similarities of experience within the group. Finally, the facilitators' role is to help the group to identify ways forward both individually and as a group.

An example of utilising the recovery approach to work through a difficult period in the development process occurred when group members became particularly passive, saying little in discussions; we found ourselves asking lots of questions in an attempt to generate some flow to discussions. This occurred just after Christmas and other members of the clinical team had noted ongoing weight loss in most group members. Rather than take responsibility for managing this problem on an individual basis as professional–patient, a decision was made to share these problems with the group. The general trend in weight loss was named alongside the time of year and the reduction in participation in the group. This initially raised anxiety in the group but by adopting the stance of non-judgemental curiosity about what was happening and what could help, it resulted in a very valuable discussion. This included identifying the emotional challenges of managing Christmas with families and the disappointment of starting another year still struggling with an eating disorder. Gradually individuals in the group took a risk to acknowledge this affected how much responsibility they could currently manage around food and meals and that they currently felt unsafe and frustrated at the expectation of being responsible. Most positively, individuals were able to identify they needed more support around these difficulties on a temporary basis. The team involved in meal support acknowledged they could not increase staffing resources but could adapt their expectations of patients. As a group it was concluded that for a few weeks the clinical team would take more responsibility for making decisions about meals and portion sizes and prioritise the supervision of meal preparation and eating rather than their current role of focusing on encouraging normal social interactions and flexibility around meals.

We framed this process for the group within the recovery approach, highlighting the importance of thinking about what group members need and emphasising the ability to *share* responsibility as a strength, especially when it is requested. These discussions were made easier because the majority of the group members involved had attended the foundation sessions, which had provided the opportunity to think about responsibility from both the medical model and the recovery approach; and to consider phases of recovery within the structure of the recovery star. The process could then be understood in recovery star terms, i.e. because much of your resources are being used up managing your mental health (emotions) at the moment, you need more support to manage your physical health (food/weight) to balance this. This example is given before describing the foundation sessions because it demonstrates the importance of shared knowledge, how this can contribute to meaningful discussions and real life application of the ethos of the recovery approach and the recovery star.

Foundation session 1 of 5

This first session has the function of introducing the importance of collaboration and the expectation of participation. This can be achieved by moving around the group and asking each person to say something about their interpretation of what has just been presented. Time may not allow this for every section, therefore choose one to focus on so participants get used to the idea from the start that they will be directly invited to speak at least once in every group if they have not volunteered any opinions or experiences. If all group members are able to engage this is not necessary but in the pilot work it was found to help quieter members who often had extremely valuable contributions. This initial group can set up reasons for the group and introduce the recovery star as a way of working which values collaboration and offers experience based and personal value driven recovery vs medical recovery which is defined more in terms of symptom reduction.

1. Introducing the group.

Presenting research highlighting difficulties in areas other than food/weight and introducing the recovery approach.

2. Psycho-education about research into general and social functioning in eating disorders using the example of one of the outcome measures: Work and Social Adjustment Scale (WSAS) (for more details see Tchanturia *et al.*, 2013a).

It is important to know where in life patients feel their main difficulties are, and that research suggests it is in the domains of work, relationships and leisure on the scale between 0–8 (Tchanturia *et al.*, 2013a). We also share graphs of the main finding from the research paper (Tchanturia *et al.*, 2013b) and ongoing audit at the end of the chapter (Appendix 1).

Useful questions

*   What do you think of this research finding?
*   Are you surprised or have you heard this before?
*   Is your experience the same or different? How?

3. Complete Work and Social Adjustment Scale (WSAS) and invite reflections to the group on why individuals have rated themselves as they have.

Encourage participants to give examples if they can of why their rating makes sense to them.

4. Summary of differences between medical model and recovery model.

The pilot groups utilised a useful summary table highlighting the differences between the two models taken from '100 ways to support recovery' (http://www.mentalhealthrecovery.com/recovery-resources/documents/100_ ways_to_support_recovery1.pdf). We typically give it as a handout with an invitation to respond to the descriptions; it is worth acknowledging to the group that some of the language is technical. During the early stage of development of the recovery group the majority responded with a preference for the recovery model. Even when members stated they did not understand most of the terms they reported that it 'felt' better to read a list including phrases like 'hopes and dreams'; 'understanding'; 'value-centred' as opposed to 'psychopathology' and 'focus on the disorder'.

Having established the recovery approach sounds 'nicer' it was then found useful to explore treatment experiences generally. Experience from the pilot groups suggests that patients understand that inpatient treatment often fits the medical model and can recognise that at certain points in the course of their illness the handing over of control was necessary to feel safe, experience relief from responsibility and to restore physical safety. It is useful to raise the question of how do you begin to take this back in a safe way and how can the recovery approach help with this. This allows the facilitator to encourage the group to begin to think in more realistic terms about what receiving recovery based treatment might feel like.

5.   Introduce recovery star as useful tool.

If time permits the recovery star can be given as a handout and briefly introduced as offering a way to think about different aspects of life and recovery which the group will be based on.

Foundation session 2 of 5

The aims of this session are to focus on exploring what 'recovery' means and understanding the recovery approach further.

1.   Group brainstorm on what 'recovery' means to attendees.

It provides a good opportunity to role model acceptance of difference in terms of meaning, values, hopes, goals. In the spirit of collaboration facilitators would also add their ideas which often prompted further discussion. Facilitators made a conscious choice to speak from personal experience, without sharing details and while maintaining professional boundaries. Participants seemed to value finding out about 'normal' struggles, experiences and challenges. For example, describing the need to take time to adjust after a few years of intense training/working/ living while gaining professional qualifications.

The facilitators can begin to observe with the group any themes which seem to emerge, some that were noted during the pilots include:

- Recovery is a process not a destination.
- It seems to involve feeling a certain way about self or life.
- Different people have different expectations of what recovery means.
- It is about being able to do certain things you have stopped doing or have never done.
- Time is important.
- Hope is important but can also be risky.
- It involves ups and downs.

2.   Explain the recovery approach – give handout and ask for feedback.

Handouts for this session were prepared from the collaboration between patients attending early groups and us to emphasise that responsibility is shared. The document we produced is included at the end of the chapter (Appendix 5).

3.   Explore with the group the implications of the recovery approach for their *individual* recovery process.

At this point the focus is shifted away from the theoretical to specific, and group members are asked to think about how they will personally experience recovery based treatment. This exploration can be varied depending on the areas of importance for the individual members.

Our group members often joined straight from inpatient treatment where they had limited responsibility and choice, e.g. meals chosen from a standard rolling menu, enforced rest periods after meals, restrictions on time off the ward. This session provided an opportunity to acknowledge the hopes and difficulties of moving to treatment where meals were chosen on a weekly basis, shopped for and prepared by staff and patients alongside each other, portions were not exact nor decided by a dietician, fewer restrictions on time, rest was encouraged not enforced and individuals could leave the ward at any time and some had to travel in daily to attend.

Useful questions

- What would be different in the relationship with staff?
- What might it be like to collaborate with staff rather than them making decisions or taking control?
- What will it feel like to be given more choice and responsibility?
- Is there anything worrying about being in recovery based treatment?
- How will you feel taking responsibility for your recovery?
- Do you know what is personally meaningful to your recovery and what values you have?

- What will you need as support while you are making your recovery journey?
- Which aspects of life are important for you to focus on?
- What do you hope for from this treatment?

At this point fears and concerns can be identified and spoken about. In the pilots this usually led to a discussion about phases of recovery, recognising that different approaches and levels of control/responsibility are valuable at different times. This helps keep the discussion balanced so that the medical model is not overly devalued for patients or staff and acknowledges the fluidity of the recovery process.

It may be useful to open up further discussion of shared responsibility at this point using the group as a starting point. For example, all these sessions and discussions provide opportunities for staff to demonstrate recovery based collaboration by being accepting and responsive to opinions, ideas and concerns. Handling shared responsibility for the group in a way which feels manageable to individuals provides an experiential basis for sharing responsibility in other areas of life. For example, everyone has the task of turning up on time, engaging by being curious, sharing experiences/opinions where they can, respecting differences, having ideas and questions. Patients have the specific task of focusing on their personal recovery, taking from sessions what is useful, communicating problems, providing feedback, asking for topics they are interested in to be covered, etc. Facilitators have the specific tasks of supporting patients to use the group, responding to requests for particular topics, bringing expert knowledge where they have it or accessing reliable resources if they don't, etc. Describing this highlights how the group is more effective when everyone takes responsibility for their role and tasks in a collaborative effort.

4. Generate discussion around the recovery approach and in particular its emphasis on the whole person where strengths are acknowledged and issues related to food and weight are only a small part of a bigger picture. Highlight that the recovery approach views social life, leisure, relationships, identity, trust and hope as important areas to focus on.

Encourage group members to share the impact the eating disorder has had on these areas of their lives, what they may have missed out on or lost and what they would like to discover or regain.

5. Link to recovery star.

It is important to keep linking discussions back to the recovery star highlighting how the group overall will be using it to keep a wide perspective on recovery. This helps patients keep it in mind so they are better prepared for the later session where they are asked to rate themselves on it.

Foundation session 3 of 5

The main aim of this session is to provide a reflective space encouraging engagement in activities with the objective of supporting individuals to develop a picture of their own recovery and what it means to them.

1.   Reminder of last session and idea of recovery as a broad concept.

The facilitator can highlight that the previous session looked at recovery more generally and that this group is shifting the focus towards what this might mean for them as individuals.

2.   Complete a mind map to visualise what makes up recovery for an individual.

Facilitators will need examples of mind maps to show the group what they could look like and to provide some blank versions for people to use if they want to. In the pilot groups facilitators also completed mind maps for themselves resulting in five to ten minutes of quiet focused working time to encourage more reluctant participants to engage since facilitators are also taken up in the task, creating a 'have a go' attitude to group tasks.

3.   Everyone is then invited to share their experience of completing a mind map of recovery, how easy or difficult they found it, any revelations, surprises or learning, the thoughts and feelings evoked. The experiences from the pilot group suggest this can be a very varied discussion which at times prompted strong emotions for participants which included anger and disappointment in themselves, immense sadness for what has been lost to the illness as well as hope and optimism.

Throughout all the sessions the emphasis is not just on the completion of tasks and use of tools but the *experience* of trying to use them. Facilitators' questions and contributions can emphasise curiosity about this and acceptance of difference in the group where participants may span a wide range of stages of recovery.

4.   Identify a metaphor which represents what an individual is aiming for in their own recovery to encourage hope and support motivation.

This could be an image, a song lyric, a poem or an object. The idea is to provide a shortcut to remind and motivate the individual to continue working towards their own individual goals of recovery.

 Responses from the groups suggest this can be quite difficult for some participants. It was accepted that it may be important to allow this to take time, to develop the right individual metaphor. It may be best to approach this as planting the seed of an idea, encouraging individuals throughout later sessions to keep thinking about what might represent their recovery. The idea is that if an individual takes time to discover their metaphor then it is likely to have more personal meaning for them.

While considering individual metaphors it may also be worthwhile to be developing a shared group metaphor for recovery. It was from this session in the first pilot that one particular group developed the idea of a tree of recovery which needed roots to provide a foundation for growth in the branches and leaves. In a series of open sessions the group collaborated on representing this tree in a piece of art for the step up room. Other groups have written inspirational words for recovery on stones kept in a bowl in the room.

5.   Reintroduce link to recovery star.

As before link the discussion and themes back to the recovery star which will be used as a tool to think about recovery in the context of a range of life domains. Inform group that the next session will focus on understanding the ten domains of the recovery star.

Foundation session 4 of 5

The main focus is on explaining and exploring the recovery star (see Appendix 2 and Appendix 5).

1.   Show recovery star.

Give each person a copy of the recovery star.

2.   Explore each of the ten dimensions and brainstorm what activities/issues/ skills might be assigned to each dimension.

In the initial pilot group this was one part of a session; however, it usually took up the whole time therefore the foundation sessions were increased from four to five to allow for this. Experiences varied: at times the discussion started quickly and ideas were generated rapidly, at others it could take ten minutes just to decide which domain to discuss first. The format involves having the titles of all ten domains written up on flip chart paper stuck on walls around the room:

1.   Managing mental health.
2.   Relationships.
3.   Physical health and self-care.
4.   Addictive behaviour.
5.   Living skills.
6.   Responsibilities.
7.   Social networks.
8.   Identity and self-esteem.

9. Work.
10. Trust and hope.

Facilitators can invite the group to start in a number of ways – start with the domain you have most ideas about, or the one that you face most challenges in or the one you find easiest.

If the group really struggles to get started the facilitator/s may have to be more directive and choose one domain giving some ideas of activities or issues which might be involved in it. It is worth, however, tolerating a bit of a struggle initially in order to maintain the ethos of collaboration where participants' engagement is both necessary and valued – this is about how *they* make sense of these domains rather than being *told* what these domains involve.

Facilitators then take an active collaborative role in moving around the room writing ideas under particular domains as directed by the person who offered them or by asking which domains it should be applied to, suggesting where ideas may fit more than one category, e.g. lack of trust affects relationships, social networks and mental health. In this way the facilitator supports the group to begin viewing the domains as interconnected.

It can be useful to observe with the group what they do or don't do with this discussion. For example, we noticed the group had not spoken about the domain of physical health and self-care. Nearing the end of the session when prompted to think about what aspects of life might come under that domain the group could not identify anything. We took a risk to tell the group of our surprise and name the 'elephant in the room', that for them this was a key area in eating disorder recovery as it included weight monitoring, learning to feed self adequately, balanced nutrition, keeping self safe by permitting physical health checks, blood tests, bone scans, etc. Only after this were group members able to name that on reflection they were actually aware of it, that it seemed too obvious to talk about but more importantly they acknowledged it felt scary and threatening.

3.   Highlight how each dimension overlaps with others – none are discrete and isolated.

This can help to foster hope in that working on one area can positively influence other domains, in the same way strengths in one domain can be drawn upon to help in areas of difficulty. It was also found useful to take a few minutes to reflect on which categories attracted the most thoughts and ideas and to begin thinking with the group about which domains should be covered in the open sessions. For example, after one pilot group brainstorm it was recognised that self-esteem and identity was an area of particular interest and challenge. Also that having self-esteem was not the same as having a sense of identity therefore the open sessions could usefully explore both separately in two connected sessions.

4. End by explaining they will be invited next week to complete a star for themselves.

It is important to emphasise that the next session will spend time looking at what different ratings may mean and strategies to help individuals rate themselves.

Foundation session 5 of 5

The focus of this final foundation session is to increase understanding of how to use the ladder to self-rate on the recovery star and for each to complete their own star.

This session can be particularly challenging for participants and facilitators, partly due to the known detail focus in individuals with anorexia nervosa (Lang *et al.*, 2014) which complicates and over-analyses the process. Difficulty could also relate to resistance to self-ratings due to high levels of perfectionism and self-criticism (see Chapter 6 and Lloyd *et al.*, 2014) resulting in it feeling like a painful, shaming process. The structure of this session is designed to mediate against a problematic detail focus. The recovery approach itself, with its emphasis on recognising strengths, helps to mediate self-criticism, and facilitators can also help participants consider where they are being too harsh in their ratings.

1. Recap on previous week.
2. Introduce the ladder of change and the five stages – Stuck, Accepting help, Believing, Learning, Self-reliance.

The aim is to encourage discussion without getting caught up in the details of the ladder, in fact the ten point ladders which accompany the recovery star workbook we have tested only once with the first group and we realise that it creates very detailed discussions and deviates the focus from the 'bigger picture'. We tried with our groups to move away from detail by sharing that for us it is hard to read through all the ten point descriptions of any ladder and it might be more useful to focus on the overall themes of each stage.

The brainstorm is supported by having a large blank version of the ladder drawn out to be filled in during the session (see Figure 10.1 below).

The group can then be encouraged to identify how they might be thinking and feeling if they were currently in the stage being discussed. After a few pilot groups had been run, this amalgamation was shared with the current group for review and discussion and an interesting alternative to the ladder emerged from this lively thoughtful discussion. Instead of a process through stuck, accepting help, learning and self-reliance the group began to view their process as journeying through *surviving*, *coping*, *managing*, *living* then *enjoying* various aspects of their lives. These innovative ideas and inspirational moments emerged out of collaboration between professionals and patients as experts together supported by the recovery approach and the recovery star tool.

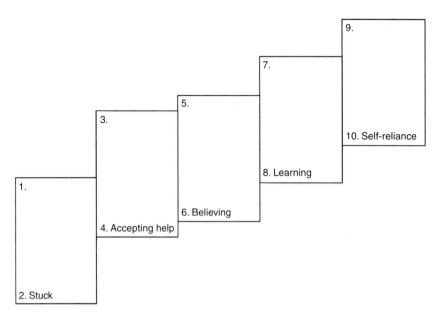

Figure 10.1 The ten point ladder of change

3.   Recovery star is individually completed.

Having prepared group members and allowed them to provide their own structure and rating scale, based on the kinds of experiences they may recognise, they are asked to rate themselves against this for each domain. Similar to the mind maps, facilitators also completed their own recovery star.

   Experience from our groups suggests that some will still struggle with getting lost in details, will feel confused or unclear, or describe diverse feelings. For example, one person struggled to rate self-esteem and identity as she described a strong sense of who she was but had low self-esteem. This prompted others to share similar dilemmas about rating themselves as they identified both strengths and challenges in certain domains. It can be worth cautioning the group against a sense of needing to get the rating right/perfect and encouraging the alternative of going with gut instinct of what feels *about* right for this domain for you *at the moment*. Also highlight that this is about personal experience not measuring themselves against a standard set for them by professionals.

4.   Reflection of what group members have learned and identified from completing their own recovery star – what are the areas of strengths, where are the areas to develop, what help might be needed, are there transferable skills?

If time permits it can be worth sharing that one of the ideas suggested by the recovery star is that a balance across domains would lead to a rounded shape if all the rating points are linked up in a join the dots way. Sharp points and troughs, unbalanced star shapes can suggest that too many resources are being put into one domain at the expense of another. For example, excelling in the work domain at the expense of a social network or mental health. In this way the recovery star can be used to give hints and ideas about how to redirect resources and strengths to promote balanced recovery and identify possible ways forward. It also highlights that everyone has limited resources and has to consider how to share them across different areas of their life rather than assume they can give 100 per cent to all areas all the time.

Foundation sessions conclusions

The knowledge sharing, group formulation of ideas about recovery, introduction to shared responsibility for the group and the meaningful use of the recovery star as a self-rating tool are valuable components from the foundation sessions. As more groups are run the learning continues and it is likely the format will be revised further. Each clinician will need to consider which aspects they will find most useful to emphasise, where time for discussion is valuable and where information can just be given.

The open sessions (sessions 6–14)

These are to be designed to respond to the identified needs of the patients who are attending the group.

This can include bringing tools, strategies and materials. We kept encouraging patients to bring their knowledge and experiences as well as particular questions they had.

This can incorporate inviting guest speakers from the multidisciplinary team including recovery workers, as well as people from the wider clinical community and external agencies as appropriate. It is hard to describe the ten open sessions as they are different every time and can cover a range of issues. For example, in different groups we had invited guests: dietician, librarian, representative from job centre, someone who had depression, person with experience of eating disorder, researcher doing brain imaging, medical doctor specialising in sleep disorders; it really depends on the group and what members will find useful.

More examples from past groups:

- Recovered persons attending for Question and Answer or to share their stories.
- Reading a range of recovery stories and discussing them (in the reference section we have included helpful materials).
- How to build and maintain a social network (materials based on social psychology and communication based research but after brief introduction we encourage group discussion and experiential learning in addition to

psycho-education – we try to give handouts to read outside of the group and use group time for the discussions).

- Building a toolkit to cope with difficult times (large number of handouts and toolkits developed by group members; some examples are included at the end of this chapter, Appendix 5). In this group we encourage patients to take responsibility for typing the work done by group members from the clipboard and disseminating amongst the peers and group facilitators.
- Watching body language videos with the aim to improve communication styles. Again discussion and finding key points in the group space is important (https://www.ted.com/talks/amy_cuddy_your_body_language_shapes_who_you_are.).
- Exploring addictive behaviours and how to resist temptation.
- How to write a CV and present yourself at interviews. In these sessions we have used the group expertise and experience when it was possible. Some group members might not have any experience with job interviews; many of them feel they have no skills at all. Some of the group members still have part time or even full time jobs after the hospital programme and without realising it have lots of important points to contribute and share with others.
- Dietician invited for question and answer session. This session could be used very effectively when group members plan and prioritise questions which are most important.
- Individually group members have dietician input but preparation for this one off group has therapeutic importance. For example, what questions are generated and which ones are common, how to use time and tap into most relevant themes.
- Sleep hygiene – the charge nurse facilitated this session. This session relates strongly to the self-health care domain and raises awareness of a theme which could be forgotten and yet has high relevance.
- Health care – ward manager with nursing background invited to facilitate this session.
- Time management again more linked to the 'bigger picture' of recovery.
- Developing a metaphor for the recovery journey and creating something to represent this (the recovery tree). In different groups we try to explore the most relevant format to create a powerful metaphor to ground the work we did for 15 sessions in the form of art/story/logbook/object.
- Making Christmas cards to sell in the art gallery. This is very small scale 'fundraising' but involves the group working together, having a goal, managing produced work, after money raised managing a small budget and how to spend it. The importance of this session was that it is an ecologically valid real life scenario simulation of social decision making in the group in the safe therapeutic environment.
- Applying for grants to support recovery activities (Maudsley Charity had several calls).

- Mindfulness (one off sessions delivered by experts and their thoughts, tailoring it for eating disorders).
- Creating an image of an inspirational place.
- Vocational opportunities – inviting occupational therapy colleagues, and when possible outside speakers from job centres.
- Research and novel findings in treatment of eating disorders. In our department patients participate in a variety of the projects. Frequent questions are: What are novel research findings in treatment studies for anorexia? What do we know about how the brain works when a person has eating disorders? What we know about recovery from eating disorders?
- Recovery lecture – in South London and Maudsley NHS Trust we have a recovery college and, depending what the group would like to hear about, it can be a person with experience of recovery from mental illness or a recovery lecturer with clinical experience.
- Applying for recovery/research grants – as scientist-practitioners we apply for research grants and increasingly need consultations with our patients. Several of our patients express interest in reading our research proposals and contributing to it. From time to time we bring to the attention of the group members the opportunities we have.
- Assertive communication skills.

Recovery stories

The recovery approach emerged out of learning and feedback from users of mental health services. It seeks to achieve a balance of power between professionals and patients and aims to instil and sustain hope; learning together from various narratives of recovery helps to support these objectives. We found useful resources from the Scottish Recovery Network and the b-eat website including a collection of recovery stories and guidance for those wishing to share their own recovery story (see resources at the end of the chapter, p. 215). The pilot group utilised this collection of recovery stories in a couple of open sessions which took the format:

1. Each person is asked to select a story to read and is informed that they will be asked to give a brief summary and identify one useful thing about recovery that they took from it.
2. Choose one to read (including facilitators).
3. Allow five to ten minutes to read the narrative.
4. Each person then takes a turn in:
    - giving a brief description of the journey they have read about
    - sharing with the group one thing they found useful/helpful from the narrative.
5. Time for open discussion and reflections of the various recovery journeys.

6.   Facilitator draws group to a close by summarising any themes from discussion.

Many NHS trusts are developing recovery resources, involving StaR (support time and recovery) workers or setting up recovery colleges; these are good places to find people willing to speak about their recovery. This route is useful since it often means the recovered person has received some training and has access to support; other possible sources include Beat (eating disorders charity) as well as previous patients from your own service.

We often invite people with experience of mental illness (not only eating disorders because group members found it very useful to hear different experiences). The speakers are sharing something very personal, meaningful and precious for them and the facilitator needs to safeguard their emotional well-being throughout this process. In the early groups this took the form of an initial meeting with the facilitators and the recovery worker to identify what felt important and/or difficult to share. The facilitators could then use clinical skills to deflect the group away from difficult topics if the recovered person seemed to be struggling to manage this. This preparatory meeting can also help by anticipating any difficult responses they may face from group members. For example, it was useful to sensitively caution against being too evangelical about what worked for them and highlight that it is more useful to invite the group to take what they find useful from the narrative. From this meeting it was identified that an interview approach may work well. As a result group members were invited to submit questions anonymously in advance, which second author CB adapted and organised into questions which were used to 'interview' the recovered person in the session. Following this, group members gave feedback that they learned a lot from hearing how Claire had rephrased some questions, that they knew what they wanted to ask but had not known how to go about asking it in a sensitive way. Feedback from the recovery worker was that it had felt comfortable and easy.

In general all recovery group members were respectful of speakers, grateful for their honesty, openness and willingness to share their recovery journeys. The response in these sessions was often a renewed openness from group members, a depth of emotion and connection between those still suffering and those who had suffered with the possibility of real hope emerging. In summary, from our point of view it seems very worthwhile to include this in the open sessions.

Session 15

In this session we typically include a review of the 15 sessions overall, encouraging patients to identify what they have learned, found helpful and how they may use information positively from these sessions to support their ongoing recovery journey.

Open sessions conclusions

Unlike other groups we run, the flexible, varied nature of the open sessions meant those attending for longer or returning to treatment avoided having to attend groups presenting the same information they had received before. The ethos of shared responsibility reduces the pressure on the facilitator to keep coming up with new topics or tools while providing added variety, making this variety more manageable.

Evaluation of the programme before and after the group

Outcome measures

We try to audit outcomes for all groups to generate evidence and benchmark benefits of the group work, try to critically evaluate what works and what does not. For this reason we outlined what we use currently for the recovery group evaluation.

Work and Social Adjustment Scale (WSAS; Mundt *et al.*, 2002; see Appendix 1)

The WSAS is a simple five-item self-report scale developed to measure degree of functional impairment. The items cover different areas of functioning: ability to work, home management, social leisure, private leisure and ability to form and maintain close relationships. Each item is rated on a 9-point Likert-type scale, ranging from 0 (no impairment) to 8 (very severe impairment). The maximum total score is 40, with higher scores representing greater impairment. The WSAS has demonstrated good internal consistency and test-retest reliability (Mundt *et al.*, 2002). We found that people with eating disorders (ED) particularly adults with anorexia nervosa have significant problems with social, private leisure and relationship items (Tchanturia *et al.*, 2013a, 2013b; Harrison *et al.*, 2014).

Motivational Ruler (see Appendix 3)

This readiness ruler has been adapted from the one developed by Rollnick *et al.* (2008) for use as a tool in motivational interviewing. This is a simple two-item self-report scale which assesses the importance of change to the patient and the patient's confidence in their ability to change. Each item is rated on an 11-point Likert-type scale, ranging from 0 (change is least important/low ability to change) to 10 (change is most important/high ability to change).

Patient Satisfaction Questionnaire (see Appendix 4)

This is a 15-item self-report questionnaire which aims to assess the patients' experience of the programme and elicit areas which they consider to be helpful as well as areas for development.

APPENDIX I

As can be seen in the table below (for more details, see Tchanturia *et al.*, 2013a), the self-reported work and social adjustment scale shows the main problems in self-reported functioning. The most difficulties are in social leisure and close relationships. These results were replicated in the Harrison *et al.*, 2014 study on the larger group of patients, again showing highest impact of eating disorder in the relationship and social leisure domains. This measure and session about Work and Social Adjustment Scale (WSAS) can facilitate discussions and useful explorations about how these domains could be improved with or without an eating disorder.

Table 10.1 WSAS between-groups comparisons

Variable	AN group n = 77 M (SD)	HC group n = 83 M (SD)	Test statistics t (df), p	Effect size (d)
WSAS total	25.31 (8.93)	0.72 (2.8)	−23.86 (158), <0.001*	3.8
Work	5.26 (2.56)	0.24 (0.97)	−16.64 (158), <0.001*	2.65
Home management	3.53 (2.63)	0.13 (0.62)	−11.43 (158), <0.001*	1.82
Social leisure	6.26 (1.85)	0.17 (0.58)	−28.59 (158), <0.001*	4.54
Private leisure	4.83 (2.47)	0.08 (0.42)	−17.26 (158), <0.001*	2.75
Close relationships	5.43 (2.08)	0.1 (0.46)	−22.77 (158), <0.001*	3.62

Note: * $p < 0.001$.

The WSAS scores show reductions in the step up programme (Figure 10.2), but, as can be seen for the four years, it varies a lot. Over time we have more difficult/complex patients (time one scores are higher, as we can see); time spent in the step up programme is shorter, very much defined by the economic climate. One thing which is consistent in Figure 10.2 below is that patients report a reduction of the impairment most of the time.

We try to address problems in the social/communication area in different ways. Here we are showing one of the examples of the handout generated in one of the recovery group sessions: where can people network?

The group identified problems with communication and, after long admissions, not having a social life and having problems getting back into the community. We had a long discussion about exploring opportunities to meet new people (Figure 10.3). Group members flagged up that they don't think about it, and having thinking space and strategies to explore opportunities of how to meet people was useful.

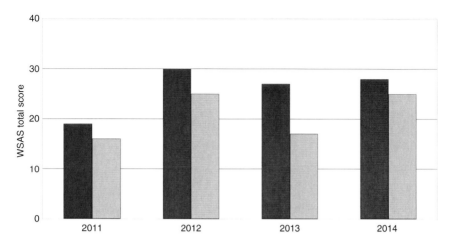

Figure 10.2 Work and Social Adjustment Scale results before recovery group and after the group. Bars represent how patients rate themselves in time 1 and time 2 assessments

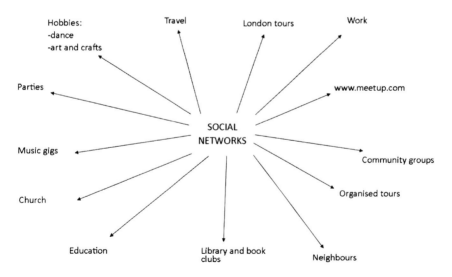

Figure 10.3 How to meet new people

APPENDIX 2

Step up recovery ladder: eating disorders

Developed from group discussions in recovery star groups 2011–2013

Step up recovery ladder: eating disorders		
1	This works for me	Black and white
	Satisfied	Don't care
	Invincible – it won't happen to me	I don't have any problems
	Not seeing any other way	Feeling alone
	Not thinking anything could be different	Hopeless
		Too daunting
	Unhelpful risks	Angry
	Denial	I don't have any control so change is not possible
	Self-destruct	
	Comfortable	Lack of action/concern
	Fear – of being stuck/of changing	I don't have any problems
	Disappointment – self/others	I want to change but don't know how
	Familiar habits = safe	Isolation
	Angry/frustrated – self/others	Why is everyone talking to me about this?
	Feeling you are letting others down	
2	Resisting	Leave me alone
3	Not sure how to ask for help	Beginning to recognise own fragility – it could happen to me
	Wanting to prove I can do it on my own	
		Helpful risks
	Fluid/changeable	Beginning to trust others
	Powerless	Starting to talk to others
	Shame	Seeing the bigger picture
	Loss of dignity	Ambivalence
	Change feels unfair	Listening to others' concerns and viewpoints
	Trust	
	Feeling childlike	Considering life consequences of staying the same/changing
4	Resentment	
	Accepting there is a problem	Acknowledging unhelpfulness of current situation
	Courage	
	Expectations – self/others	Awareness of impact on self and others
	Desire to do it perfectly	
	Contemplating help	Building trust
	Fear of judgement	Beginning to accept/ask for some help
	Feeling a fraud	Struggle to let others help – want to do it my way
	Beginning to see how it could work for you	
		Asking for advice
		Exploring opportunities
		Choices and options

5	Beginning to trust self	Realising I don't always need it (illness/
	Accessing support	support)
	Actively making changes	HOPE
	Working with others	Accepting the need to take
	Hoping for hope	responsibility
	Facing challenges	Beginnings of optimism and hope
	Adventurous and curious about own	Beginning to want change
	potential and possibilities	Faith in others
	Believing in past successes	Changes enforced by others can
	Believing change is possible	provide trials and experiments
	Believing in learning	Noticing small changes
6	Recognising and accepting need for	Growing hope
	support	Feeling better in self
		Developing hope/confidence
		Every mistake is a treasure

7	Realising I don't always need it	Stepping out on my own
	Learning I can trust myself	Challenging self
	Building evidence	Drawing from previous experiences
	Every mistake is still a treasure	Not trying to change everything
	Growing awareness	at once
	Learning to recognise the red flags	Learning your limits
	Learning to know myself	Learning to tolerate mistakes
	Let go of 'I should'	Pacing yourself
	Learning my limitations	Developing responsibility
	Separating my identity from the	Getting to know yourself
	illness	Creating yourself
8	Acknowledging the battle inside	Practice

9	Knowing when you need help, how	Flexibility
	and where to access it	Managing unpredictability
	Drawing on learning	Knowing how to cope
	Trusting own judgement	Always learning
	Flexibility in thinking	Managing
	Good knowledge of strengths	Reasonable expectations of self
	and limits	Reasonable reliance on self
	Managing responsibility	Knowing how, when and who to seek
10	Recognising struggles and really	support from
	accepting the need for support	

	Recovery star ladder	**Step up ladder**
9 to 10	Self-reliance	Enjoying
7 to 8	Learning	Living
5 to 6	Believing	Managing
3 to 4	Accepting help	Coping
1 to 2	Stuck	Surviving

APPENDIX 3

Motivational ruler

1. **Importance to change**. Ask yourself the following question: How important is it for you to change? What are your desires, reasons and needs for change? What score would you give yourself out of 10?

0   1   2   3   4   5   6   7   8   9   10

2. **Ability to change**. Ask yourself the following question: How confident are you in your ability to change? What score would you give yourself out of 10?

0   1   2   3   4   5   6   7   8   9   10

APPENDIX 4

PATIENT SATISFACTION QUESTIONNAIRE
– HELP US IMPROVE OUR CLINICAL SERVICE

Please help us improve our step up service by answering some questions about the care you have received. We are interested in your honest opinions, whether they are positive or negative – all responses will be kept confidential and anonymous. Please answer all the questions. Thank you very much: we really appreciate your help.

Circle your answers:

1. How would you rate the quality of the clinical service you have received?

4	3	2	1
Excellent	Good	Fair	Poor

2. Did you get the kind of clinical service you wanted?

1	2	3	4
No, definitely not	No, not really	Yes, generally	Yes, definitely

3. To what extent has our clinical service met your needs?

4	3	2	1
Almost all of my needs have been met	Most of my needs have been met	Only a few of my needs have been met	None of my needs have been met

4. If a friend were in need of similar help, would you recommend our clinical service to him or her?

1	2	3	4
No, definitely not	No, not really	Yes, generally	Yes, definitely

5. How satisfied are you with the amount of help you have received?

1	2	3	4
Quite dissatisfied	Indifferent or mildly dissatisfied	Mostly satisfied	Very satisfied

6. Do you think that staff have been able to listen to and understand you during your treatment?

4	3	2	1
Yes, to a great extent	Yes, to some extent	No, not really	No, not at all

7. Have the services you received helped you to deal more effectively with your problems?

4	3	2	1
Yes, they helped a great deal	Yes, they helped	No, they really didn't help	No, they seemed to make things worse

8. Would you say that you and the staff were in agreement about the goals of treatment?

4	3	2	1
Yes, all of the time	Yes, some of the time	No, not really	No, none of the time

9. In an overall, general sense, how satisfied are you with the service you have received?

4	3	2	1
Very satisfied	Mostly satisfied	Indifferent or mildly dissatisfied	Quite dissatisfied

10. If you were to seek help again, would you come back to our service?

1	2	3	4
No, definitely not	No, I don't think so	Yes, I think so	Yes, definitely

11. Can you tell us which interventions you received were the most helpful?

12. Can you tell us which interventions you received were the least helpful?

13. Can you tell us what was good about the service?

14. Can you tell us what could be improved about the service?

15. Do you have any other comments to make about the service you received?

APPENDIX 5

The patients and clinical team in the recovery star group produced this document for newly arrived patients in the step up treatment programme where we started these recovery groups. This is one of the examples, because we have several hand-outs and information leaflets produced collaboratively to help newly admitted patients.

The step up to recovery ethos

The step up to recovery programme is based on a particular approach to the treatment of mental health problems called the recovery approach. The recovery approach is being used increasingly by a range of services to support individuals with a range of problems including addictions, escaping domestic violence and mental and physical health issues. The current increase in its use is a response to service user feedback about their experience of treatment but the ideas behind it have been around for a long time.

The recovery approach views recovery as an individual process or journey which everyone goes through following a setback in life. The recovery approach is not a model or method of treatment provided by expert professionals to non-expert patients. It is designed to support the person and assumes individuals are competent to manage their life; therefore it gives the responsibility for recovery to the person who is recovering rather than the professionals around them. Recovery is seen as a process of self-discovery and growth where the recovering person is at the centre of the process; the process involves focusing on the whole person rather than just their diagnosis and symptoms. The person recovering is seen as the expert on their life, their beliefs and values, their goals and hopes for an acceptable quality of life. A core belief of the recovery approach is that it is possible for an individual to regain a meaningful life despite significant setbacks.

A key element of the recovery approach is to foster hope and resilience in the person who is recovering. This means recognising and accepting problems or areas of difficulty which require support or where change is needed to manage illness and take back control over life. This is balanced with identifying and appreciating skills and strengths; individuals are encouraged to trust their abilities and have real hope for the future. During recovery it is important that opportunities for success are facilitated, experienced and celebrated. Recovering involves making a personal commitment to change, finding role models who inspire hope, and looking forward with optimism. Instead of avoiding risk, the recovery approach encourages people to utilise support networks to manage dilemmas and crises and views 'mistakes' as valuable learning opportunities. Resilience helps in this process of personal growth; by taking positive risks and learning new ways of managing unfamiliar feelings, confidence and self-esteem can be rebuilt.

The recovery approach offers a different view of mental health problems; it offers individuals the opportunity to think again about the experiences associated with having an eating disorder. Recovering from a serious mental health problem, such as an eating disorder, is not a stigma to be ashamed of, it is a significant accomplishment which gives people unique skills, strengths, knowledge and insight which those who have not experienced it do not have.

The Mental Health Foundation (http://www.mentalhealth.org.uk/help-information/mental-health-a-z/R/recovery/) suggests that recovery is supported by:

- good relationships;
- financial security;
- satisfying work;
- personal growth;
- the right living environment;
- developing one's own cultural or spiritual perspectives;
- developing resilience to possible adversity or stress in the future;
- being believed in;
- being listened to and understood;
- getting explanations for problems or experiences;
- having the opportunity to temporarily resign responsibility during periods of crisis.

There are a number of tools which support patients and staff to adopt a recovery approach. The step-up to recovery programme uses the **recovery star** tool which covers the following ten areas:

1. Managing mental health.
2. Physical health and self-care.
3. Living skills.
4. Social networks.
5. Work.
6. Relationships.
7. Addictive behaviour.
8. Responsibilities.
9. Identity and self-esteem.
10. Trust and hope.

APPENDIX 6

Feedback comments from Step Up audit: people discharged 2011–2013
(Each bullet point is a comment from a different person)
Can you tell us which interventions you received on the ward were most helpful?

* listening to other patients helped me;
* key-working sessions;
* having a daily structure and regular eating times;
* OT (occupational therapy) – pottery, cooking, being made to come in a couple of weekends;
* the skills, e.g. how to cook a meal, to know what is appropriate on the portion side;
* Being put back in the dining hall when step up wasn't working and then being given a second chance. Coming in weekends for a while even though I was on step up. Some staff not giving up on me and helping me to find ways to beat the illness and change my behaviour.
* psychology sessions, OT, psychology groups, family therapy;
* psychology.

Can you tell us which interventions you received on the step up were least helpful?

* some group discussions repetitive;
* some groups felt less relevant to me;
* book group;
* Being around anorexics frightened me because I had been in those shoes. I lost weight and noticed all those anorexic signs coming back.
* meal support;
* one to ones with staff.

Can you tell us what was good about our service?

* good understanding of difficulties encountered;
* The staff's attitude towards the patients. This programme allows you to develop as a person and doesn't just concentrate on the ED.
* being heard;
* structured groups/meals out/routine;
* Personal responsibility given to us. High level of individuality. Some of the groups. Variety of places and things to eat at lunches. Flexibility in food as time went on. Friendly staff.
* Talk about things other than EDs – often the best distraction rather than constantly talking about problems. Having some influence over how programme

is run. The staff cared and didn't give up – I am such an all over the place person I find it hard to communicate.
- The staff I found extremely proactive, and have helped a great deal. Again the structure and regular eating helped a lot.
- tailored to meet individual needs, specialised team; experienced;
- staff intervention regarding self-injury.

Can you tell us what could be improved about the service?

- More one to one time.
- Staff communication, clear guides about what Step Up is, how it works and having a clear plan of how they can help you as an individual.
- Less groups in the morning. More psychology on step-up. Evening meals cooked rather than ward food. Planned social activities aren't very attractive/appealing.
- I think the funding and time could have been more plentiful as with all health services.

Do you have any other comments to make about the service you received?

- It's inspirational being around someone who has actually recovered. Rosemary is my keyworker and she's been brilliant, really helping me broaden my scope of the 'world' outside of the ED.
- A big thank you – it has helped me make a lot of changes and I have also met wonderful people – staff and patients. My main worry is that my brain hasn't made the same progress as my weight and I would have liked some more psychology to try to help that.
- You are helping a lot of people and that is amazing.
- Feels that at the beginning of treatment on step-up, the lack of structure and long periods of nothing to do made it difficult for me. I found myself getting very down and depressed and feeling quite isolated. I needed more help/support in structuring my afternoons from the outset.
- Although I have been on treatment longer than expected I am very grateful to have been given this opportunity and time and feel that the service I have received has really helped me.
- I am truly grateful to the service for all the help I have received and hugely improving the quality of my life. With support I have made changes and challenged my illness. However, I feel that a firmer approach would have been helpful to ensure I was able to get the most from my treatment – particularly during my time on step up. I think this would have helped me to consistently make progress and meet the goals of my treatment fully.

Final thoughts

In this chapter we presented our work with challenging patients in the challenging times moving from hospital admissions (most of them have been ill for a long time and have long repeated admissions in inpatient programmes) to the community with the idea of coping better with illness and life demands. Recovery is a very difficult and highly relative concept, as we tried to highlight in the chapter. In the medical model 'normalising' nutrition, body mass index, physical and psychological health is the leading goal but clinical reality sometimes is to modify this goal and think how it is possible to keep someone with a long history and severe anorexia outside of the hospital with a reasonable quality of life; how we can support and help them with skills to cope with life outside of the institution; how we can work motivationally on their strengths and resources; how we can create hope, positive thinking and confidence. When we think about future developments of this work these are the questions we have in mind and constantly ask ourselves and think collaboratively with patients. From our point of view the strengths of the recovery group are thinking *together with*, not for, the patients who have an eating disorder.

Acknowledgements

We would like to thank our colleagues, Amy Brown, Nikola Kern, Lynn StLouis from South London and Maudsley Eating Disorder Adult Service in support, ideas and valuable input in development of this group protocol and practical input in the implementation.

Resources

Beat – http://b-eat.co.uk.
Pat Deegan – http://www.patdeegan.com/.
Mental Health Foundation – http://www.mentalhealth.org.uk/.
Devon Recovery – http://www.recoverydevon.co.uk/.
WRAP – http://www.mentalhealthrecovery.com/.
Scottish Recovery Network – http://www.scottishrecovery.net/.
Story Sharing Guidance – http://www.scottishrecovery.net/Download-document /66-Story-Sharing-Guidance.html.
Journeys of Recovery – http://www.scottishrecovery.net/Download-document /81-Journeys-of-Recovery.html.
Rethink – http://www.rethink.org.
Summary of differences between medical model and recovery approach here: http://www.mentalhealthrecovery.com/recovery-resources/documents/100_ ways_to_support_recovery1.pdf.
Body language video here: https://www.ted.com/talks/amy_cuddy_your_body_ language_shapes_who_you_are.

Bibliography

Anthony, W. A. (1993). Recovery from mental illness: The guiding vision of the mental health system in the 1990s. *Psychosocial Rehabilitation Journal*, 16(4), 11–23.

Darcy, A. M., Katz, S., Fitzpatrick, K. K., Forsberg, S., Utzinger, L. and Lock, J. (2010). All better? How former anorexia nervosa patients define recovery and engaged in treatment. *European Eating Disorders Review*, 18(4), 260–270.

Davidson, L. (2005). Recovery, self management and the expert patient: Changing the culture of mental health from a UK perspective. *Journal of Mental Health*, 14(1), 25–35.

Davidson, L., O'Connell, M., Tondora, J., Styron, T. and Kangas, K. (2006). The top ten concerns about recovery encountered in mental health system transformation. *Psychiatric Services*, 57(5), 640–645.

Davidson, L., Rakfeldt, J. and Strauss, J. (2010). *The Roots of the Recovery Movement in Psychiatry: Lessons Learned*. West Sussex, UK: Wiley-Blackwell.

Department of Health (2007). *Commissioning Framework for Health and Well-Being*. London: Department of Health.

Department of Health (2009). *New Horizons: A Shared Vision for Mental Health*. London: Department of Health.

Department of Health (2011). *No Health Without Mental Health: A Cross-Government Mental Health Outcomes Strategy for People of All Ages*. London: Department of Health.

Hambrook, D., Brown, G. and Tchanturia, K. (2012). Emotional intelligence in anorexia nervosa: Is anxiety a missing piece of the puzzle? *Psychiatry Research*, 200(1), 12–19.

Harrison, A., Genders, R., Davies, H. and Tchanturia K. (2011). Experimental measurement of the regulation of anger and aggression in women with anorexia nervosa. *Clinical Psychology Psychotherapy*, 18(6): 445–452.

Harrison, A., Mountford, V. and Tchanturia, K. (2014). Social anhedonia and work and social functioning in the acute and recovered phases of eating disorders. *Psychiatry Research*, 218, 187–194.

Hay, P. J., Touyz, S. and Sud, R. (2012). Treatment for severe and enduring anorexia nervosa: A review. *Australian and New Zealand Journal of Psychiatry*, 46(12), 1136–1144.

Jenkins, J. and Ogden, J. (2012). Becoming 'whole' again: A qualitative study of women's views of recovering from anorexia nervosa. *European Eating Disorders Review*, 20, e23–e31.

Lang, K., Lopez, C., Stahl, D., Tchanturia, K. and Treasure, J. (2014). Central coherence in eating disorders: An updated systematic review and meta-analysis. *World Journal of Biological Psychiatry*, 1, 1–14.

Lloyd, S., Fleming, C., Schmidt, U. and Tchanturia, K. (2014). Targeting perfectionism in anorexia nervosa using a group based cognitive behavioural approach: A pilot study. *European Eating Disorder Review*, 22(5), 366–372.

McKeith, J. and Burns, S. (2010). *The Recovery Star: User Guide* (2nd edition). London: Mental Health Providers Forum. http://www.mhpf.org.uk.

Morris, R., Bramham, J., Smith, E. and Tchanturia, K. (2014). Social and emotional functioning in anorexia nervosa. *Cognitive Neuropsychiatry*, 19(1), 47–57.

Mundt, J. C., Marks, I. M., Shear, M. K. and Greist, J. H. (2002). The work and social adjustment scale: A simple measure of impairment in functioning. *The British Journal of Psychiatry*, 180, 461–464.

National Social Inclusion Programme (2007). *Capabilities for Inclusive Practice*. www.rcn.org.uk.

Prochaska, J. O. and DiClemente, C. C. (1986). Toward a comprehensive model of change. In Miller, W. R. and Heather, N. (eds), *Treating Addictive Behaviors: Processes of Change*. New York: Plenum Press, pp. 3–27.

Rollnick, S., Miller, W. R. and Butler, C. C. (2008). *Motivational Interviewing in Health Care: Helping Patients Change Behavior*. New York: Guilford Press.

Slade, M. (2009a). *Personal Recovery and Mental Health Illness*. Cambridge: Cambridge University Press.

Slade, M. (2009b). *100 Ways to Support Recovery: A Guide for Mental Health Professionals*. Rethink Recovery Series: volume 1. London: Rethink.

South London and Maudsley NHS Foundation Trust (2010). *Social Inclusion and Recovery Strategy, 2010–2015*. London: SLaM.

South London and Maudsley NHS Foundation Trust & South West London and St Georges Mental Health NHS Trust (2010). *Recovery Is for All: Hope, Agency and Opportunity in Psychiatry – A Position Statement by Consultant Psychiatrists*. London: SLaM/SWLSTG.

Straughan, H. and Buckenham, M. (2006). In-Sight: An evaluation of user-led, recovery-based, holistic group training for bipolar disorder. *Journal of Public Mental Health*, 5(3), 29–43.

Tchanturia, K., Davies, H., Harrison, A., Fox, J. R. E., Treasure, J. and Schmidt, U. (2012). Altered social hedonic processing in eating disorders. *International Journal of Eating Disorders*, 45(8), 962–969.

Tchanturia, K., Hambrook, D., Curtis, H., Jones, T., Lounes, N., Fenn, K., Keyes, A., Stevenson, L. and Davies, H. (2013a). Work and social adjustment in patients with anorexia nervosa. *Comprehensive Psychiatry*, 54(1), 41–45.

Tchanturia, K., Smith, E., Weineck, F., Fidanboylu, E., Kern, N., Treasure, J. and Baron Cohen, S. (2013b). Exploring autistic traits in anorexia: A clinical study. *Molecular Autism*, 12(4), 1–44.

Tickle, A., Brown, D. and Hayward, M. (2014). Can we risk recovery? A grounded theory of clinical psychologists' perception of risk and recovery-oriented mental health services. *Psychology and Psychotherapy: Theory, Research and Practice*, 87(1), 96–110.

Touyz, S., Thornton, C., Rieger, E., George, L. and Beumont, P. (2003). The incorporation of the stage of change model in the day hospital treatment of patients with anorexia nervosa. *European Child and Adolescent Psychiatry*, 12(1), 65–71.

Turton, P., Demetriou, A., Boland, W., Gillard, S., Kavuma, M., Mezey, G., Mountford, V., Turner, K., White, S., Zadeh, E. and Wright, C. (2011). One size fits all: Or horses for courses? Recovery-based care in specialist mental health services. *Social Psychiatry & Psychiatric Epidemiology*, 46, 127–136.

Wagner, E. H., Austin, B. T., Davis, C., Hindmarsh, M., Schaefer, J. and Bonomi, A. (2001). Improving chronic illness care: Translating evidence into action. *Health Affairs*, 20(6), 64–78.

Warren, B. J. and Lutz, W. J. (2000). A consumer-oriented practice model for psychiatric mental health nursing. *Archives of Psychiatric Nursing*, 14(3), 117–126.

Watkins, P. N. (2007). *Recovery: A Guide for Mental Health Practitioners*. London: Elsevier.

Weinstein, J. (2010). *Mental Health, Service User Involvement and Recovery*. London: Jessica Kingsley Publishers.

Final thoughts

It is a very ambitious task to cover ALL the groups taking part or developing in our clinic. Having said that, I very much hope that the reader will get some flavour of the broad variety of the clinical and research work we do as the psychology team to understand the mechanisms and maintenance factors of eating disorders, trying to support patients in their recovery with best evidence-based practice.

Our clinical sense is that group therapy is a very important part of the treatment, but, as we highlighted in the opening chapter, evidence and research as to what works the best and for whom is still in the very early stages.

We tried to develop the group programmes in the context of the National Health Service (NHS) in the UK taking into account clinical and economic pressures for short hospital admissions, and for the group programmes we did our best efforts to manualise treatment or at least have clear protocols for groups. Our main goal is to make sure that we capture our knowledge of psychopathology and symptoms in our group programmes and support patients with the best research evidence available at present. We also hope that some of the ideas toolboxes, suggested outcome measures and our results will serve clinicians and researchers to develop these ideas further and do a better job for our patients. As we highlighted in our systematic review of the group-based literature in Chapter 1, there are gaps in our clinical research work about group programmes for eating disorders.

Group therapy is hard to deliver well, for several reasons: first of all therapists need to be confident, competent and very experienced because even with our brief group interventions the group dynamics are hard to manage without clinical experience and good/regular supervision.

The second big problem which makes group programme implementation difficult is patients' engagement and poor motivation. In the intensive programmes we have nutritionally and physically very compromised patients; most of them have a long history of illness, high comorbidity (e.g. 70 per cent of the patients have clinical depression); autism spectrum disorders (an ASD comorbidity of 37 per cent is a very rough estimate that we audited in our adult inpatient service), most of our patients are socially anxious, have high social anhedonia, are shy and long-time isolated.

The third important contributor to consider, when we reflect on difficulties designing and delivering group programmes, is time. In the current NHS, hospital admissions and time to treat in the intensive care programmes are getting shorter and clinical teams are under huge pressure to do work in a limited time. Brief group interventions are a response to this demand, but as the clinical team we were very reflective about how to do it in the best interests of our patients. We tried to translate our clinical and research knowledge to have psychoeducational and experimental components in the groups.

We have in the clinic longer-term groups as well but in this book we focused mainly on brief group interventions highlighting the main ones we offer in the inpatient and residential programmes. As was mentioned in Chapter 1, patients are not very enthusiastically engaged in the groups but once they are the majority of them recognise the benefits of it.

One of my Masters students, Katie Sparrow, helped me to analyse several years' worth of qualitative feedback audit we collected within our inpatient treatment programme. Figure FT.1 below shows what we found. Interestingly, several overlapping themes emerged when we started to look at the patients' feedback. As

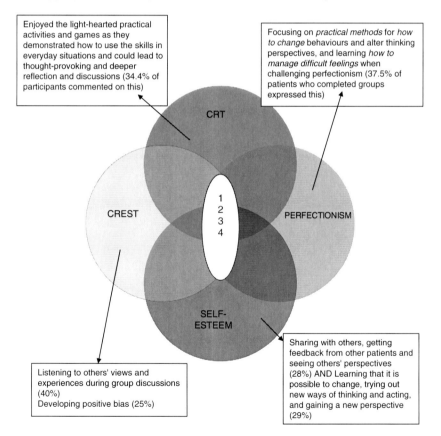

Figure FT.1 The most common theme in each of the four groups and overlapping themes which were common across all these groups

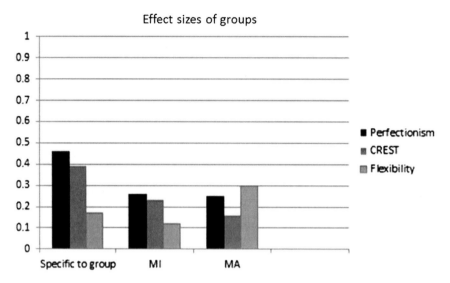

Figure FT.2 Magnitude of change between time 1 (pre-group) and time 2 (post-group) assessments

you can see there are unique themes in feedback for every single group (we chose these four groups simply because the audit data was better quality – with a return rate above 70 per cent).

There were also themes which were shared amongst all four groups when we looked carefully at the feedback. These shared themes between the groups were (based on the patients' subjective views):

1. Sharing thoughts with others and listening to others' perspectives/group discussions/the interactive or communicative aspect of the group (42.3 per cent).
2. Acquiring practical strategies for how to change and completing practical tasks (31.6 per cent).
3. Learning something new/acquiring new knowledge (21.9 per cent).
4. Learning about and trying out new ways of thinking and acting/goal setting (17.4 per cent).

Facilitating or supervising most of the groups described here, my impression is that clinical teams and patients sometimes need more motivation and enthusiasm at the beginning but once committed we all acknowledge that groups raise confidence and help hospitalised patients to feel less isolated and give more skills to be around other people. In Figure FT.2 we presented the magnitude of change between time 1 (before groups started) and time 2 (when groups finished) on group-specific measures and motivational aspects: MI – Motivation Importance to change; MA – Motivation Ability to change. As can be seen from the figure, group-specific and motivational changes are present in all groups. We are mindful that the number of sessions is limited but further research will help us to establish what is the good proportion of each intervention.

Overall we think that the brief group programme is an important component of the treatment programme and we very much hope this book will stimulate more research and clinical work in this very under-researched area.

Acknowledgements

We would like to acknowledge the Swiss Anorexia Foundation and the Maudsley Charity for funding to help us to evaluate the group programmes we have implemented and shared with you with the hope that we will generate stronger evidence in the future.

Index

action-oriented exercises 75
active listening 62
affect regulation systems 133, 137–8
affirmation 114, 173–4
'all or nothing' thinking 164
Allan, S. 6, 134, 138–9
anhedonia 1, 121
anorexia nervosa (AN) 1–3, 51–2, 74, 107, 134, 139, 141, 146, 167, 185
autistic traits 3

Baillie, Claire x, 202; *co-author of Chapter 10*
Baker, Laura x, 53; *co-author of Chapter 4*
'banking' of positive experiences 91–2
b-eat (charity) 127, 202
Beattie, Blake 100
Bhatnagar, K.A.C. 7
biased thinking 163–4
'bigger picture' thinking 28, 31–4, 39, 47–8, 52, 56–60, 64, 114, 128, 197
'Blokus' game 57
board games 56–7
bodily sensations 79, 86, 139
body image 162, 166–80; distortion of 175; and identity 176–7; media effects on 170–2; questionnaire on 181
body language 104
body mass index (BMI) 28, 116, 168–9, 185
'body positioning' game 54
Body Wise groups 162–5; session outlines 165–80
Bone, M. 13
brain plasticity 30
Brennan, M.A. 5
brief group psychotherapy, benefits from 1–3, 221

'Broaden and Build' theory of positive emotions 93–4
Broberg, A.G. 12
Brown, Amy x; *co-author of Chapters 5 and 9*
Bruch, Hilde 107
bulimia nervosa (BN) 108
'Buzz' game 55

card games 35, 63
Centre for Clinical Interventions 123
Checkerboard Illusion 175
Chen, E. 13
circulatory system 178
Clark, S. 12
Clinical Perfectionism Questionnaire (CPQ) 115–17
cognitive behavioural therapy (CBT) 107–9, 115, 122; group provision of 133–5
Cognitive Flexibility Scale (CFS) 39
Cognitive Remediation and Emotion Skills Training (CREST) 74–89, 94
cognitive remediation therapy (CRT), group format for 26–66; content of sessions 29–33; differences from individual format 46; patient characteristics in 28; provision for adolescents 51–66
colour, 'compassionate' 150
communal meals 25
compassion, role of imagery in 148–9
compassion focused therapy (CFT) 133, 144, 152–3
compassionate behaviours 146–7
compassionate blueprints 152, 159–60
compassionate colour 150
compassionate letter-writing 151, 157–8
compassionate others 149

compassionate self-correction and thought balancing 143–5
competition, levels of 66
Connors, M.E. 15
counting squares in an image 58–9
Crafti, N.A. 13
Csikszentmihalyi, Mihaly 78, 93, 96
Cuddy, Amy 104

Dean, H.Y. 11
'describing' tasks 31–2
Detail and Flexibility (DFlex) questionnaire 47–8
diaries of positive events 94–5
'different waya of doing things' game 64–5, 69–70
'difficult meal time' game 64, 68
digestive system 178
dissociation 135
distress, mindful acceptance of 124–5
distress intolerance 123–4
'do the opposite' game 55
Doris, Eli x; co-author of Chapter 3
Doyle, Suzi x–xi; author of Chapter 7
'dream job' game 64

eating disorders not otherwise specified restrictive type (EDNOS-R) 51
eating programmes: aims of 25; stages in 25
Ebbinghaus Illusion 175
ego syntonic disorder 28
elicitation of positive emotions 98
'emotion continuum' 85–6
emotional experience 80–3
emotional expression 2, 121
emotional intelligence 1, 74–5
emotional pain as distinct from emotional suffering 82
emotional reasoning 164
emotions: acceptance of 145–6; as distinct from mood 93; experienced in the body 79, 86; expression or suppression of 84–7; function of 155; helping us communicate 155–6; identification of 83–4; interaction with thoughts and images 148; language of 79–80; management of 81, 85–7; and needs 87–9; negative 81–2, 93, 97, 155; optimal balance of 97; positive 78–80, 83–4, 93–7, 155; preparing us to act 155; word lists for 90
endocrine system 178

Espie, Jonathan xi, 53; co-author of Chapter 4
Evans, Jane xi; author of Chapter 8
exit interviews 65

facial expressions 2, 155
facilitators: reflections of 66; role of 188–91, 194–8, 202
Family Therapy for Anorexia Nervosa (FT–AN) 51
'favourite person' exercise 96
feedback 39–40, 46–7, 65; from CREST 89
'feeling fat' 172–4
Fennell, Melanie 109, 114
Fernandez-Aranda, F. 14
'fight or flight' response 155
flashbacks 135
Fleming, Caroline xi, 5; co-author of Chapters 5 and 6
flexibility workshops 26
flexible thinking 31, 52, 60, 65–6, 71
'flow' 96–7, 187
Frederikson, Barbara 78, 93–4, 97
Frost Multi-Dimensional Perfectionism Scale (FMPS) 115–16
frustration tolerance 187
Fursland, Anthea 109

Gale, C. 133
Genders, R. 10
geometric figures 64
Ghandi, Mohandas 100
Gilbert, P. 137, 150
'glass half empty' and 'glass half full' approaches 95
goodbyes 152
Goss, K. 6, 134, 138–9
Goss, K. 6
gratitude 84; letters of 103
group rules 136
group therapy 133–5, 218–19; applied to social problems 2; encouragement of patients to attend 2; literature on 3–19; number of studies of 17–18; problems with 218; summary of research on 17–19

'hand tapping' game 60–1
handwriting tasks 29–30
Harrison, A. 204
Hay, P.J. 185
head–heart lag 144

healthy weight 169
homework 31, 33–4, 40, 64, 68; barriers to engaging with 80

'ice-breakers' 48–9, 54, 110
'ideal nurturer' exercise 149–50, 153
identity, sense of 3; and body image 176–7
illusions and illusion cards 34, 59, 66
imagery 147–9
interpersonal skills improvement 3
'invisible circles' game 63
isolation, feelings of 3

Jackson, Jesse 100
Johnson, Charley 100
Johnson, Spencer 31
Juarascio, A. 7–8

Katzman, M.A. 10
Kelly, A.C. 133–4
Kirkley, B.G. 15

Laberg, S. 14
'ladder of change' concept 184–5, 197, 296–7
Lavender, A. 9
Layous, Kristin 78, 94
Lázaro, L. 9
Lee, D.A. 149
Legenbauer, T. 10
letter-writing exercises 151, 153, 157–8
Lieb, R.C. 16
Lloyd, Samantha xi, 107, 118; co–author of Chapter 6
'London landmarks' game 58
Lounes, N. 47
lymphatic system 178
Lyubomirsky, Sonia 78, 94

Maiden, Zoe xi–xii, 53; co-author of Chapter 4
'maintaining factors' of illness 51
MANTRA 24
Marner, T. 15
Maudsley Hospital 24–5, 185
media impact on body image 170–2
'medical model' of mental health 215
memory games 62
Mental Health Foundation 212
mentalisation, development of 60
mind maps 38, 110, 114, 194
'mind reading' 164–5
mindful acceptance of distress 124–5

mindfulness 139–40, 151; exercises in 142–5, 153
models, body size of 171
mood 93, 95
Morgan, J.F. 6
Mother Teresa 100
Motivational Ruler (MR) 39–40, 78, 89, 115–16, 203, 208
mottos 65
Mountford, Victoria xii; co-author of Chapter 9
'multi-coloured ball' game 55–6
multi-tasking 34, 56, 62–4
muscular system 178
Mussell, M.P. 14

National Health Service (NHS) 184, 202, 218–19
Nevonen, L. 12
'new pastime' game 64
Nichols, Donovan 100
normal weight, shape and attitudes, meaning of 169
Nowoweiski, D. 10

'occupational' tasks 36–7, 63
Ohmann, S. 8
'one, two, three' game 61–2
optical illusions 59, 174–5
outcome measures 26, 38–40, 47–8, 115, 203–5

pain, emotional 82
Patient Satisfaction Questionnaire 203, 209–10
perceptions and preconceptions 174
perfectionism 107–18; model of 111–12; ways of learning 111
'photoshopping' 171
play-dough 62–3
'pop-up' groups 122–3
portfolios of positive outcomes 91
positive experiences 94–6
positive psychology 93, 173
positivity 78–9, 91–3
Prestano, C. 11
Pretorius, N. 9
Proulx, K. 10
proverbs 37–8, 72
psycho-education 30, 171
punctuality in attending sessions 136

'Qwirkle' game 56

recovery, different definitions of 185
'recovery approach' to mental health
    problems 186, 190–4, 201, 211–12
Recovery Star tool 184–99, 212
Reeve, Christopher 100
reflective discussions 53–4
reintegration into the community 3
resources, *intellectual*, *physical*, *social*,
    psychological and *spiritual* 94
Revised Social Anhedonia Scale
    (RSAS) 78, 89
Richards, P.S. 11–12
Rollnick, S. 203
Roy-Byrne, P. 15

'safe place' imagery 147
Salisbury, J.D. 16
sayings 37–8, 72
Schmidt, Ulrike 24
self-compassion 135–44, 147–8, 150
self-criticism 141, 152
self-defeating behaviour 176
self-esteem 114
self-soothing 150
Seligman, Martin 78, 91
Shafran, Roz 109, 111, 115
sharing of activities 96
Simic, Mima xii; *co-author of Chapter 4*
Simple Pleasures toolkit 82–3, 95, 99
single-session groups 121–32
'slap clap click click' game 56
'snap' card game 63
social anhedonia 1
social rank theory 134
soothing and self-soothing 138–9,
    144–9, 153
South London and Maudsley (SLaM)
    Intensive Treatment Programme 51–4
Sparrow, Katherine xii, 219; *co–author of
    Chapter 1*
'spot the difference' game 58
Steele, Anna L. 108
'Step up to recovery' programmes
    185–6, 211–14
Stevens, E.V. 16
'Stroop' exercise 60

suffering, emotional 82
supervision, observations from 66
support networks 131
support and recovery (StaR) workers 202
'switching' exercises 59–64

'Taboo' game 58
Tasca, G.A. 13
Tchanturia, Kate xii–xiii, 6, 10, 46, 53,
    109, 118, 187; *editor, author of Chapter
    2 and co-author of Chapters 1, 3 to
    6 and 10*
'texting an alien' game 57
thinking styles 36, 40, 64, 68, 113, 145;
    see also biased thinking
Thompson, T.L. 16
'three circles model' 133, 137–8
'three good things' exercise 80, 91, 102
'three Ps' for maintaining positive
    change 132
Toronto Alexithymia Scale
    (TAS–20) 78, 89
Treasure, Janet 24
'twisted fairy tales' 60

Usbourne Activities 59

Vandereycken, W. 15
Vanderlinden, J. 15

Wade, Tracey D. 108
Waisberg, J.L. 13–14
Wallace, William 101
Westerberg, C. 15
Williams, Kate 24
Wiseman, C.V. 13
Wood, L. 9
Woods, M.T. 13–14
word association 56
word-search and colouring-in
    exercises 63
Work and Social Adjustment Scale
    (WSAS) 190, 203–5

Zuchova, S. 8
Zuroff, David C. 107